DISCIPLE

REMEMBER WHO YOU ARE

Study Manual

The Prophets • The Letters of Paul

Writers of
DISCIPLE: REMEMBER WHO YOU ARE
Study Manual

Richard Byrd Wilke
Julia Kitchens Wilke

Consultants to the Writers
William J. A. Power, Old Testament
Leander E. Keck, New Testament

Maps by **Nell Fisher;** all illustrations by **Mitch Mann;** cover design by **Mary M. Johannes.**

Nellie M. Moser, Editor of DISCIPLE; Katherine C. Bailey, Assistant Editor; Linda O. Spicer, Secretary; Phillip D. Francis, Designer

For more information about DISCIPLE or DISCIPLE training events, call toll free 800-251-8591 or 800-672-1789.

13 14 15 16 – 16 15 14

Contents

As You Continue DISCIPLE 4

The Prophets 5

1. God's People Weep 6
2. God Sent Messengers 14
3. Starved for the Words of the Lord 22
4. God's Faithfulness 30
5. God's Requirement 38
6. God Pleads 46
7. God Rules the World 54
8. God's Anguish 62
9. God Will Not Abandon 70
10. The Day of the Lord Has Come 78
11. God Cleanses and Renews 86
12. God Will Save 94
13. God's Vision for a New World 102
14. God's City of Peace 110
15. God Will Restore Zion 116
16. God's Mission for Israel 124

The Letters of Paul 131

17. Called Through God's Grace 132
18. The Letters of Paul 140
19. The Lord Is Coming 148
20. Honest Labor 154
21. Seeing the Good 160
22. The Body of Christ 168
23. Crisis in Confidence 176
24. God's Saving Righteousness 184
25. Salvation for All 192
26. New Life in Christ 200
27. Fruit of the Holy Spirit 208
28. Christ Above All 216
29. Whole Armor of God 224
30. Leadership in the Church 232
31. From Generation to Generation 240
32. Remember Who You Are 248

As You Continue DISCIPLE

You have committed yourself to thirty to forty-five minutes of disciplined study six days a week and to participate in a two-and-one-half-hour weekly group meeting for thirty-two weeks. Faithfulness in daily study will prepare you to participate fully in group discussions because you will have had time to read thoughtfully, to make careful notes, and to reflect deeply on what you have been reading.

Daily Study

The amount of Scripture to be read daily varies from day to day and week to week. Some weeks require reading many chapters of Scripture; some weeks, fewer chapters. The important thing is to read and study daily. And taking notes as you read Scripture and listen to Scripture is an absolutely essential part of your daily study. Make it a daily habit also to read footnotes in your study Bible. When you begin studying a different book in the Bible, read the introduction to that book.

The Prophets

We will study the prophets in their historical sequence rather than in their biblical sequence. The prophets spoke in the context of history with its kings, nations, power struggles, and often brilliant achievements. So we pay attention to the history in order to understand the message of the prophets.

You will discover you will be reading some Scripture passages more than once. Generally, these passages report on the kings to whom the prophets related. Often, more than one prophet related to the same king. So each time we study a different prophet, we read about the king or kings to whom the prophet related. And we read from a different perspective because each prophet is different and the relationship between the king and that prophet is set in a different context.

Much of the literature in the prophets is poetry. As you read, stay alert to word pictures and to symbolic meanings in words. Look for the message under the words. Watch for words or phrases that signal connection to other events, persons, or situations.

The big backdrop for the prophets is God at work in history. Keep your eye on that.

The Letters of Paul

Like the prophets, the letters of Paul are not treated in their biblical sequence. They are treated in the sequence in which they were written. However, this sequence is to be understood in a fluid sense because opinions vary on the dating of Paul's letters. Paul's writing tends to be involved and sometimes abstract. As you read, take time to think about the language he uses and the tone of the language. Watch for his frequent use of the Hebrew Scriptures. In the letters of Paul as in the prophets, community and identity as God's people are central to the message.

Study Manual Format

The familiar elements of the study manual format are here. Two sections have new titles: The commentary section is titled "The Word of the Lord"; and the discipleship or ministry section, "Marks of Obedient Community." The statement of "Our Human Condition" and the "Marks of Obedient Community" are always in tension. See them and struggle with them together. In line with the overall emphasis on community in this study, the "Marks of Obedient Community" section most often addresses the community rather than just the individual.

Many suggestions in the "If You Want to Know More" section call for using a Bible dictionary to look up suggested topics and the maps in your study Bible or a Bible atlas to locate places.

Geography and history play a particularly important role in the lessons on the prophets and Paul. In nearly every weekly group meeting some work will involve using maps and a chart of history. Suggestions for research include persons, places, or events important to the history or geography related to the lesson and are chosen to help group members get the most out of the maps and the chart, as well as to enrich their reading of Scripture.

One recurring suggestion in the "If You Want to Know More" section of the letters of Paul calls for writing a letter with a particular focus or purpose. The letters are not necessarily meant to be sent but rather to offer a way of responding to or reflecting on the week's study in writing. Mostly the letters would be considered private, though the group may occasionally invite members to read their letters.

Individual research is not meant to result in a report to the group, though occasionally that may be appropriate. Rather the exercise benefits the person who does it by equipping that person to bring information into the discussion at appropriate points.

DISCIPLE

THE PROPHETS

RETURN

"Let us test and examine our ways,
and return to the LORD."
—Lamentations 3:40

1 God's People Weep

OUR HUMAN CONDITION

We go our own way until we hurt. Then in shock and confusion we ask, What happened? With guilt we wonder, Where did we go wrong? We want to blame others. But confronted by the outcomes of our actions, we ask, Where can we turn for relief?

ASSIGNMENT

We begin by walking through the rubble of Jerusalem, reading Lamentations. (Read the laments aloud.) Later, looking back through our tears, we will, week by week, read the warnings of the prophets. The grief, confusion, and hope we hear expressed in Lamentations we will hear also in the prophets. Now, read quickly the chapters from Deuteronomy to remember the life-and-death admonitions of Torah. Deuteronomy helps us know what went wrong. The destruction of Jerusalem and the exile into Babylon will forever shape our faith, as it has the faith of the Jews, for we will remember; we will repent; we will slowly envision a new future.

Day 1 Lamentations 1–3 (laments over Zion, God's warnings fulfilled, confession, God's steadfast love)

Day 2 Lamentations 4–5 (punishment of Zion); Psalms 74 (prayer for deliverance); 78 (God's deeds, Israel's faithlessness); 79 (plea for mercy for Jerusalem); 80 (prayer for Israel's restoration)

Day 3 Deuteronomy 5–11 (the Law at Sinai, a chosen people, warnings and consequences, God's requirements)

Day 4 Deuteronomy 12–18 (place of worship, warning against idolatry, sabbatical year, Passover, kingship)

Day 5 Deuteronomy 23; 25–28 (miscellaneous laws, first fruits, altar on Mount Ebal, blessings and curses)

Day 6 Read and respond to "The Word of the Lord" and "Marks of Obedient Community."

Day 7 Rest

PRAYER

Pray daily before study:
"Hear my prayer, LORD,
and listen to my cry;
come to my aid when I weep"
(Psalm 39:12, TEV).

Prayer concerns for this week:

RETURN

Day 1 Lamentations 1–3 (laments over Zion, God's warnings fulfilled, confession, God's steadfast love)

Day 2 Lamentations 4–5 (punishment of Zion); Psalms 74 (prayer for deliverance); 78 (God's deeds, Israel's faithlessness); 79 (plea for mercy for Jerusalem); 80 (prayer for Israel's restoration)

Day 3 Deuteronomy 5–11 (the Law at Sinai, a chosen people, warnings and consequences, God's requirements)

Day 4 Deuteronomy 12–18 (place of worship, warning against idolatry, sabbatical year, Passover, kingship)

Day 5 Deuteronomy 23; 25–28 (miscellaneous laws, first fruits, altar on Mount Ebal, blessings and curses)

Day 6 "The Word of the Lord" and "Marks of Obedient Community"

THE WORD OF THE LORD

We are about to plunge into the prophets and the agony of Israel. The experience will be painful, filled with anguish and struggle. The prophets, in the name of God, will proclaim dire warnings, dramatize disasters to come—always pleading with the people to repent. When the people suffer, the prophets will weep. So will we.

We may become weary, reading the endless warnings. We may question our tightly held theologies. But the Word will never let the light go out.

The Agony in the Laments

Why begin this study with the book of Lamentations? First, because our human tendency, like that of ancient Judah, is not to take shouts of warning seriously. But after reading Lamentations, we know the warnings were altogether fulfilled. The predicted punishment took place. So, when we read the prophets, we cannot be complacent.

Second, people often define their lives by some major event, a disaster or a life-shaping tragedy. The Jews can never forget that day in 587 B.C. when Babylon ravaged Jerusalem. Biblical theology is shaped by the day David's dynasty came to an end and Solomon's sanctuary was destroyed. Israel experienced a watershed of history when its people were slaughtered and survivors dispersed into foreign lands. Both Jews and Christians must read the Hebrew Bible through the eyes of post-exilic Judaism.

Third, when you and I suffer grief, where can we go for help? We go to those who understand pain and sorrow because they have experienced it. We may cry, Is there any sorrow like my sorrow? What a relief to find others who hurt and who shake the doors of heaven for answers. In the depths of Israel's pain, we will find that the Lord who punishes is also the Lord who cares and sustains.

Anguish in History

The Assyrians had demolished the Northern Kingdom, first with a heavy invasion in 732 B.C., then in 722 B.C. with siege, destruction, and exile. The Babylonians ravaged the Southern Kingdom with the same one-two punch—first an invasion in 597 B.C. and later in 587 B.C. following the awful siege, the complete destruction of Jerusalem. Jerusalem had believed itself to be impregnable. Now it lay in ruins.

Walk through the smoldering remains of the city in 587 B.C. Step carefully over the broken stones and burning embers. Listen to the soft wails of raped women, starving children, mourning elders. Smell the stench. Young men and women able to walk were marched off into exile. A few scholars, some artisans, a handful of priests and nobility went into slavery with them. Just as Assyria had scattered Israelites

NOTES, REFLECTIONS, AND QUESTIONS

The terms *Hebrew Bible* and *Hebrew Scriptures* both refer to the body of writings Christians call the *Old Testament*. The three terms mean the same. This study manual uses all three terms.

from the Northern Kingdom over a century earlier, Babylon carted off the people of Judah from the Southern Kingdom after the siege of Jerusalem. The people of God had been slaughtered or scattered.

Solomon's Temple, carefully handcrafted centuries before, now lay in rubble, cedar beams smoldering amid the stones. In better days, the priests had offered there a continual stream of prayer and praise. Now the priests were dead or exiled, the gold and silver vessels carried away. Once during religious festivals, massive throngs gathered at the Temple. But now,

"The roads to Zion mourn,
for no one comes to the festivals" (Lamentations 1:4).

Walk into the Judean hills, a land of grazing and mixed farming. Crops had been confiscated or burned. The pastures were empty, for the animals had long since been eaten. Ancient landmarks were strewn about, homes and barns torn down. The Babylonians axed the centuries-old olive trees, set their stumps afire. They salted the fields so nothing would grow. Gone was the land of milk and honey, Abraham's promise, Moses' dream, Joshua's possession. The land was each family's inheritance. Gone was the land of promise.

The defeat marked the end of the monarchy. The king had become the sacred link between God and nation. The monarchy symbolized the body politic, uniting all the tribes of Israel into a cohesive nation. The golden age of David was recorded indelibly in the collective mind. When the Northern Kingdom, Israel, broke away after the death of Solomon, it was a tragic weakening of the nation. But the Southern Kingdom, Judah, carried on David's tradition. For four hundred years, each succeeding king had been a direct descendant of David, a sign of the providence and plan of God. Years before, Assyria had captured the last king of Samaria, putting an Assyrian governor in charge. Now David's descendant, King Zedekiah of Judah, was a prisoner. Babylon killed his sons while he watched, gouged out his eyes, and led the pitiable figure away into exile. With the collapse of the monarchy, God seemed to have abdicated divine protectorship, condemning Israel to the chaos of history.

Something happened to the soul of Judah. The theology of being a chosen people was tossed into turmoil. What had happened to God's protection? Judaism would spend generations trying to understand. Priests and prophets, wise leaders and ordinary people would thread theologies to make sense of catastrophe. Jewish and Christian communities continue the struggle to understand punishment and pain.

Grief Laid Bare

Lamentations uses words that touch every human sorrow. The experiences are all voiced. *Shock:* The elders "sit on the ground in silence" throwing "dust on their heads" (Lamentations 2:10). *Weeping:* "Let tears stream down like a torrent /

NOTES, REFLECTIONS, AND QUESTIONS

day and night!" (2:18). *Bodily pain:* "My stomach churns; / my bile is poured out on the ground" (2:11). *Loneliness:* "How lonely sits the city. . . . How like a widow she has become. . . . She weeps bitterly in the night" (1:1-2). Notice the personification: The survivors are depicted as a bereaved woman. Judah or Jerusalem is a daughter, now in tears.

If any reaction is lacking, it is the normal effort to deny what actually happened. The destruction was so complete, the suffering so severe, that disbelief was impossible.

"My soul continually thinks of it
and is bowed down within me" (3:20).

Like grieving people, Lamentations tells the details over and over. Guilt is expressed. So is shame. Self-pity is prevalent, and anger, projected toward God and others, explodes.

"Look, O LORD, and consider!
To whom have you done this?" (2:20).

The writer demands that others must suffer (3:64).

Repentance is required, for we cannot be healed without it. "Woe to us, for we have sinned!" (5:16). And with the healing balm of God's love comes the ability to trust again.

"The LORD is my portion, . . .
therefore I will hope in him" (3:24).

Acceptance of reality and the willingness to go on help heal wounded souls.

"Why should any who draw breath complain
about the punishment of their sins?" (3:39).
"It is good that one should wait quietly
for the salvation of the LORD" (3:26).

The Laments

A lament is a Hebrew poem, designed to verbalize suffering and pain, to be used at funerals, and to express grief within worship. Psalms 79 and 80 are laments. The prophetic books use laments as warnings—wailing, as it were, before the fact. The prophets sing the dirges long before the funeral.

Lamentations consists of five closely structured laments, one per chapter. They were meant to be chanted in worship. All around the world, Jews still read Lamentations on the ninth of Av (July/August) to remember the destruction of Solomon's Temple (587/586 B.C.) and the loss of the rebuilt Temple in A.D. 70. But the laments, like the Psalms, are meant to be read by anyone who needs to express sorrow.

The poems employ every possible literary device to drive home pain and sorrow. The Hebrew word that begins a lament, often translated "alas" or "woe" or "how," is spoken with a sad clicking of the tongue.

Hebrew poetry has parallel lines, saying the same thing in similar ways. A lament uses a three-beat, two-beat form so that the second part of the line or sentence is shorter, creating a falling rhythm. This long-short style seems to limp or weep with the content. Laments are hymns sung in a minor key.

NOTES, REFLECTIONS, AND QUESTIONS

A *dirge* is music or words intended to be sung or read at a funeral. A *lament* is a song or poem expressing deep grief and loss. In common usage, the terms *dirge* and *lament* are used interchangeably. Both kinds of writing can employ any slow, mournful form and rhythm.

Traditionally, the book of Lamentations is associated with Jeremiah, "the weeping prophet." The writer of Chronicles says Jeremiah wrote a lament and sang it when King Josiah died (2 Chronicles 35:25). The feelings and the thoughts of Lamentations are like those of Jeremiah; but the style is so deliberate, so carefully constructed, and so completely after the fact that Lamentations must have been written by later poets.

The first four laments use an acrostic pattern, employing each of the twenty-two letters in the Hebrew alphabet in sequence. Thus even the construction shows completeness of grief. Chapter 5 echoes the device by using twenty-two short verses, but it is not an acrostic poem. This closing chapter, however, returns to a normal three-three beat to introduce tones of hope. Thus the laments provide full emotional relief for grief, from remorse and despair to repentance and faith.

Prophetic Themes

The Israelites, in desperate straits, looked at their pitiable condition and asked, Why did this happen to us, God's chosen? Did God forget the promise to protect us from our enemies? Why did God destroy those things most sacred—the Temple, David's kingdom, Jerusalem, even take away the land of promise?

The questions escalate: Why have we been punished? For the sins of our mothers and fathers? For our own sins? Why was the punishment so harsh? Are we not the children of Abraham, the covenant people of Moses? Is there any hope at all for us?

For now, we can only hint at answers, for we have not yet probed the questions deeply. But Lamentations, like the prophets, agrees on several basic principles.

• *God is in charge.* There is no suggestion that God was weak, overwhelmed by other more powerful gods or by some force of evil. No, clearly the events that happened were under God's control. Did God *allow* the destruction? Yes, for the lament says, God "has withdrawn his right hand" (Lamentations 2:3), that is, pulled back his protective power. But more prominent is the insistence that God actually selected foreign armies to deliver divine punishment (1:14). The underlying conviction is that God punished Israel (1:15). God did not act casually or accidentally; God acted purposefully and intentionally.

• *The destruction was punishment.* "The crown has fallen from our head," a reference to both the fall of the king and the fall of the chosen nation; "woe to us, for we have sinned" (5:16).

The laments do not detail the sins and transgressions as the prophets do; they refer simply to rebellion. We will see this theme strongly dramatized by the prophets. But who sinned, forebears or the punished? Both, comes the answer. The ancestors were guilty. But the people suffered for their own sins as well. The experience was communal.

Did God forget Israel was special? No, God remembered. It was God's remembrance of righteousness that caused the destruction. The people forgot. They forgot Mount Sinai and Torah. The people of promise were special *within* the covenant. If they forgot the covenant, broke the commandments, forgot the poor, God would punish. Since nothing is

NOTES, REFLECTIONS, AND QUESTIONS

An *acrostic* uses letters, usually the first letter in each line, to form a pattern. The pattern in Lamentations is the Hebrew alphabet, with letters repeated in sequence to express the full range of grief, from beginning to end.

Hebrew Alphabet

Name	*Letter*	*Sound*
Aleph	א	AH or silent
Bet	בּ	B
	ב	V
Gimel	ג	G
Dalet	ד	D
Hey	ה	H
Vav	ו	V
Zayin	ז	Z
Chet	ח	CH
Tet	ט	T
Yod	י	Y
Kaf	כּ ך	K
	כ	CH
Lamed	ל	L
Mem	מ ם	M
Nun	נ ן	N
Samech	ס	S
Ayin	ע	AH or silent
Pey	פּ ף	P
	פ	F
Tsade	צ ץ	TS
Qof	ק	K
Resh	ר	R
Shin	שׂ	S
	שׁ	SH
Tav	ת	T

more precious to God than justice and mercy, God would come down hard on injustice and cruelty, even if it meant destroying the Temple, the king, and the land of promise.

• *God has not abandoned Israel.* The despairing survivors, sitting in the ashes, cry plaintively, "Is it nothing to you, all you who pass by?" (1:12). Is there any hope for comfort? No, not from human sources. But the poets and prophets know God is never without new possibilities. The laments are laced with hope built on the dependability of God's Word.

"The LORD has done what he purposed,
he has carried out his threat" (2:17).

There is good news in that, for even God's punishment proves the Almighty is dependable.

God's Steadfast Love Will Yet Save

What can we do when hope seems gone, when even the voice of God is silent? In the heart of the laments we are told,

"This I call to mind,
and therefore I have hope:
The steadfast love of the LORD never ceases,
his mercies never come to an end;
they are new every morning;
great is your faithfulness" (Lamentations 3:21-23).

So Israel learns to trust the love that never ends, for "the LORD is good to those who wait for him" (3:25).

In the fifth lament, the cadence of the poem turns to a major key: "Restore us to yourself, O LORD, that we may be restored; / renew our days as of old" (5:21).

Deuteronomy

Scholars say Deuteronomy is built on Mount Sinai, the Ten Commandments, the sermons of Moses, and the spiritual insights of Exodus and wilderness faith. But it was a living word, oral, and taught for centuries. Like all civil law, it received interpretation for new situations.

The point of Deuteronomy is that Moses made clear who the covenant people were and the God to whom they belonged. Moses told where the blessings would come from (28:1-14) and warned where the pitfalls lay (28:15-68).

At least part of Deuteronomy was in written form and found in the Temple during the reform of Josiah (620 B.C.). Reading it caused the king to repent and tear his clothes, for it showed how far Judah had strayed.

The book probably was finalized in Jerusalem after the Exile by the scholarly priests and prophets who returned from Babylon. The theology is clearly that of the prophets. It is as if Deuteronomy warned in advance from the time of Moses and then shouted "I told you so" after the destruction and exile. The rules for behavior were not new; they were drawn from the basic commandments. The Lord of the Hebrews pours forth justice (righteousness) and compassion. Stealing, adultery,

NOTES, REFLECTIONS, AND QUESTIONS

The books of Joshua through Second Kings, called The Former Prophets in the Hebrew Scriptures, are also often called "the Deuteronomistic history." Deuteronomy and the books of Joshua through Second Kings were organized and put into their final form after the Exile by a group of editors or collectors known as "the Deuteronomists." In trying to understand the writings of the prophets, it is crucial to understand the content of these books because they offer an after-the-fact theological perspective on the history of the people of God. The history and social practices of the chosen people in the land given to them by God are measured against the standard of Deuteronomy.

false witness offend God's nature, violate the covenant community, and betray the harmony God desires for the world. A great responsibility rests on the shoulders of Israel.

The prophets remember. They remember their beginnings. They remember the salvation event, and they know the conditions for survival. They understand Israel has a uniqueness, a special identity carefully prescribed by the Lord. So when the prophets speak, they compare what Israel is doing with what Israel is supposed to be doing. They give warning after warning, but Israel does not listen. All the counsel of Moses in Deuteronomy does not prevent the punishment.

Yet, God does not abandon the covenant people. Hints in Deuteronomy and glimmers of hope in Lamentations become full-blown visions in the prophets. God will bring the remnant home.

MARKS OF OBEDIENT COMMUNITY

The community of faith learns God's word is trustworthy. God means exactly what God says. When we remember God's law and God's love, we remember who we are and who we are meant to be. God judges, and God saves. So we can repent, realign our lives to God. We are never so lost as to be outside God's compassion. We can turn in confidence to God.

How do you understand the idea that the God who judges us, causing us pain, is also the God to whom we go for relief from that pain? What is your experience of this God?

How does your fellowship deal with suffering, especially suffering caused by sin or stupidity?

When have you experienced "return"?

IF YOU WANT TO KNOW MORE

Pretend you just asked a grieving friend, "What happened?" and then reread Lamentations 4. Notice the attention to detail as the tragedy is recounted.

Read Deuteronomy 29–34 to hear Moses' third sermon, to understand the covenant better, to learn how Moses chose Joshua, and to hear Moses' final instruction and blessing.

NOTES, REFLECTIONS, AND QUESTIONS

The community of faith relies on the trustworthiness of God's word.

HEAR

"Hear, O Israel: The LORD is our God, the LORD alone. You shall love the LORD your God with all your heart, and with all your soul, and with all your might. Keep these words that I am commanding you today in your heart."

—Deuteronomy 6:4-6

2 God Sent Messengers

OUR HUMAN CONDITION

We are drawn to the promises and practices of the culture that surrounds us. We try to walk in two worlds. We choose compromise—surely small compromises won't matter. A single loyalty asks too much. We look away; we don't want to hear.

ASSIGNMENT

We must know the history in order to understand the work of the prophets. We must hear them in context. We have much to read; so read quickly, noting important events and key figures. Associate prophets with their king counterparts and with the issue of conflict. Try to figure out what makes a prophet a prophet.

Note: As we come to different prophets in this study, we will reread Scripture involving the related kings. For example, here we read 2 Kings 15. We will reread portions of that chapter in later lessons.

Day 1 Deuteronomy 6 (the Shema); 1 Samuel 8:1–10:16 (Samuel anoints Saul); 2 Samuel 12 (Nathan and David); 1 Kings 11–14 (Solomon, Ahijah and Jeroboam, Shemaiah and Rehoboam)

Day 2 1 Kings 16:29–19:21; 21–22 (Elijah and Ahab, Micaiah and Jehoshaphat)

Day 3 2 Kings 2; 4–5; 9 (Elijah and Elisha, Naaman's leprosy, Jehu anointed king, end of house of Ahab)

Day 4 2 Kings 15–19 (Uzziah king of Judah, Ahaz, kings of Israel, Israel taken captive to Assyria, Hezekiah's reforms, Sennacherib invades Judah)

Day 5 2 Kings 20–25 (death of Hezekiah, Manasseh, kings of Judah, Josiah's reforms, fall of Jerusalem, Judah taken captive to Babylon)

Day 6 Read and respond to "The Word of the Lord" and "Marks of Obedient Community."

Day 7 Rest

PRAYER

Pray daily before study:

"You have taught me ever since I was young,
and I still tell of your wonderful acts. . . .
Be with me while I proclaim your power
and might
to all generations to come" (Psalm
71:17-18, TEV).

Prayer concerns for this week:

1) Loss of life & property.
2) Jeremy move to SC - Guidance & strength
3) New boss Michel; Prayer for her new position.
4)

Deut. 6:4 Hear O Israel.

HEAR

wed

Day 1 Deuteronomy 6 (the Shema); 1 Samuel 8:1–10:16 (Samuel anoints Saul); 2 Samuel 12 (Nathan and David); 1 Kings 11–14 (Solomon, Ahijah and Jeroboam, Shemaiah and Rehoboam)

Fear the Lord & obey all his commands.

700 wives of Royal birth, 300 concubines! Ruled 40 yrs. (Solomon)

Good leaders put the best interests of the followers above their own. (Jeroboam & Rehoboam)

Trust God's word instead of hearsay. (Ahijah)

Disregard messages that contradict the Bible.

Thur Man of God deceived by old prophet.

Day 2 1 Kings 16:29–19:21; 21–22 (Elijah and Ahab, Micaiah and Jehoshaphat)

The Fifth Mountain - Paulo Coelho

Small thing becomes important. Vinyard like Haman wanted Mordecai killed; Saul wanted David killed; David & Bethsheeba;

Fri

Day 3 2 Kings 2; 4–5; 9 (Elijah and Elisha, Naaman's leprosy, Jehu anointed king, end of house of Ahab) Jehu king of Israel

Elijah → Elisha transition.

Elisha perform a miracle with God's help. Raises dead son.

Feeding a hundred twenty (20) loaves of barley.

Leprosy washed away (Naaman) → similar to what we must do to have our sin washed away.

Gehazi (servant) wrongly implied that money could be exchanged for God's free gift.

Sat.

Day 4 2 Kings 15–19 (Uzziah king of Judah, Ahaz, kings of Israel, Israel taken captive to Assyria, Hezekiah's reforms, Sennacherib invades Judah)

Sun

Day 5 2 Kings 20–25 (death of Hezekiah, Manasseh, kings of Judah, Josiah's reforms, fall of Jerusalem, Judah taken captive to Babylon)

The Lord hears Hezekiah's prayer & adds 15 yrs.

Josiah good king. Removed all idol worship [illegible].

Monday

Day 6 "The Word of the Lord" and "Marks of Obedient Community"

THE WORD OF THE LORD

No other civilization, no other religion ever produced people quite like the Hebrew prophets. Of course, sages and soothsayers, seers and fortunetellers were scattered throughout the ancient world. Every tribe, every city, every nation had its gods and goddesses served by priests and prophets who conducted rituals, spoke in ecstatic language, even advised their rulers.

But the Hebrew prophets of the ninth, eighth, seventh, and sixth centuries B.C. were a different breed. Planted in the same Mediterranean soil as other nations, Israel produced prophets so disciplined, so determined to serve the God of Mount Sinai that they stand out with historic uniqueness.

Who Is a Prophet?

The Hebrew word *nabi,* translated "prophet," means simply "one who speaks for" or "one who represents." In the Bible, *nabi* means "one who speaks for God" or "God's messenger."

The word first appears in Scripture when King Abimelech called Abraham a prophet. The king perceived that Abraham and Sarah were in touch with God and on a special spiritual journey (Genesis 21:22). Moses was called a prophet unequaled among prophets (Deuteronomy 34:10-12). Both Abraham and Moses interceded for the guilty. Prophets speak to people for God and to God for people. Intercession is one of their primary functions.

Miriam was named a prophet when she sang God's victory song at the Red Sea (Exodus 15:20-21). Aaron was designated a prophet for Moses (7:1). On one occasion seventy elders "prophesied" standing at the tent of meeting (Numbers 11:25). Eldad and Medad, also elders, didn't go to the tent but "prophesied" anyway in the camp (11:26). Moses said he wished all the people were prophets like them (11:29).

Judges like Deborah, called a "prophetess," were in touch with God; but she was primarily an inspired executive and military leader (Judges 4:4-5). The prophet Balaam, strange clairvoyant, gave divinely inspired forecasts of the outcome of battles to be. His temptation to sell out and the reprimand by his donkey illustrate the importance of prophetic integrity (Numbers 22–24).

Prophets and Kings

In many ways, Samuel was the first of the true prophets of Israel. His calling to be a prophet was clear and dramatic (1 Samuel 3:1-10). He performed one of the main duties of a prophet—to help Israel *remember its identity* and to *demand loyalty to the one God.* Like the great prophets to follow, Samuel dealt with the monarchy—warning, correcting, chastising, condemning. He anointed Saul (10:1), and later David (16:13), as king of Israel. Though he moved in and out

NOTES, REFLECTIONS, AND QUESTIONS

Several terms are used for the prophets and the biblical books named for prophets:

- *Former Prophets*—in the Hebrew canon, Joshua through Second Kings, referred to by scholars as Deuteronomistic History because they follow the perspective of Deuteronomy
- *Latter Prophets*—in the Hebrew canon, Isaiah through Malachi except for Lamentations and Daniel, *Latter* because they follow the *Former* in sequence
- *Major Prophets*—in the Christian canon, Isaiah through Daniel
- *Minor Prophets*—Hosea through Malachi; the terms *Major* and *Minor* refer to length, not to importance of the books
- *Preexilic Prophets*—those who prophesied before the Exile or whose writings addressed Israel and Judah before the Exile
- *Postexilic Prophets*—those who prophesied after the Exile or whose writings addressed the people of Judah after the Exile
- *Canonical Prophets*—those prophets whose prophecies are preserved in the Bible
- *Precanonical Prophets*—those prophets mentioned in the Bible but whose prophecies are not preserved (for example, Nathan, Elijah, and Elisha)

of "schools" or groups of prophets, Samuel was God's prophet.

Some schools of prophets spoke in "prayer language." Saul joined them once, so that the saying went out "Is Saul also among the prophets?" (10:10-13). But Samuel was never known for these ecstatic experiences. Though he did seem to have a special sense: He knew Saul's donkeys had been found (9:18-20). But the Bible indicates that the word *seer,* once used of Samuel, was no longer appropriate (9:9). Samuel's primary virtue was knowing and doing the will and work of God.

The Hebrew prophets were not fortunetellers seeking information about future events by studying sheep's entrails. They didn't link people up with zodiac signs or determine their future from the stars. They weren't supposed to converse with the dead, although a medium did it once for King Saul (28:6-14). The law of Moses clearly forbade such practices (Deuteronomy 18:10-13).

We cannot define the prophets apart from the *monarchy.* We must know the actions of the kings if we are to understand the message of the prophets. Each king had schools of prophets attached to his shrine or living adjacent to his palace. They offered prayers, gave counsel—often "yes men" who said what the king wanted to hear. But in and out of that circle moved an occasional prophet who felt the call of God in his soul and spoke as if he were the holy God of Israel.

Nathan

The prophet Nathan was court adviser to King David. Whereas King Saul had listened to Samuel's continual stream of counsel, David said his own prayers, made his own decisions. Nathan was merely one of David's advisers—until King David saw Bathsheba bathing (2 Samuel 11:2-5).

When David's morality collapsed, Nathan the prophet came to the king. Using the subterfuge of telling a story about a poor man with a pet lamb, Nathan showed great courage (12:1-15). He lifted the role of prophet to a new and higher level as he looked King David in the eye and said, in effect, "You are an adulterer, murderer, thief, and liar." When Nathan said sternly, "You are the man!" (12:7), he was standing on the Ten Commandments given by God to Moses on Mount Sinai.

The issue for Nathan was deeper than the king's breaking the commandments of God. The issue for Nathan was the king's breach of covenant. David had betrayed kingship by killing his soldier instead of protecting him, by stealing a man's wife instead of providing security for her home. He betrayed the trust of kingship by acting in self-interest. David sowed seeds of covenant deterioration that would one day bring down his monarchy.

Now look at Solomon, anointed by Nathan and the priest Zadok. What did King Solomon do wrong? He sealed treaties by marrying the daughters and sisters of foreign kings. Such

NOTES, REFLECTIONS, AND QUESTIONS

intermarriage was expressly forbidden by Moses: "Do not intermarry with them" (Deuteronomy 7:3). Why? Because they would bring their pagan gods, their shrines, and their theologies with them, watering down God's Law. "They will surely incline your heart to follow their gods" (1 Kings 11:2). Worse, intermarriage "would turn away your children from following me, to serve other gods" (Deuteronomy 7:4). What a denial of the great Deuteronomic command, "Recite them [the laws] to your children and talk about them when you are at home and when you are away. . . . and write them on the doorposts of your house and on your gates" (6:7-9).

From Solomon's idolatry flowed grievous sins—arrogance, greed, and misuse of his people. His opulent construction in Jerusalem raped land and people. In Solomon's old age, the nation trembled on the brink of revolution. Oppression had bred discontent. And at his death, the nation split between north and south.

Ahijah

The prophet Ahijah met Jeroboam on a lonely road near Jerusalem, and Ahijah tore his new robe into twelve pieces (1 Kings 11:29-39). Then, to Jeroboam, a non-Davidic, northern "commoner" who had served as superintendent of forced labor for Solomon, the prophet gave ten pieces of his robe. His gift represented the ten tribes that would become the Northern Kingdom, to be called Israel. He withheld two pieces of his robe (presumably for Benjamin and Judah) for King David's sake and for Jerusalem's sake to symbolize the Southern Kingdom, to be called Judah (11:32).

Ahijah's symbolic action did three things—spotlighted sin, forecast the future, and helped to bring the future to pass. The civil breach took place without a single blow struck. Another prophet, Shemaiah, stopped Solomon's son Rehoboam from going to war against the new Northern Kingdom by saying, "Thus says the LORD, . . . this thing is from me" (12:24). And 180,000 Judean soldiers went home without a fight.

Like the prophets to follow, Ahijah wanted Jerusalem to be the one and only center of worship, even though he recognized political division. Unfortunately, King Jeroboam of the Northern Kingdom determined that political unity demanded national shrines. He installed worship centers with calves of gold in Bethel and Dan and set the stage for ultimate disaster. From then on, when historians wanted to refer to idolatry, they used shorthand—"the sins of Jeroboam."

Elijah

Do not lose sight of these key points—the interaction between prophet and king, the concern of the prophet for a faithful monarchy, and the prophetic effort to maintain the laws and the land. Kings were meant to be shepherds of Israel, serving in God's behalf. The prophets, with courage

NOTES, REFLECTIONS, AND QUESTIONS

The Bible does not mention a prophet in connection with King Solomon. Saul had Samuel to advise him; David had Nathan and Gad. Rehoboam had Shemaiah, and Jeroboam was advised by Ahijah; but being somewhat of a prophet himself, Solomon relied on personal, direct communication with God.

and consistency, denounced the kings whenever they violated this charge.

Just as King David had his prophet Nathan, so King Ahab of the Northern Kingdom had Elijah. The baggage of divinations, ecstatic language, even miracles of healing, seemed incidental to Elijah. He knew he was God's messenger to help Israel remember that the Lord is God and to return to the covenant.

The contest against the 450 priests of Baal was not a game for Elijah. It was life and death for Israel (1 Kings 18:17-46). Either Israel belonged to God, or it did not. Either the covenant was in effect, or it was not. If the first commandment were broken, all other commandments would be broken as well. Salvation memory was at stake. Identity as God's chosen people was at stake. The Promised Land was at stake.

Idolatry is the enemy on Mount Carmel. Idolatry is the Number 1 sin. It is so hard for us to recognize our own idolatry when our idols do not have faces of stone or gold. But it was also hard for ancient Israel to understand. They couldn't fathom that a seemingly innocent mixing of gods could be such a threat. The baals had great power, because they diluted loyalty to God and watered down law and grace.

What gods from the surrounding culture do we adopt and allow to dilute our loyalty to God?

Ahab had married Jezebel from the royal family in Sidon to seal a treaty with the seafaring Phoenicians. Jezebel brought with her all her pagan gods and an entourage of cultic prophets. The queen was trained in royal ways: The monarchy was absolute. You hired your prophets, you prayed to the gods for success, and you did as you pleased. Ahab, trained in the ways of Israel, knew in his heart that God had given each Hebrew a piece of land; that everyone, even the king, stood under the Ten Commandments; and that the king was supposed to be shepherd-servant for the people.

When Ahab wanted a little garden plot near the palace, Jezebel had its owner, Naboth, killed; and she gave the land to Ahab (21:1-16). Her gods did not care. They dealt with fertility issues like rain and childbirth, with victory in war, with protection from injury and disease. They made no moral demands.

King Ahab lived with compromise, worshiping both God and Baal, listening to Israel's prophets as well as to foreign prophets. "Have you found me, O my enemy?" (21:20) are words of both guilt and awe. Elijah's words about Naboth's vineyard pricked Ahab's heart. He knew prophets spoke for God.

A true prophet was one whose words rang true, whose predictions came to pass. Elijah said, "The dogs shall eat

NOTES, REFLECTIONS, AND QUESTIONS

The Phoenician culture emerged along the eastern coast of the Mediterranean Sea during the twelfth and eleventh centuries B.C. The Phoenicians were sea traders, famous for an expensive purple dye extracted from sea mollusks and for the development of alphabetic script. Phoenicia, with its principal cities Tyre and Sidon, was largely autonomous, not controlled by outside political forces, except for occasionally paying tribute to Assyria in the ninth century B.C. Phoenician artisans helped build Solomon's Temple.

Jezebel" (21:23). His words were fulfilled when Jehu's horses crushed her body and the dogs devoured her (2 Kings 9:30-37). The prophet Micaiah, alone and in opposition to four hundred court prophets, decreed disaster in battle for King Ahab (1 Kings 22:13-28). The court prophets ridiculed Micaiah and one slapped him, but the kings expected Micaiah to speak God's truth. When an arrow pierced a space in Ahab's armor, the prophet's words came true (22:34-35). Deuteronomy asks, " 'How can we recognize a word that the LORD has not spoken?' If a prophet speaks in the name of the LORD but the thing does not take place or prove true, it is a word that the LORD has not spoken" (Deuteronomy 18:21-22).

Elisha

Elijah's mantle, with a double share of his spirit, was passed to Elisha (2 Kings 2:9-14). Notice two attributes apparent in the prophet Elisha—his compassion for the poor and his ministry to foreigners. Elisha, often in the company of a group of prophets, learned that a widow of a prophet was destitute. Creditors were coming to take her two children into slavery. God, through Elisha, wondrously provided enough oil so she could pay her debts (4:1-7). Concern and care for the weak was basic to Torah (Deuteronomy 24:12-15, 17-21).

Elisha healed an Aramean commander, Naaman, who had leprosy. Naaman tried to pay him, but Elisha refused to accept money—a fact that characterized the great prophets of Israel. They could not be bought or bribed. They were determined to act without shadow of compromise (2 Kings 5).

Called to Be Messengers

So what shall we say about the prophets? They believed they were called of God to be messengers at any risk to themselves. They were people of unswerving devotion to God as they remembered ancestral promises and Mosaic principles. By word and symbolic action they challenged kings to total allegiance to God. Their words rang true, their warnings fulfilled. With unspeakable courage, they condemned idolatry, knowing it would cloud collective memory and soften the nation's sense of justice. Idolatry would lead to immorality. Fiercely the prophets pleaded for a return to God lest the monarchy fail, lest the God who had saved them be forced to punish them.

The prophets held in their memories God's actions in the past—freedom from slavery, providential care each day in the wilderness, clear laws for harmonious community, and a land of promise where each family would live on its inheritance with justice and compassion. Then they read the signs of their times and courageously portrayed the truth for others in every conceivable way. Unfortunately, most people either refused to see and hear or were unwilling to pay the price of obedience.

NOTES, REFLECTIONS, AND QUESTIONS

MARKS OF OBEDIENT COMMUNITY

Loyalty to the one God characterizes obedient community. And loyalty is kept intact through our collective memory. The prophets knew that Israel must belong totally to God or it was lost. So, like the prophets, we must understand idolatry, that tendency we have to stray to other loyalties. We know that false gods will destroy us.

The prophets read the signs of the times. How can they help us read the signs of our times?

What will help us confront the idolatry we excuse or explain away?

What are warning signs that a church is losing or has lost biblical memory that gives it identity and purpose?

What response can the faith community make to such signs?

Obedience to God's teaching is at the heart of loyalty to God. Yet in modern society we often want to avoid both the word *obey* and the idea of *obedience*. Why?

How is your faith community giving its members the collective biblical memory that defines it?

IF YOU WANT TO KNOW MORE

We have spotlighted dramatic episodes in First and Second Kings. Read about the nameless prophet (1 Kings 13).

NOTES, REFLECTIONS, AND QUESTIONS

The obeying community chooses loyalty to God as its first commitment.

The study manual uses the familiar designations B.C. and A.D. Occasionally the video presenters use the scholarly designations B.C.E. (Before the Common Era) and C.E. (Common Era). Think of the term *Before the Common Era* as that time in history when our religious ancestor, Judaism, existed but Christianity had not yet come into being. The *Common Era*, then, is that time in history when Judaism and Christianity began to share history together. The term *common* here means "shared."

FAMINE

> "The time is surely coming, says the Lord GOD,
> when I will send a famine on the land;
> not a famine of bread, or a thirst for water,
> but of hearing the words of the LORD."
>
> —Amos 8:11

3 Starved for the Words of the Lord

OUR HUMAN CONDITION

We seek help but get silence. We reach out but experience absence. Where is the assurance we took for granted, the attention we were used to? What can fill this emptiness?

ASSIGNMENT

First, skim Amos, getting a feel for the overall message. Then read carefully, deliberately. Shout the powerful preachments aloud, with indignation, especially 4:1-8; 5:8-15; 5:21-24; and Chapter 8. Watch for vivid prophetic allusions to other events or practices in Scripture. Some political context for Amos is given in 2 Kings 14:23-29.

Day 1 Amos 1–9
Day 2 Amos 1–2 (judgment on Israel's neighbors, Judah, and Israel)
Day 3 Amos 3–6 (judgment on Judah and Israel, the day of the Lord)
Day 4 Amos 7 (visions of judgment, Amaziah); 2 Kings 14:23-29 (Jeroboam II)
Day 5 Amos 8–9 (no escape from judgment, prophecies of restoration)
Day 6 Read and respond to "The Word of the Lord" and "Marks of Obedient Community."
Day 7 Rest

PRAYER

Pray daily before study:

"As a deer longs for a stream of cool water,
so I long for you, O God.
I thirst for you, the living God" (Psalm 42:1-2, TEV).

Prayer concerns for this week:

FAMINE

Day 1 Amos 1–9

Day 2 Amos 1–2 (judgment on Israel's neighbors, Judah, and Israel)

Day 3 Amos 3–6 (judgment on Judah and Israel, the day of the Lord)

Day 4 Amos 7 (visions of judgment, Amaziah); 2 Kings 14:23-29 (Jeroboam II)

Day 5 Amos 8–9 (no escape from judgment, prophecies of restoration)

Day 6 "The Word of the Lord" and "Marks of Obedient Community"

THE WORD OF THE LORD

Tekoa was a small Judean village six miles south of Bethlehem. The town sat on a ridge that separated the rocky pastures and marginal cropland on the north from the barren Negeb wilderness on the south. The terrain was harsh, breeding independent, hard-working people like Amos.

Amos was a shepherd, but he also tended an inferior kind of fig tree called a sycamore that required a careful prick of the emerging fruit to allow it to ripen clean and insect free, making it edible. Not like the lush figs from the Jezreel Valley, this fig was eaten by the poor and fed to animals.

This shepherd-farmer did not belong to a school of prophets, was not linked to a sanctuary, was never paid for prophecy. Without credentials, he proclaimed, "I am no prophet, nor a prophet's son" (Amos 7:14). Yet God said to him, "Go, prophesy to my people Israel" (7:15).

Still, Amos was no untutored rustic. He was the first of the great literary prophets who not only preached with power but also wrote with dramatic clarity. Amos chose words carefully. His poetic allusions rivet the mind. His Hebrew parallelisms soar and sing. His laments sound like the mournful wail of the funeral dirge. Most of the words are his, perhaps set down by his own hand.

Go to Bethel

Amos carried the stigma of a southerner going north, a Judean intruding into Israel's affairs. He was obligated to announce destruction and death—not a happy task. But worse, he had to preach doom and gloom when most Israelites were basking in success and believing God was blessing them richly.

Now, if Amos were to travel into the Northern Kingdom to deliver one searing sermon, where would he go? To Bethel, of course, the king's shrine, the house of the priest, the center of idolatry. So Amos walked six miles to Bethlehem, another six to Jerusalem, then up the trader's trail, crossing the Judah-Israel border, eleven more miles to Bethel.

Bethel was steeped in tradition. Abraham pitched his tents there (Genesis 12:8; 13:3). Jacob dreamed of God, set up a sacred pillar of rock, and named it Bethel, "house of God" (28:10-22). Samuel made annual pilgrimage to its sanctuary (1 Samuel 7:16), and in the days of Elisha a school of prophets lived there (2 Kings 2:3).

When the kingdom divided (922 B.C.), Jeroboam son of Nebat thought it necessary to have the people of the north worship at national shrines, Bethel and Dan, rather than go to the Temple in Jerusalem (1 Kings 12:25-30). No sooner had Jeroboam designated Bethel a royal sanctuary than he added a golden calf, full of fertility cult meanings. The mixing of Egyptian, Canaanite, and Hebrew religious concepts watered down Torah, violated the laws of Sinai, and spawned idolatry

NOTES, REFLECTIONS, AND QUESTIONS

Generally a shrine is any place where sacred objects are kept, but gradually the term came to indicate any site of worship. In ancient Israel non-Hebrew shrines housed idols, altars, or other cult objects. Most of them were high, open-air sites called "high places." Many Hebrew shrines were sacred sites associated with the patriarchs. They usually had a resident priest or prophet. The prophet Samuel tended the shrine at Shiloh and later at Ramah. Kings of Israel established shrines close to their capitals to assure easy contact with the priest or prophet and therefore with God. The principal Hebrew shrines during the time of Amos were Bethel in the north, associated with the king of Israel, and the Jerusalem Temple in the south, the ultimate shrine, always associated with the kings of Judah, descendants of David.

so feared and hated by the prophets. Now, centuries later, as Amos would show, that idolatry led to injustice and immorality (Amos 5:4-7).

Speaking for God

Amos lived during the reign of two great kings, Uzziah of Judah (783–742 B.C.) and Jeroboam II of Israel (786–746 B.C.). Under these long-tenured monarchs, except for occasional border disputes, the period was tranquil and both tiny nations flowered.

Foreign powers were struggling with internal problems or fighting with enemies on other fronts. Egypt, after earlier military expansion, had slipped back into its own Nile Valley. Syria, with its capital Damascus still flourishing, nevertheless watched neighboring nations nip at its outlying territories. The Assyrian Empire floundered under weak kings. So with the superpowers Egypt and Assyria asleep and Syria threatened, Israel saw a window of opportunity and pushed its boundaries toward the north, east, and south. Trade flourished because all the main trade routes from Mesopotamia to Egypt passed through Israel's toll stations. People thought themselves quite religious, honoring Hebrew festivals, presenting gifts to Canaanite gods, giving tithes, offering prayers, and celebrating their blessings.

If Jeroboam II had run for office in mid-eighth century B.C., his slogan would have been "Peace and Prosperity." Israel basked in a golden moment. Pride and plenty ruled the land. Cities sparkled with elegance. The rich enjoyed both winter and summer homes, decorating their bedsteads with inlaid ivory, adorning their couches with damask pillows. They entertained one another with sumptuous feasts. Wine was not only sipped at meals but guzzled at orgies. The men slipped money under the table. The women grew greedy and demanding.

Into this arena strode the southern shepherd. In front of the priest Amaziah, a school of prophets, and an assortment of business and civic leaders, Amos proclaimed God's coming judgment. He pointed first to Syria, Israel's hated neighbor, announcing that the Judge of all nations would destroy the brutal king Hazael and his son Ben-hadad (Amos 1:3-5). Damascus, its capital, would be consumed by fire because of its evil deeds. "Good news," thought the Israelites.

Next came Gaza, the seacoast home of ancient enemies, the Philistines (1:6-8). Fire would fall upon cities named for their gods, Ashdod and Ashkelon. Amos spoke of Tyre, the upper coastal region, often friendly, sometimes politically allied, occasionally intermarried (1:9-10). But, said Amos, Tyre forgot friendship. Fire on them. The cheers subsided. One by one, as Amos described them, the neighbors seemed less wicked. When he prophesied against Edom, Ammon, and

NOTES, REFLECTIONS, AND QUESTIONS

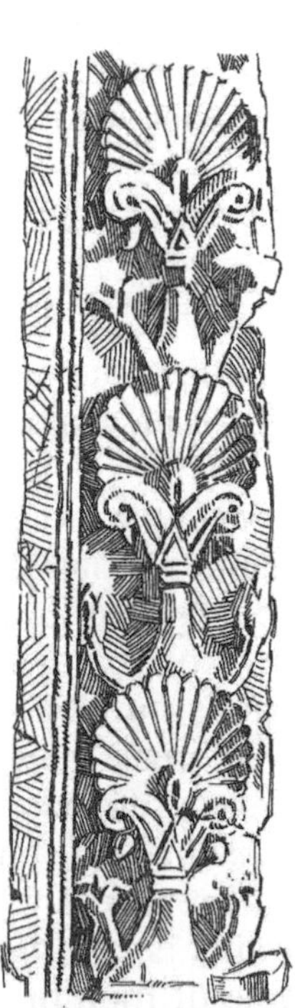

From the ninth or eighth century B.C., ivory carvings like this one with spread palm leaves, from King Ahab's "ivory house" (1 Kings 22:39) in Samaria, were used to ornament walls and furniture.

NOTES, REFLECTIONS, AND QUESTIONS

Moab—Semitic people, almost kinfolk—on the eastern side of the Jordan, the listeners became sober (1:11–2:3).

Now the sermon began to hit home. Amos denounced his own homeland, Judah, separate but still Hebrew (2:4-5). He recalled God's saving actions, going back to Moses and Egypt, to Joshua and victory over the Amorites. Judah's history was Israel's history too. Amos said Judah had rejected the law of the Lord (2:4). But, thought the people, Jerusalem has sacrifices in the Temple. Judah had been led astray by lies (2:4). But, thought the listeners, they study the law of Moses.

Now Amos did what he came to do. In God's name he took aim at Israel. Their prosperity was built on the backs of the poor. You "sell the righteous for silver, / and the needy for a pair of sandals" (2:6). You "trample the head of the poor into the dust of the earth" (2:7). How? With inequities. You "take a bribe" so the poor do not receive justice. In fact, you shove them aside at the court (the gate of the city) (5:12). The law of Moses said, "Cursed be anyone who deprives the alien, the orphan, and the widow of justice" (Deuteronomy 27:19).

How do you make the quantity of food less and the cost of food more? You sell grain in "cheat baskets," slightly smaller than regular two-thirds-bushel size. You shave your balances when you sell, weight them when you buy. You put your thumb on the scales. You exchange money with a surcharge. You put dust and chaff sweepings in with the wheat (Amos 8:5-6).

Sometimes religious people give food baskets to the poor but create social structures that oppress them. What are some economic devices that steal from the poor?

Under covenant law, the disabled were to be given special consideration. But, said Amos, you "push the afflicted out of the way" (2:7).

Your sexual sins defy the laws of God. A man and his son sleep with the same woman. Defilement. You take a poor man's cloak in pledge, lay it down beside an altar, and sleep with a prostitute. Abomination.

You teach serious-minded young people—youth you might have nurtured—to break their holy vows. You who are prophets and priests, fathers and mothers, you should be teaching the words of God; but you are neglecting your task. You silence your preachers who might bring you back to God (2:11-12). A famine is coming, said Amos,

> "not a famine of food or a thirst for water,
> but a famine of hearing the words of the LORD"
> (8:11, NIV).
>
> "In that day the . . . young women and the young men
> shall faint for thirst. . . .
> they shall fall, and never rise again" (8:13-14).

NOTES, REFLECTIONS, AND QUESTIONS

In what ways do you perceive young people starving for God's Word?

What could the faith community do to feed them?

Greed controls your lives, claims Amos. You can hardly wait for sabbath to end so you can begin making money again. You are eager for religious festivals to finish so you can get back to work (8:5). You have turned a blessing into a curse and a curse into a blessing. Your rich people lavish comforts on themselves while the homeless go hungry in the streets.

When you go to worship, your heart is not in it. You go to Bethel with guilt on your hands and greed in your hearts. You love to make offerings, give tithes, and sing songs, but you are not in love with the God of Sinai (4:4-5). When God drops the plumb line alongside you—your attitudes and actions—you will be shown up as crooked (7:7-8). Nothing is so unforgiving as a plumb line; it reveals every distortion.

Because worship had become hypocrisy, because the sacrifices at the altar were separated from the sanctity of justice and compassion, God cried out through Amos:

> "I hate, I despise your festivals,
> and I take no delight in your solemn assemblies. . . .
> Take away from me the noise of your songs. . . .
> But let justice roll down like waters,
> and righteousness like an ever-flowing stream"
> (5:21-24).

When does our worship become empty ritual rather than obedience to God?

The saddest part for God was that Israel was so special. God judges all the nations, but Israel was God's pride and joy. Nevertheless, Amos must prophesy against Israel. Notice that Amos uses *Samaria* (the capital), *Carmel* (the mountain), *Bethel* (the shrine), and *Jacob* (the patriarch) all as poetic and personified references to Israel.

The Day of the Lord

Just as a trumpet calls a city to emergency, so the prophet announced God's forthcoming actions (Amos 3:6-8). Because the people had been given special privileges (the Law, the covenant, the salvation history), they would be given severe punishment for their unfaithfulness. They boasted about "the day of the Lord" when they thought God would bring restoration of David's kingdom, peace, and victory for Israel. Amos turned understanding of the expression "the day of the Lord" upside down.

"Alas for you who desire the day of the LORD!
Why do you want the day of the LORD?
It is darkness, not light" (5:18).

Amos publishes the obituary in advance, relentlessly repeating the message. Israel is drawing inexorably to its end. How soon will it come? Like summer fruit, it is dead ripe (8:1-3). The Hebrew uses a fearful pun; *qayits* (fresh fruit) sounds like *qets* (end). The end of Israel is near.

Can they repent? Will God allow a glimmer of grace? Perhaps. Amos, most scathing of the prophets, leaves the door open just a crack. "Seek the LORD and live" is the faint cry (5:6). But they must turn away from "Bethel," house of God, for it is really "Beth-aven," house of nothing, or house of idolatry (5:5).

But *will* Israel repent? No. They are apostate, unfaithful. So the God "who made the Pleiades and Orion," who recreates each day afresh, who draws from the ocean to give us rain and thus sustains life, will make "destruction flash out against the strong" (5:8-9). Why? Moses had given the answer: "Because you did not obey the LORD your God, by observing the commandments and the decrees that he commanded you" (Deuteronomy 28:45).

God holds out hope only after the ordeal. The prophets never see complete and final disaster. Even Amos has a word of restoration. After the punishment will come the healing.

"I will raise up
the booth of David that is fallen,
and repair its breaches" (Amos 9:11).

The land, after the rebellion, will bear so bountifully again that the reaping will not be finished when it is time to plow (9:13). God will not utterly forsake God's people.

Notice three aspects of God's response to Israel's idolatry and injustice.

- *God's thoughts*. God looks over the situation and is offended. God smells the stench of injustice, robbery, disenfranchisement, poverty, and enslavement.
- *God's instruments*. God does not act directly. Instead, God uses agents to punish. The soil turns against the people (8:8); the earth shakes (9:1, 9); the locusts devour (4:9). Enemy nations destroy. Assyria will be God's punishing rod against a transgressing Israel (7:9, 11).
- *God cannot deny reality*. Human deceit destroys community. Sin breaks down the network of society.

MARKS OF OBEDIENT COMMUNITY

We know we are nourished by the words of the Lord. They are our bread and milk. Without the word, our community starves. We lose our memory, our identity, our guide, our hope.

NOTES, REFLECTIONS, AND QUESTIONS

The faithful community lives on the words of the Lord, lives in the word of the Lord, and lives by the word of the Lord.

Surely there is "a famine on the land" today. How would you describe it?

Some say there is a famine "of hearing the words of the LORD" in the church. How do you evaluate that?

Amos warned that the faithlessness of the people would result in God's withdrawing his word from them. A judgment of famine. God could be reached only through repentance.

What faithlessness in us and in our community of faith would today bring Amos's warning that God would have nothing more to say to us?

How would you describe the eagerness and willingness of your congregation to hear the words of the Lord, even the words you don't like?

What is blocking your hearing God's word?

What can we do to teach the Scriptures within our rural community, town, or city so children, youth, and adults will know the "words of the LORD"?

IF YOU WANT TO KNOW MORE

In a Bible dictionary, look up Jeroboam I son of Nebat and Jeroboam II son of Joash. Compare their policies.

The prophets preached against the backdrop of history and geography, kings and nations. As you come across names of kings, countries, and cities, read about them in a Bible dictionary or Bible atlas. For example, Hazael, Ben-hadad, Aram, and Damascus.

NOTES, REFLECTIONS, AND QUESTIONS

This jasper seal, with the finely-cut figure of a lion, was found at Megiddo and dates from about 775 B.C. Above the lion is inscribed the name of the owner, "to Shema," and below the lion, his title, "servant of Jeroboam"—"Belonging to Shema, servant of Jeroboam," probably Jeroboam II, king of Israel from 786–746 B.C.

REDEEMING LOVE

"I will take you for my wife forever; I will take you for my wife in righteousness and in justice, in steadfast love, and in mercy. I will take you for my wife in faithfulness; and you shall know the LORD."

—Hosea 2:19-20

4 God's Faithfulness

OUR HUMAN CONDITION

We desire harmony, order, relationship, but we are divided in our loyalties. Cover all bases. Make the necessary compromises. Seek the right connections. We are drawn to pursuits that promise power, success, control.

ASSIGNMENT

Don't try to reconcile Hosea 1 and 3. They are different accounts of Hosea's marriage problems (and of Israel's infidelity).

Hosea was a long-time prophet active during the reigns of various kings. As you read 2 Kings 15, identify one or two acts of each king.

Like other prophets, Hosea can be scathing. Yet Hosea's pathos, his compassion, can be as tender as a mother's kiss, as gentle as a lover's touch. God's searching, reaching love is never more poignant in the prophets than in Hosea 2:18-23; 11:1-4, 8-11; and 14:4-9.

Day 1 Hosea 1–3 (Hosea's marriage to Gomer, faithless Israel)

Day 2 Hosea 4–6 (God accuses Israel, coming judgment on Israel and Judah)

Day 3 Hosea 7–9 (futile reliance on other nations, chastisement of Israel)

Day 4 Hosea 10–11 (Israel's sin and captivity, God's compassion); 2 Kings 15:1-31 (Uzziah king of Judah, various kings of Israel)

Day 5 Hosea 12–14 (God's compassion, call for repentance, assurance of forgiveness)

Day 6 Read and respond to "The Word of the Lord" and "Marks of Obedient Community."

Day 7 Rest

PRAYER

Pray daily before study:

"LORD, I know you will never stop
being merciful to me.
Your love and loyalty will
always keep me safe" (Psalm 40:11, TEV).

Prayer concerns for this week:

REDEEMING LOVE

Day 1 Hosea 1–3 (Hosea's marriage to Gomer, faithless Israel)

Day 2 Hosea 4–6 (God accuses Israel, coming judgment on Israel and Judah)

Day 3 Hosea 7–9 (futile reliance on other nations, chastisement of Israel)

Day 4 Hosea 10–11 (Israel's sin and captivity, God's compassion); 2 Kings 15:1-31 (Uzziah king of Judah, various kings of Israel)

Day 5 Hosea 12–14 (God's compassion, call for repentance, assurance of forgiveness)

Day 6 "The Word of the Lord" and "Marks of Obedient Community"

THE WORD OF THE LORD

Hosea's book is filled with difficulties. Certain Hebrew words are obscure. Poetic allusions have distant meanings. Ancient editors have reworked the text. The book collects Hosea's oracles, sermons, laments, symbolic actions, poems, and explanations. All are loosely bound together without strict chronology or continuity.

Hosea was a contemporary of Amos. But he did not carry Amos's stigma of coming to the north from the south. Hosea spoke to his own beloved people, Israel. Nor did he confine his work to one trumpet blast at Bethel. Hosea prophesied for more than twenty years. Like Amos, he preached during the prosperity and peace of Jeroboam II but continued into the period of confusion, anarchy, and destruction afterward. Unlike Amos, who was sent packing after his pronouncements, Hosea not only announced desolation; he also watched as it transpired.

He continued to prophesy as Jeroboam's son Zechariah (not the prophet) was killed by Shallum after a six-month reign. Within one month, Shallum was killed by Menahem, who ruled for seven years fighting Assyria. His son Pekahiah was murdered by one of his officers, Pekah, who ruled five years. Hosea preached while Israel was falling apart.

Remember the prophets have two overarching spiritual enemies—injustice and idolatry. Amos focused more on social injustice, the breakdown of human relationships. Hosea pointed more to idolatry, the failure to love God. The two issues, love of neighbor and love of God, are opposite sides of the same coin (Hosea 4:1-2).

A god is something or someone we serve, to which or whom we give our time and energy. Service to false gods leads to corruption of life. Service to God leads to harmony with life.

Unfaithful

The descriptions of Hosea's wife, Gomer, are confusing. Hosea 1 is written as biography; Hosea 3, as autobiography. Was Gomer a prostitute before Hosea married her, or simply a woman with a tendency to be unfaithful (1:2)? Did she become a woman of the streets or a prostitute at the shrine of the baals? Did God's love for Israel induce Hosea to buy his wife back, or did Hosea's unrequited love for her teach him about God's unbounded mercy? No matter. In this experience of marital infidelity, Hosea felt the broken heart of God over God's unfaithful people. In the cost of bringing Gomer home, Hosea understood that God would never abandon Israel, no matter the price.

Here, early in the prophets, the marriage between a man and a woman is compared to the love relationship between God and God's people. In fact, the allegory in Hosea 2 is so interwoven that often we cannot tell if we are dealing with Hosea and Gomer or with God and Israel.

NOTES, REFLECTIONS, AND QUESTIONS

Secular historical dates for rulers and prophets often do not match dates or time periods given in the Bible. Scripture sometimes rounds off numbers. Sometimes numbers are symbolic rather than actual years. In some cases, different ancient manuscripts have different numbers in a passage. In the case of the kings of Israel and Judah, the problem of difference in dating is complicated because we cannot tell when the biblical writers are counting co-regencies or when they are counting the time a king was in power before actually being made king.

Today the prophet's picturing his wife's unfaithfulness as a symbol of Israel's unfaithfulness might be interpreted as debasing womanhood. We would hesitate to use such an analogy. Still the image of a broken marriage drives home to us the prophetic message of the brokenness between God and Israel. The point of it all—Israel, men and women, had gone awhoring.

Hosea gave his children frightening symbolic names. The first son was called Jezreel (1:4). Just as Jehu, at Jezreel, had assassinated the sons of Ahab, ending the house of Omri, so the descendants of Jeroboam would be assassinated, ending the house of Jehu. The event came to pass and is recorded in 2 Kings 15:8-12. Jezreel also meant that "the bow," the military might of Israel, would be broken in that rich valley, which was a battleground for the armies of history. Tiglath-pileser III finally broke Israel's bow in the Valley of Jezreel in 732 B.C.

Lo-ruhamah, "Not pitied," the daughter's name, was even worse. God would not take pity on Israel. Assyria would capture most of its territory in 732 B.C. Then, without pity, Assyria would lay siege to Samaria, the capital, razing it in 722/21 B.C.

The third child, a son, was given the saddest name of all, Lo-ammi, "Not my people." Once Israel had been God's people, rescued from slavery in Egypt, instructed in the wilderness. Now Assyria would slaughter some and scatter the rest into exile so there would scarcely be a people at all.

Look carefully at Hosea 2. Gomer ran to other lovers, probably as a cult prostitute at Bethel or Gilgal or Dan. Hosea's heart was broken. She was his beloved, the mother of his children. He asked two of the children, now called "My People" and "Pitied," to plead with their mother to come home (2:1-2), but to no avail. Would Israel ever repent? Not until the nation was punished, for her feeble efforts to change were always like the early morning dew, quick to disappear (6:4).

Read Chapter 2 as if Hosea were talking about Gomer; then read it again as if God were talking about Israel. Especially if Gomer were a cult prostitute receiving the wool and the flax, the grain and the wine offered to the baals, the two images are so intertwined they almost merge. In Hosea's mind, the two experiences blend into one reality of betrayal (2:13).

What Were the Baals?

The baals were nature gods. Baal was god of the storm, the wind and the rain. In a land desperate for rain as the source of life, where the slightest failure meant drought and famine, the people were drawn to Baal worship.

In Canaanite religion, Mot, god of death, not only controlled normal human mortality, but also caused summer drought and unexpected disasters. The god of life-giving forces (Baal) was in constant conflict with death powers (Mot). Baal, often depicted as a bull, died each year; but

NOTES, REFLECTIONS, AND QUESTIONS

before dying, he mounted a cow to insure fertility. Baal also came back to life each spring. The bull image was used in Egypt and Assyria, as well as in Canaan, always as a symbol of life-giving fertility for crops, flocks, and families. The baals promised power, prowess, ambition, and success to their devotees.

Asherah, a female goddess, was imported from the coast. She was particularly popular in Tyre and Sidon and was the deity worshiped by Queen Jezebel. (Remember in Elijah's battle on Mount Carmel, he dealt with 450 prophets of Baal and 400 prophets of Asherah.) Asherah's symbols were trees, pillars, poles, and wooden images of a female figure with large breasts. In popular religion she was sometimes thought of as a mother figure, where all nature found nourishment, and other times as consort of Baal or even mistress of the God of the Hebrews.

Worship consisted of going to the "high places," a pillar or tree on a hilltop, and trying to placate these fertility gods and goddesses. Worship included offerings of agricultural produce—wool, flax, olive oil, wine, grain, bread, and water (Hosea 2:5, 9). Sometimes, in desperate appeals, firstborn children were offered. The prophets were aghast, but occasionally even an Israelite king would cause his firstborn to "pass through fire," a euphemism for child sacrifice.

Why Worship the Baals?

Why were people drawn to these fertility gods? Life was so precarious, so fragile in Canaan. Rainfall was marginal and uncertain. Grasshoppers, locusts, and windstorms could destroy a crop. Families could not feed themselves or maintain their little flocks of sheep and goats.

Suppose you had wandered forty years in the Sinai as nomads. You didn't know how to farm, particularly in the hilly land of Canaan. You now lived in villages, sometimes as neighbors to established farm families who knew when the early rains might come. They lived in rhythm with nature, knowing the seasons, harvesting the crops, taking offerings to the high places. Their gods were nature gods of fertility, so that union between Baal, the lord of life, and Asherah, the mother of fertility, meant winter would change into spring, cows would calve, and crops would be plentiful.

If you thought it might help your farm feed your babies, and if you could still offer sacrifices to the God of Abraham, wouldn't you go to the high places of Canaan? When people had sexual intercourse with the sacred prostitutes beside the bull of Baal and the pillar of Asherah, they reenacted the drama of the gods, which, they believed, released power to guarantee fertility. In a nonscientific age, a farmer dared not ignore Baal rites that could have an impact on his future. In a nearly powerless predicament, how could people gain some semblance of control?

NOTES, REFLECTIONS, AND QUESTIONS

This bronze bull, roughly five inches high, from about 1200 B.C. was found at an open-air cult site between Dothan and Tirzah and may be a representation of Baal.

What Was the Result?

Of course the prophets hated the worship of false gods, pillars, and images. Of course Hosea was offended by the sexual interchange that violated the strict laws of Moses on marriage and family. But still more tragic, Baal worship gave devotees a sense that "God is with us." The establishment used Baal worship as a way of maintaining the status quo. The nobility and priests reinforced their own power and influence without divine condemnation—in fact, with support from the gods. Not only would they lose sight of God's rule—the way the world really runs—but they would try to run the world another way, their way, the way of elbowing a neighbor and oppressing the weak. Queen Jezebel, whose Asherah prophets ate at her table, had the gods at her command to do as she pleased. Thus the prophets saw idolatry as the root of greed and community destruction. The priests became murderers, drunkards, prostitutes (Hosea 4:9-12). The merchants cheated (12:7), and the kings assassinated to gain power. God did not stand in their path; rather the gods, properly placated, stood ready to help them achieve their selfish purposes.

The net result was not the harmony and fertility the people hoped for. The people were running away from the God of order and running toward the ways of confusion. The prophets knew that idolatry led to immorality. Immorality shattered community. The people, by worshiping false gods, would destroy themselves by "swearing, lying, and murder, / and stealing and adultery" (4:2). Even the soil (which they had tried to make fertile) turned unproductive: "The land mourns, / and all who live in it languish" (4:3).

The Kings

The priests encouraged the kings and other officials to flirt with foreign alliances. A pro-Assyrian party and a pro-Egyptian party believed Assyria or Egypt could help them (Hosea 5:13; 8:9; 12:1). When Assyria was weak, Israel fought against Aram (Syria), centered in Damascus. Later, in 734–733, Israel and Syria joined forces to build a coalition against Judah and were encouraged by Egypt. When Assyria attacked Damascus in force, some officials wanted to deal quickly with Assyria, and some wanted Egypt or Judah to come to their aid. The foreign policy was a quicksand of indecision. Gone was Israel's integrity. Israel, sometimes referred to as Ephraim, did not stand steadfast, trusting in God (7:11).

Did you notice that Hosea did not name the kings of Israel he served after Jeroboam II died (1:1)? He named the kings of Judah for the next several years. Why? Four of the five kings of Israel were assassinated in those years. They usurped the throne by violence. No Samuel came to anoint a king like David. No Nathan came to anoint a king like Solomon. God was not even consulted.

NOTES, REFLECTIONS, AND QUESTIONS

"They made kings, but not through me;
  they set up princes, but without my knowledge.
With their silver and gold they made idols
  for their own destruction.
Your calf is rejected, O Samaria.
  My anger burns against them" (8:4-5).

NOTES, REFLECTIONS, AND QUESTIONS

Punishment

Notice how God relates the punishment to the crime. "You have played the whore"; therefore everything is polluted, adulterated (Hosea 9:1). The security of the home has been violated. The result is a miscarrying womb, dry breasts; the children of harlotry will be aborted (9:14). You wanted to wander like a wild ass (8:9). So be it. You "shall become wanderers among the nations," a hopelessly scattered people (9:17).

Cause and effect—that's how Hosea saw it. The more Israel, the vineyard of God, flourished, the greater became the idolatry (10:1). You made the calf to worship; you shall carry the calf (as exiles) to Assyria (10:5-6). You didn't let God choose your kings; the kings will float away like a chip on the water (10:7). You plow wickedness; you reap injustice (10:13). Gomer broke the bonds of marriage; she ended up in the chains of slavery. You sow the wind, and you reap the whirlwind (8:7).

Redemption

Would God forsake Israel? No, that would be impossible. Forsaking Israel would violate the steadfast love of God. Could Hosea abandon Gomer? No, he bought her back for fifteen shekels of silver, a homer of barley, and a measure of wine (Hosea 3:2), a highly symbolic figure, equivalent in money and produce to the thirty shekels prescribed by the Law as the full and proper value of a person given as a vow to God (Leviticus 27:4). For a symbol of a bedraggled Israel, Hosea paid top price to show how much he valued her. The cost of redemptive love is high.

Hosea, with a depth of pathos as yet unheard in Scripture, and with his heart breaking, understood God as a parent who weeps. The Lord says,

"When Israel was a child, I loved him,
  and out of Egypt I called my son.
The more I called them,
  the more they went from me. . . .
Yet it was I who taught Ephraim to walk,
  I took them up in my arms. . . .
I was to them like those
  who lift infants to their cheeks" (Hosea 11:1-4).

Now God pours forth his unending redemptive love:

"How can I give you up, Ephraim?
  How can I hand you over, O Israel?" (11:8).

God must somehow redeem Israel, even if the saving act

comes after punishment and tragedy. God wants to reach out again, just as in Egypt, and bring Israel "home." That day will come, just as Gomer was reunited with Hosea.

"They shall again live beneath my shadow,
they shall flourish as a garden" (14:7).

Who *really* provides the rain; who *really* gives fertility to the fields; who *really* will protect Israel from their enemies? "It is I [says the Lord] who answer and look after you" (14:8).

MARKS OF OBEDIENT COMMUNITY

We know we belong to God. We know God loves us, provides for us, comforts us like a parent loves a child, like a lover loves a mate. We know there are "baals" that would draw us into infidelity; but today they are not idols of wood or stone, so they are hard to spot. Today's false gods are subtle, but we know we are tempted by them. Today we even find it hard to grasp the concept of idolatry because our false gods look so different and have different names.

What becomes idolatry for the community of faith today?

What helps us identify the "baals"?

How might we be bringing our gods into our worship of God, deceiving ourselves about what we are doing?

How can we discard our idolatrous loyalties?

What sources of strength help us resist idolatry and focus on righteousness?

IF YOU WANT TO KNOW MORE

Look up Jezreel in a Bible dictionary and locate Jezreel and the Valley of Jezreel on a map.

The image of God as husband or parent is found in several places in the prophets. Read some examples: Isaiah 49:14-16; 54:8; Jeremiah 2:2; 31:20; Ezekiel 16:8-14.

NOTES, REFLECTIONS, AND QUESTIONS

Obedience in community declares the winsome, forgiving, redeeming love of God calling people back to God.

OBEY

"He has told you, O mortal, what is good;
and what does the LORD require of you
but to do justice, and to love kindness,
and to walk humbly with your God?"

—Micah 6:8

5 God's Requirement

OUR HUMAN CONDITION

When confronted with our injustice in our daily dealings, we defend it or explain it away by comparing it to other injustices. We offer extravagant promises to change our ways and rely on our belief that our actions will be forgiven, not punished.

ASSIGNMENT

As you read, be aware of the changing political landscape and the economic and social realities that caused the prophets to speak out.

One note of explanation: Usually the prophet's time frame is established by naming *Judah*'s king (Davidic) even if *Israel* (Northern Kingdom) is discussed.

In Micah, listen for echoes of Mount Sinai and Torah.

Day 1 Northern kings: 2 Kings 14:23-29 (Jeroboam II); 15:8-12 (Zechariah); 15:13-16 (Shallum); 15:17-22 (Menahem); 15:23-26 (Pekahiah); 15:27-31 (Pekah); 17; 18:9-12 (Hoshea)

Day 2 Southern kings: 2 Kings 15:1-7; 2 Chronicles 26 (Azariah/Uzziah); 2 Kings 15:32-38; 2 Chronicles 27 (Jotham); 2 Kings 16; 2 Chronicles 28 (Ahaz)

Day 3 2 Kings 18–20; 2 Chronicles 29–32 (Hezekiah)

Day 4 Micah 1–3 (judgment on Samaria and Judah, social evils and wicked leaders denounced)

Day 5 Micah 4–7 (peace and security through obedience, God challenges Israel)

Day 6 Read and respond to "The Word of the Lord" and "Marks of Obedient Community."

Day 7 Rest

PRAYER

Pray daily before study:

"The LORD judges the peoples;
judge me, O LORD, according to my righteousness
and according to the integrity that is in me"
(Psalm 7:8).

Prayer concerns for this week:

OBEY

Day 1 Northern kings: 2 Kings 14:23-29 (Jeroboam II); 15:8-12 (Zechariah); 15:13-16 (Shallum); 15:17-22 (Menahem); 15:23-26 (Pekahiah); 15:27-31 (Pekah); 17; 18:9-12 (Hoshea)

Day 2 Southern kings: 2 Kings 15:1-7; 2 Chronicles 26 (Azariah/Uzziah); 2 Kings 15:32-38; 2 Chronicles 27 (Jotham); 2 Kings 16; 2 Chronicles 28 (Ahaz)

Day 3 2 Kings 18–20; 2 Chronicles 29–32 (Hezekiah)

Day 4 Micah 1–3 (judgment on Samaria and Judah, social evils and wicked leaders denounced)

Day 5 Micah 4–7 (peace and security through obedience, God challenges Israel)

Day 6 "The Word of the Lord" and "Marks of Obedient Community"

THE WORD OF THE LORD

Three events happened almost simultaneously—the death of Jeroboam II in Israel (746 B.C.); the death of Uzziah in Judah (742 B.C.); and the rise of the great soldier Tilglath-pileser III, nicknamed "Pul," in Assyria (745–727 B.C.). As Amos and Hosea had predicted, God was raising up an agent of punishment. Israel plummeted toward disaster, anarchy, and death.

Kings of Israel

The mood of stability was shattered when Jeroboam II died. His son Zechariah was assassinated after six months by Shallum, who in turn was murdered by the violent Menahem. This cruel monarch served ten years, sometimes slaughtering his own people (2 Kings 15:16), often fighting losing battles with Assyria. He took money, lots of money, from the rich who had profited so much during the glory days of Jeroboam II and gave it as tribute to Assyria (15:19-20). Menahem died, and his son Pekahiah ruled two years before he was killed by Pekah. Hold King Pekah in your memory, because he joined forces with King Rezin of Syria (Aram) and rebelled against Assyria. They tried to coerce Judah to join them, failed, then attacked Judah in an effort to depose the Davidic King Ahaz (734 B.C.) and put in power a sympathetic substitute. The whole episode was a last-gasp effort. King Tiglath-pileser III crushed Syria and Israel in 732 B.C., put a puppet, Hoshea—who killed Pekah—in power, and began exiling the people of Israel. Hoshea paid tribute as a subservient but then foolishly rebelled. Samaria was pulverized in 722/21 B.C.

Kings of Judah

Now the spotlight shifts. To get a fix on the Southern Kingdom, Judah, during the time of the prophets Micah and Isaiah, we need to focus on four kings. The line was cleanly father to son, all descendants of King David:

- Uzziah (783–742 B.C.), also called Azariah
- Jotham (ruled alone, 742–735 B.C.)
- Ahaz (735–715 B.C.)
- Hezekiah (715–687 B.C.)

Uzziah took over at age 16 and quickly became an aggressive ruler who took advantage of the world power vacuum as did the corresponding king, Jeroboam II, in Israel. Uzziah expanded the borders eastward and southward as far as Solomon's old port of Elath on the Gulf of Aqaba. During Uzziah's forty-year rule, trade flourished; and as in Israel, the rich became powerful and the poor were squeezed.

Toward the end of his life, Uzziah became arrogant. He even tried to offer a sacrifice in the Temple, knowing that only priests had that privilege. He was struck down with leprosy and thereafter isolated to separate living quarters

NOTES, REFLECTIONS, AND QUESTIONS

This palace relief from Nimrud, carved during the reign of Tiglath-pileser III (740 B.C.), shows the king riding in his chariot after a military victory.

(2 Chronicles 26:16-21). Jotham, his son, was co-regent for eight years, then king for seven or eight more years. He continued the policies of his father.

But when Jotham's son Ahaz became king (2 Kings 16:1), the power structure of the Near East began to change. Tiglath-pileser III had turned Assyria into an awesome world power. Young King Ahaz was ill-prepared for international politics. He refused an appeal by Syria and Israel to join forces against Assyria (Syro-Ephraimite War). When they attacked, trying to coerce him to join their modest coalition, Ahaz pleaded to Assyria for help. Ahaz even sent to the king of Assyria a present of silver and gold from the Temple. During the brief dispute with Syria and Israel, Ahaz lost soldiers and land. Edom picked off the outlying territory of Elath. Assyria considered Ahaz a confused weakling.

Later, after Tiglath-pileser had demolished Damascus and wounded Israel (732 B.C.), Ahaz met with Tiglath-pileser in Damascus and then ordered the Temple priest, Uriah, to copy the altar that was in Damascus and build a replica right in Solomon's Temple at Jerusalem (2 Kings 16:10-16). Whereas, his father and grandfather had avoided most Baal worship, even destroying some of the high places, Ahaz, in his desperate plight, "did not do what was right . . . , but he walked in the way of the kings of Israel. He even made his son pass through fire" (16:2-3). All of Ahaz's efforts to get the gods to help him were futile. Judah quickly became a vassal state of Assyria.

Hezekiah, a son of Ahaz, became king upon Ahaz's death (715 B.C.) and ruled until 687 B.C. On one hand, he purified worship in the Temple. He celebrated Passover with a pomp and gladness not seen since King Solomon's time (2 Chronicles 30:26). Hezekiah gave hospitality to refugees from Israel who were fleeing Assyria's wrath. He built the famous tunnel of Hezekiah to insure water for Jerusalem in the event of siege.

But, in an effort to win independence for Judah, Hezekiah listened to both Egypt and Babylon. He quit paying tribute to Assyria. When King Sargon II of Assyria died (705 B.C.), Hezekiah rebelled.

The new king, Sennacherib, quashed this modest rebellion with a vengeance. He captured forty-six Judean fortified cities, including Lachish, Judah's second largest city (2 Kings 18:14-16). He received all the gold and silver Hezekiah could strip from the Temple and the palace. Sennacherib claimed, in an official Assyrian inscription, that he had confined Hezekiah in Jerusalem "like a bird in a cage." He came right up to the walls of Jerusalem and laid siege in 701 B.C.

Why do we care about these ancient kings? Because the God of the Bible works in history, weighing the nations in a balance. Because we cannot understand the prophets without knowing the social, political, and economic context in which they spoke. Because the insights God provided through the prophets in their day have relevance to our troubled times.

NOTES, REFLECTIONS, AND QUESTIONS

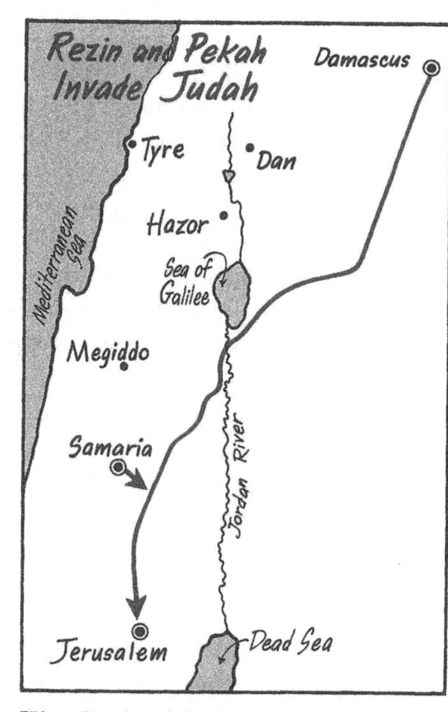

King Rezin of Syria (Aram) and King Pekah of Israel tried to coerce King Ahaz of Judah into joining them in a rebellion against Assyria. When Ahaz refused, Rezin and Pekah invaded Judah and attacked Jerusalem (2 Kings 16:1-9).

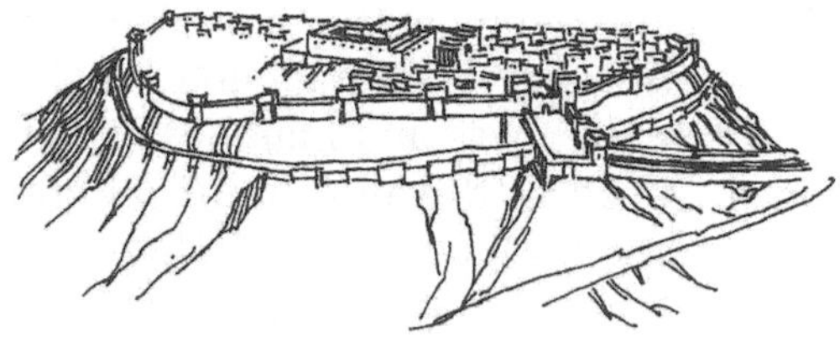

The city of Lachish as it may have appeared before being attacked by Sennacherib in 701 B.C. The higher wall was stone, the lower wall crushed bricks and stone. The large building in the center of the city was probably a temple.

NOTES, REFLECTIONS, AND QUESTIONS

Micah

Micah came from Moresheth, a small farming village nestled in the Judean foothills twenty-five miles southwest of Jerusalem. The town was sometimes called Moresheth-gath because it neighbored the old Philistine city of Gath. Toward the east, Micah could see the sheep grazing and the terraces covered with grapes; toward the western coast, he looked at the rich level fields of barley, wheat, and olive groves.

So close to the coastal plain, however, Micah's village often was overrun by the armies that periodically raced up and down that natural highway to Egypt.

Micah, like Amos, never lost his rural mindset. Unlike Amos, who spoke out in Samaria, Micah prophesied in his own capital, Jerusalem. In Moresheth, he may have been an elder, a kind of country judge who sat "at the gate," meting out justice for the local citizens. He used a lot of legal imagery in his preaching. But he was no city prophet like Isaiah with natural access to the centers of power. Instead, with unsophisticated boldness and with blunt, straightforward, sometimes rough, language, he went to the city and denounced the establishment:

> "Listen, you heads of Jacob
> and rulers of the house of Israel!
> Should you not know justice?—
> you who . . . tear the skin off my people,
> and the flesh off their bones" (Micah 3:1-2).

Micah's call to preach was not dramatic, but it was real:

> "As for me, I am filled with power,
> with the spirit of the LORD" (3:8).

His theology was not focused on Mount Zion, the Temple, and the monarchy of David as was Isaiah's. Rather, his faith was grounded in Exodus—freedom from Egypt, protection in the wilderness, the Law of Mount Sinai, and a land of promise where God had given each family a plot of inheritance.

We will understand the Book of Micah best if we see it like a pendulum, swinging from doom (Micah 1–3) to restoration (4–5), back to doom (6:1–7:7), and then to restoration (7:8–8:20).

The book begins with a courtroom scene of scathing denunciation for both Israel and Judah. The Lord is summoned as a witness and marches out of the Temple with huge strides. When God walks on the mountains, they melt. God, the witness, is asked, "What is the transgression of Jacob [Israel]? . . . of Judah?" (1:5). God's answer: The centers of power, the capitals, Samaria and Jerusalem. They represent the sin of a divided kingdom and the heart of idolatry. Then God the witness becomes God the Judge and pronounces sentence: "I will make Samaria a heap in the open country" (1:6).

Then follows a lament, a funeral hymn, for Judah's future fall (1:8). In order to sing it properly, Micah puts on a simple loincloth and walks into Jerusalem, barefoot and naked, a sign of mourning. All the towns of Judah will soon weep and be stripped naked.

Specifically, what were the transgressions Micah denounced? Government policies and taxes robbed the peasant farmers, forcing them to sell their land and become indentured servants. The rich and powerful landowners lay awake at night devising schemes to strip the children of promise of their inheritance (2:1-2).

The people didn't want to hear what Micah had to say; they preferred the lies of the false prophets. The priests taught only for a handsome fee. The prophets preached peace when they ate well but lashed out against those who didn't pay them (3:5). When they gave oracles, they remembered how their bread was buttered.

The sanctuary prophets were not shameless charlatans. Surely they were sincere patriots, lovers of the people, devoted to state and sanctuary. They simply were so much a part of the sins of the society they couldn't see the plumb line of God. That's why they didn't speak out. That's why they resented the criticism.

Where do you see signs we in the church have become so much a part of and comfortable with the secular society that we cannot hear or see what God requires?

The judges took bribes (3:11). Taking money from the working people, they built enormous monuments and public works in the city. Micah insisted all were built with blood money (3:10). The merchants and traders used "wicked scales" and "dishonest weights," another way of cheating the poor (6:11). Lies, misrepresentation of goods, and false advertising were ways of thievery and deceit (6:12). What will happen to these greedy people? They will never be satisfied. Even when they eat, they will never have enough (6:14-15).

Idolatry was rampant. Micah claimed the people went to the high places of Baal and brought their false gods into the Temple. They followed the ways and repeated the sins of Omri and Ahab and Jezebel of Samaria (6:16).

Micah's was the voice of the countryside; but he was no mere populist, pitting farmer against city dweller. He discerned the internal dissolution of his country as it abandoned religious and political integrity. Evil policies and practices would so cut the national nerve that Judah would be easy prey for its enemies.

God's Case Against the People

In Micah 6, God enters the courtroom again. God wants the universe to know "the LORD has a controversy with his people" (6:2). The defense asks, Did God do wrong in freeing

NOTES, REFLECTIONS, AND QUESTIONS

you from slavery, in giving you Moses, in saving you, time after time (6:3-5)?

Almost innocently, the people ask what they should bring to the Lord in appreciation (6:6). What about a massive offering? What if they brought thousands of rams and ten thousand rivers of oil? What if they, perish the thought, offered their firstborn sons, as King Ahaz had (6:7)?

In a mighty answer, the prophet tells exactly what the Lord requires. In a single sentence God states Amos's demand for justice, Hosea's appeal for faithfulness to the covenant, and Isaiah's plea for quiet faith:

"He has told you, O mortal, what is good;
and what does the LORD require of you
but to do justice, and to love kindness,
and to walk humbly with your God?" (Micah 6:8).

Micah, perhaps more than any other prophet, gave the hard word about Jerusalem: God "will make you [Jerusalem] a desolation, and your inhabitants an object of hissing" (6:16). The time is soon coming when you can't trust a friend or a member of your own family (7:5-6).

The people will be led off into exile (1:16), and "Jerusalem shall become a heap of ruins" (3:12).

But Jerusalem, though sorely attacked in the Assyrian siege, did not fall in 701 B.C. Was Micah wrong? Or was his prophecy simply premature? The prophecy was totally fulfilled under the Babylonians in 587 B.C. So some said, "See, Micah was no prophet" (701 B.C.); while others much later said, "See, he saw the final end" (587 B.C.).

Before Amos, Hosea, Micah, and Isaiah, prophets thought of Israel in two stages—Egypt (slavery) and freedom (Moses and the Promised Land). Now the prophets envision a third stage—Egypt, meaning Assyrian and Babylonian exile (slavery), again!

Will there one day be a fourth stage, a restoration? Micah looks into the heart of God and knows that people one day will stream back to the mountain of Zion where God will judge fairly and where peace will rule (4:2). Micah prophesied, using the same words as Isaiah:

"They shall beat their swords into plowshares,
and their spears into pruning hooks"
(Micah 4:3; Isaiah 2:4).

True to his rural background, Micah added the glorious dream,

"They shall all sit under their own vines and under
their own fig trees,
and no one shall make them afraid" (Micah 4:4).

Israel's future looks bright. A deliverer is expected. Where will the Davidic king come from? Not from the royal courts of Jerusalem but from the common people, from a country village, from Bethlehem, "one of the little clans of Judah" (5:2).

NOTES, REFLECTIONS, AND QUESTIONS

Figs were cultivated in ancient Israel for food and for medicinal use. In Scripture the fig tree symbolizes peace and prosperity.

Micah, from the grazing lands of Moresheth, thought of God as shepherd.

"He shall stand and feed his flock. . . .
and he shall be the one [Lord] of peace" (5:4-5).

MARKS OF OBEDIENT COMMUNITY

The community of faith remembers that God is loving but expects just dealings and compassionate caring. We understand that injustice or cruelty brings judgment and punishment. We know that punishment is complex, communal—often unfathomable—and yet real and awful. We know that, under God, our actions influence others and theirs affect us.

Think about cause and effect. How is that a form of punishment?

Think about the innocent. Why do they often get caught up in the web of other people's sins?

Think of your DISCIPLE group, your church, individuals. How could punishment come? How could punishment come to a city? a country?

What unjust conditions or situations exist in your rural area, town, or city?

What steps might your DISCIPLE group take to work toward correcting those injustices?

IF YOU WANT TO KNOW MORE

Look at the geography of Moresheth and the Philistine plain in a Bible atlas.

Notice that the mothers of most of the Judean kings are named in Scripture. Why do you suppose that is so? Look back and identify them. Why do you think the mothers of kings of Israel are not named?

NOTES, REFLECTIONS, AND QUESTIONS

The community of faith recognizes that no actions or decisions of individuals or groups are taken in isolation and that obedience to God requires just actions and decisions.

JUDGMENT

"They have rejected the instruction of the LORD of hosts,
and have despised the word of the Holy One of Israel."

—Isaiah 5:24

6 God Pleads

OUR HUMAN CONDITION

Generally we block out all mention of judgment. We don't want anyone pleading with us to change our ways. We've had enough of instruction in how to live.

ASSIGNMENT

Isaiah 1–39 seems to be pre-Exile prophecies covering several decades in the eighth century B.C.

Notice that messianic prophecies come when times seem dark, hope almost gone.

Day 1 Isaiah 1–4 (wickedness of Judah, God's judgment); 2 Chronicles 26–27 (Uzziah, Jotham)

Day 2 Isaiah 5–8 (song of the vineyard, vision in the Temple, Immanuel); 2 Kings 16; 2 Chronicles 28 (Ahaz)

Day 3 Isaiah 9–12 (righteous rule of messiah, repentant remnant of Israel, the peaceful kingdom)

Day 4 Isaiah 28–33 (oracles against Ephraim and Judah, siege of Jerusalem, hope for the future, Egypt's help worthless, rule of justice)

Day 5 Isaiah 36–39 (Jerusalem threatened, Hezekiah consults Isaiah, Isaiah reassures Hezekiah, envoys from Babylon); 2 Kings 18–20; 2 Chronicles 29–32 (Hezekiah)

Day 6 Read and respond to "The Word of the Lord" and "Marks of Obedient Community."

Day 7 Rest

PRAYER

Pray daily before study:

"LORD, don't be angry and rebuke me!
Don't punish me in your anger!
I am worn out, O LORD; have pity on me!
Give me strength; I am completely exhausted
and my whole being is deeply troubled"
(Psalm 6:1-3, TEV).

Prayer concerns for this week:

JUDGMENT

Day 1 Isaiah 1–4 (wickedness of Judah, God's judgment); 2 Chronicles 26–27 (Uzziah, Jotham)

Is 2:5 Come, O house of Jacob, let us walk in the light of the Lord

Day 2 Isaiah 5–8 (song of the vineyard, vision in the Temple, Immanuel); 2 Kings 16; 2 Chronicles 28 (Ahaz)

IS 5:20 woe to those who call evil good & good evil.

IS 8:17 I will wait for the Lord who is hiding his face from the house of Jacob. I will put my trust in him.

Day 3 Isaiah 9–12 (righteous rule of messiah, repentant remnant of Israel, the peaceful kingdom)

hope 9:1–7 ; 11:1–9

Day 4 Isaiah 28–33 (oracles against Ephraim and Judah, siege of Jerusalem, hope for the future, Egypt's help worthless, rule of justice)

IS 29:19 Beatitudes.
30:15 repentence & rest, is salvation quietness & trust is your strength.
32:17 The fruit of righteousness will be peace. Spirit not law.
33:24 Sins will be forgiven.

Day 5 Isaiah 36–39 (Jerusalem threatened, Hezekiah consults Isaiah, Isaiah reassures Hezekiah, envoys from Babylon); 2 Kings 18–20; 2 Chronicles 29–32 (Hezekiah)

39:1 → over confidence, pride
38:1–7 Lord grants 15 yrs to Hezekiah

Day 6 "The Word of the Lord" and "Marks of Obedient Community"

THE WORD OF THE LORD

The book of Isaiah appears first among the sixteen prophetic books in the Bible, not because Isaiah lived before Amos and Hosea but because the book is so large, so majestic. It covers more than two centuries of prophetic writings and rises to incomparable poetic and spiritual heights. The full range of prophetic teachings from the peace and prosperity of mid-eighth century through the Assyrian and Babylonian destructions, even beyond the Exile to mid-fifth century, falls within its pages. If we could preserve only one book of Hebrew prophecy, encompassing maximum spiritual richness, we would save the book of Isaiah.

It appears that the book contains the work of more than one prophet. Apparently Isaiah was so great in the eyes of the prophets that his later disciples (Isaiah 8:16), continuing his teaching and prophetic tradition, honored him with their writings. We will look now at Isaiah 1–39 as the writings primarily of eighth-century Isaiah of Jerusalem, sometimes referred to as First Isaiah.

Isaiah was a nobleman, born and bred in Jerusalem, and may have been a priest. The Talmud suggests that Isaiah's father Amoz was a brother of Amaziah, king of Judah. Isaiah's writings show sophistication and culture. The same divine command that took hold of the village prophets took hold of this high-born confidant of kings. His prestige and influence gave him a powerful pulpit and access to the highest level of decision-making. According to 2 Chronicles 26:22, Isaiah wrote the history of King Uzziah. Isaiah was married to a prophetess (Isaiah 8:3) and had at least two children, maybe three. They named their sons Shear-jashub, "A remnant shall return" (7:3), and Maher-shalal-hash-baz, "The spoil speeds, the prey hastens" (8:3-4).

Isaiah's Call

Why do we hear the message (Isaiah 1–5) before we meet the messenger (Isaiah 6)? Why do we listen to Isaiah's prophecies before we hear of his call? Because the message is more important than the messenger.

King Uzziah, the power of Judah for four decades, had died (6:1). Isaiah went to the Temple—perhaps to grieve, perhaps to pray for Jotham, the new king who would rule in troubled times. The earthly Temple was transformed for Isaiah into the heavenly Temple of God. Suddenly it was filled with all the hosts of heaven.

The Holy One of Israel was present. Celestial sights and sounds filled the young man's mind (6:3). Isaiah went to the Temple to pray for the king and instead met the King of heaven. The tears of grief for Uzziah glistened with the ecstasy of Holy Presence.

Before God, who is not aware of sin? "I am a man of unclean lips, and I live among a people of unclean lips" (6:5).

NOTES, REFLECTIONS, AND QUESTIONS

A limestone plaque, found in Jerusalem, commemorates the reburial of the bones of King Uzziah sometime between the first century B.C. and the first century A.D. The plaque reads "Hither were brought the bones of Uzziah, king of Judah. Not to be opened."

The prophet needed purification before he became God's messenger. The searing coal from the altar touched his lips and signified divine absolution (6:6-7).

Why did Isaiah focus on his lips? Perhaps as a prophet he was aware of the power of the words of his mouth. Or perhaps his lips were being prepared for the message of prophecy. Then as if God were surrounded by the heavenly council of advisers, the question came to Isaiah, "Whom shall I send, and who will go for us?" And the young prophet replied, "Here am I; send me!" (6:8). Isaiah was willing. It is not always so.

Sadly, most readers stop at Isaiah's response. We don't like the words that follow. Neither did Isaiah. When he preached, the people would not listen. He would plead, but they would not repent. They would stop up their ears, put their hands over their eyes (6:10). For how long?

"Until cities lie waste . . .
and the land is utterly desolate" (6:11).

Not a happy prospect for a budding preacher. Interestingly, some scholars hold the view that Isaiah had his Temple experience after he had been preaching for a while, and that it came about because he found that no one was listening to his message.

Isaiah's Message

At first, during King Jotham's reign, a time of peace and prosperity, Isaiah sounded like Amos and Hosea. He indicted Judah for its rebellion:

"I reared children and brought them up,
but they have rebelled against me" (Isaiah 1:2).

The prophet announced that the upper classes (of which he was a part) had become greedy, disregarding the needs and rights of the poor and the weak. Isaiah saw God's covenant with King David and Mount Zion as the base for his beliefs. He firmly believed that the king, the descendant of David, was under obligation to guarantee justice for those who were poor and without power. Listen to the psalmist's prayer at the crowning of a king:

"Give the king your justice, O God,
and your righteousness to a king's son.
May he judge your people with righteousness,
and your poor with justice. . . .
May he defend the cause of the poor of the people,
give deliverance to the needy,
and crush the oppressor" (Psalm 72:1-4).

As a part of nobility, Isaiah saw the failures close at hand. Spiritual leadership was lacking.

"Your princes are rebels
and companions of thieves.
Everyone loves a bribe
and runs after gifts.

NOTES, REFLECTIONS, AND QUESTIONS

NOTES, REFLECTIONS, AND QUESTIONS

They do not defend the orphan,
and the widow's cause does not come before them"
(Isaiah 1:23).

Priests and prophets had become drunkards.

"The priest and the prophet reel with strong drink,
they are confused with wine,
they stagger with strong drink;
they err in vision,
they stumble in giving judgment. . . .
'Whom will he [the prophet] teach knowledge,
and to whom will he explain the message?'" (28:7, 9).

Lacking leadership, the people forgot who they were. They ran after "diviners" and "soothsayers" and mixed worship of false gods with worship of Israel's God. God wanted nothing to do with their many offerings, and Isaiah said so:

"I have had enough of burnt offerings of rams
and the fat of fed beasts; . . .
even though you make many prayers,
I will not listen;
your hands are full of blood.
Wash yourselves; make yourselves clean; . . .
cease to do evil,
learn to do good" (1:11, 15-17).

Early on, Isaiah warned of coming punishment. He discerned, with a prophet's eye, that the whole body was sick. So he said God had chosen an enemy nation to bring judgment on Judah. Picture in your mind the scene Isaiah describes:

"He [God] will raise a signal for a nation far away,
and whistle for a people at the ends of the earth;
here they come, swiftly, speedily!" (5:26).

The prophet never doubted the Assyrians were coming. Only wholesale repentance could save Judah. Isaiah delivers the warning; he also holds out the promise—God will save. Isaiah's most dramatic sermon on this subject was no speech at all, but rather was his son, named Shear-jashub, "A remnant shall return" (7:3). Some remnant will survive (10:20). A people shall be saved out of Assyria just as Israel was brought out of Egypt (11:16).

Ahaz

Then Ahaz became king. When threatened by the combined forces of King Rezin of Syria and King Pekah of Israel in the Syro-Ephraimitic War (734 B.C.), the young king was terror-stricken. He had forgotten the Lord. "The heart of Ahaz and the heart of his people shook as the trees of the forest shake before the wind" (Isaiah 7:2).

Isaiah, taking his own son, "A remnant shall return," met the king at the city reservoir near the pool of Siloam and declared this message from God: "Take heed, be quiet, do not fear, and do not let your heart be faint because of these two smoldering stumps of firebrands [Rezin and Pekah]" (7:4).

They are mere men, not God. God through Isaiah announced the destruction of King Rezin of Damascus (Syria) and King Pekah of Samaria (Israel). Isaiah appealed for quiet trust. He insisted that the great resource in time of trouble is faith—absolute trust in and dependence upon God, especially by the king (7:9).

Again Isaiah offered the frightened Ahaz assurance. Isaiah promised a sign: A son would soon be born whose name Immanuel meant *God is with us*. Before he was old enough to know good from evil, Syria and Israel would disappear (7:10-17). Later, Christians would see Jesus Christ in that sign.

But Ahaz could not wait (2 Kings 16). He appealed to King Tiglath-pileser III for help and later went to meet the king in Damascus. Isaiah felt Ahaz made a bad mistake in calling for help from the king of Assyria. That move showed lack of trust. It put Judah in a political bed with a potential enemy.

In 732 B.C., Assyria ravaged Syria and severely curtailed the position of Samaria, occupying some of the Israelite provinces, and for the first time implemented the Assyrian policy of interchange of captive peoples. Isaiah had been right. Isaiah knew Assyria would destroy Judah's enemies to the north if Judah would just be patient.

Perhaps in reaction to Ahaz's refusal to take his advice, Isaiah withdrew from public ministry for a time. He was following his own advice, quietly waiting to see the work of God.

Hezekiah

Undoubtedly, the prophet was pleased when Hezekiah purified the Temple, cleansing it of Ahaz's abomination. Hezekiah also removed many of the Baal "high places" from the countryside. Hezekiah gets high marks from the historians, who compared him to David, saying, "There was no one like him among all the kings of Judah" (2 Kings 18:5). However, Isaiah was troubled when Hezekiah became restless. People were complaining about paying tribute to Assyria. Egypt encouraged the small states that lay between Egypt and Assyria, like Philistia and Judah, to rebel. Isaiah condemned these rebellious ideas by walking barefoot and naked for three years (Isaiah 20:1-4). When Assyria attacked the coast, Egypt pulled back, leaving the Philistines high and dry. Judah escaped for the moment.

But with the death of the Assyrian king Sargon II, the whole area erupted in revolution. The fledgling power in Babylon sent a delegation with letters and a gift to Hezekiah, who had been sick (39:1). Egypt, experiencing revival, sent envoys, trying to join forces. Hezekiah fortified the Jerusalem walls.

In an hour of decision, Isaiah counseled Hezekiah to stay out of the revolution. (Oracles of Isaiah 28–38 show that God will handle the foreign nations.) The new Assyrian king, Sennacherib, did not know he was to be the instrument of God's anger. But his armies crushed Babylon, swept down the coast

NOTES, REFLECTIONS, AND QUESTIONS

Sargon II, who conquered Israel and destroyed Samaria in 722/721 B.C. and deported its inhabitants to Assyria, is shown here in a limestone relief from his palace at Khorsabad.

to the Nile, and into Judah as far as Jerusalem. The fortress at Lachish was put under siege and destroyed.

Now Isaiah, who had predicted destruction, made a strange turn. When everyone else thought the end had come, he announced God would save Jerusalem. The Assyrian official, the Rabshakeh, taunted Hezekiah from outside the city walls (36:4-10). But Isaiah, when consulted by the king, gave unbelievable advice: "Thus says the LORD: Do not be afraid. . . . I myself will put a spirit in him [King Sennacherib], so that he shall hear a rumor, and return to his own land; I will cause him to fall by the sword in his own land" (37:6-7; 2 Kings 19:6-7). Isaiah, who had preached earlier against the revolution, now staunchly refused capitulation—and for the same reason. Stand firm, and see the salvation of the Lord (Isaiah 37:33-35).

What happened? The accounts in Isaiah 37:36-38 and 2 Kings 19:35-37 are mysterious. A plague among the Assyrian soldiers? We don't know. No matter. God had intervened, and David's city was saved. Isaiah's prophecy was fulfilled. Unfortunately, later leaders would interpret that prophecy to mean Jerusalem never would, never could be destroyed.

Hope

The sin of the people was great, but the zeal of the Lord was greater. Isaiah, a "man of unclean lips," felt the fire of holy cleansing. So would Judah someday, for the ultimate purpose of God's fire is not to destroy but to purify.

> "I will smelt away your dross as with lye
> and remove all your alloy" (Isaiah 1:25).

Judgment will burn like a holy fire, but that holy fire will ultimately save.

> "Zion shall be redeemed by justice,
> and those in her who repent, by righteousness" (1:27).

Salvation will come through a child. Typical of Isaiah, who saw God working through the Davidic monarchy, a child will be born, a son with all authority on his shoulders (9:6-7). He will be a shoot out of Jesse, David's father (11:1).

> "Righteousness shall be the belt around his waist,
> and faithfulness the belt around his loins" (11:5).

He will reunite the two kingdoms (11:13). The peace of God will happen "on all my holy mountain," a belief of Isaiah that Mount Zion was the focus of God's saving work (11:9). In that day when "the wolf shall live with the lamb" (11:6) and "there shall be endless peace" (9:7), the people will know and love God.

For the people of Judah, this vision of God's great and final victory gave hope even amid the lament of national collapse. For the Christian community, Isaiah's promise has been the messianic vision of a child born of Davidic ancestry, who is the Savior of the world.

NOTES, REFLECTIONS, AND QUESTIONS

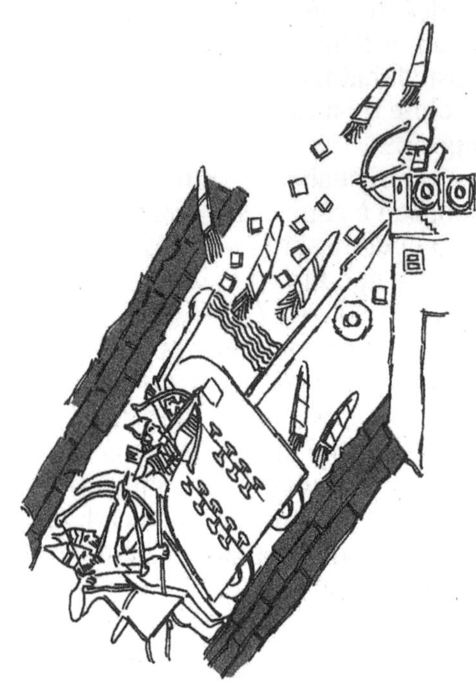

This relief from the walls of Sennacherib's palace at Nineveh details the fall of Lachish. Assyrian soldiers attack with a battering ram. One soldier pours water on the siege machine to keep it from catching fire as defenders hurl torches from the city walls.

MARKS OF OBEDIENT COMMUNITY

Sometimes the faith community can hear the words of the prophet, sometimes not. God never gives up. On God's behalf, Isaiah wooed, chastised, pleaded. Sometimes the faith community is able to respond, to repent, to return, to reclaim the heritage; sometimes not. Today, wearing a big sign or shouting "repent" seems ineffective. What are ways to help people turn toward God?

Strong outreach & living in/with the spirit.

How can we have the insight, the integrity to see ourselves as we really are?

Blessed are the poor in spirit.

What are the standards by which the community of faith is judged? the standards by which the world is judged? What, if any, are the differences?

Early workers in the vineyard. The older brother in the parable of Prodigal son.

How would you assess our capacity to "turn and be healed"?

Pray for a receptive & supple heart.

What methods and messages attract people to right living rather than encourage rebellion or indifference?

First principles. Brotherly love.

How does God save a rebellious people?

Continuous feedback.

IF YOU WANT TO KNOW MORE

Look for some hymns based on Isaiah's words. Read them aloud or sing them.

Isaiah 13–27 and 34–35 are not included in daily assignments. You may want to read those chapters.

Lessons 6, 12, and 13 are on Isaiah. As you read Isaiah, be particularly aware of those passages treasured by Christians because we see Christ in them.

NOTES, REFLECTIONS, AND QUESTIONS

The faithful community repents of its failure to hear and to respond to God's pleas for justice and righteousness.

DIVINE PURPOSE

"Look at the nations, and see!
Be astonished! Be astounded!
For a work is being done in your days
that you would not believe if you were told."

—Habakkuk 1:5

7 God Rules the World

OUR HUMAN CONDITION

Things don't make sense. Wickedness and evil seem rampant. Who is accountable? Are we? How do we hold on to a belief that behind life is a grand purpose, a plan?

ASSIGNMENT

These three prophets are among the twelve "minor" or "latter" prophets—"minor" because they are short (not unimportant), "latter" because they appear last (not least). Each book has its own unique message. Each should be read in a single sitting if possible. Look for a unifying theme. Spot a memorable verse. Watch for differences in the Kings and Chronicles accounts of the kings.

Day 1 Zephaniah 1–2 (coming day of the Lord, judgment on Judah and on Israel's enemies); 2 Kings 21:1-18; 2 Chronicles 33:1-20 (Manasseh)
Day 2 Zephaniah 3 (a righteous remnant); 2 Kings 21:19-26; 2 Chronicles 33:21-25 (Amon)
Day 3 2 Kings 22:1–23:30; 1 Kings 13:1-10 (man of God from Judah, tearing down the altar at Bethel); 2 Chronicles 34–35 (Josiah and the book of the Law)
Day 4 Nahum 1–3 (oracle of the destruction of Nineveh)
Day 5 Habakkuk 1–3 (Habakkuk and God in dialogue, Habakkuk's prayer)
Day 6 Read and respond to "The Word of the Lord" and "Marks of Obedient Community."
Day 7 Rest

PRAYER

Pray daily before study:
"Why am I so sad?
Why am I so troubled?
I will put my hope in God,
and once again I will praise him,
my savior and my God" (Psalm 43:5, TEV).

Prayer concerns for this week:

Divine Purpose

Day 1 Zephaniah 1–2 (coming day of the Lord, judgment on Judah and on Israel's enemies); 2 Kings 21:1-18; 2 Chronicles 33:1-20 (Manasseh)

Day 2 Zephaniah 3 (a righteous remnant); 2 Kings 21:19-26; 2 Chronicles 33:21-25 (Amon)

Day 3 2 Kings 22:1–23:30; 1 Kings 13:1-10 (man of God from Judah, tearing down the altar at Bethel); 2 Chronicles 34–35 (Josiah and the book of the Law)

Day 4 Nahum 1–3 (oracle of the destruction of Nineveh)

Day 5 Habakkuk 1–3 (Habakkuk and God in dialogue, Habakkuk's prayer)

Day 6 "The Word of the Lord" and "Marks of Obedient Community"

THE WORD OF THE LORD

NOTES, REFLECTIONS, AND QUESTIONS

Zephaniah: Judgment

Zephaniah, a descendant of David, moved about easily with leaders of government in Jerusalem. He knew the city well, as shown by his easy references to the Fish Gate, where fishermen from Tyre and Tiberias sold their wares; to the Second Quarter, a new residential area developed by King Manasseh; and to the Mortar, a center for commerce (Zephaniah 1:10-11). He began prophesying sometime after 640 B.C. when Josiah became king of Judah. Josiah was only eight years old, and Zephaniah may have been part of a group of reformers who tutored the young king and prayed for religious revival.

For nearly half a century, Judah had been ruled by King Manasseh (687–642 B.C.). From a secular viewpoint, the times were not too bad. After the siege of 701 B.C. was lifted, Judah lived as a vassal state under an imposed Assyrian peace. Life in the villages normalized; trade in the city prospered. Though the people of Judah paid an enormous tribute, at least the wars had stopped. But from a religious viewpoint, life was a disaster. Manasseh undid all of his father Hezekiah's reforms. In an effort to appease Assyria, Judah imported all sorts of foreign gods. People worshiped the Assyrian gods of sun, moon, and stars. The god Milcom, Ammonite god of fertility and storm, was now placed prominently in the Temple.

Zephaniah pointed to three great sins nurtured by Manasseh and his son Amon (642–640 B.C.)—idolatry, syncretism (the mixing and intermingling of all kinds of religion), and indifference. Perhaps this third sin was the worst. God was irrelevant. Zephaniah pictures God with lamps, walking the streets of Jerusalem, looking for people who ignored God's rule. What God found was complacency, like wine left too long with the dregs (1:12).

Zephaniah knew Judah was supposed to be distinct, different, a people set apart (Exodus 33:16; Numbers 23:9). But King Manasseh was practical, compromising, accommodating.

The Bible says King Manasseh not only served the longest as king but was the worst king in Judah's history (2 Kings 21:1-9). The first sixty years of the seventh century B.C. were a religious wasteland. No prophet is recorded to have spoken in Judah since Micah and Isaiah.

Now, according to Zephaniah, God was angry. All the nations, including Judah, were condemned. Sin had infected all nature, even the animals, birds, and fish of the sea. Judgment would begin in Jerusalem, then spread throughout the world (Zephaniah 1:4, 18).

The Day of the Lord

The expression "the great day of the LORD" (Zephaniah 1:14) had often meant the day of God's victory. From Israel's

An *oracle* is a message from God, either a spontaneous prophecy or an answer to a question. In the writings of the prophets, oracles are inspired pronouncements presented as direct communications from God, many beginning with "the word of the LORD" (Zephaniah 1:1) or "Thus says the LORD" (Isaiah 7:7; 10:24; Amos 1:3, 6, 9, 11, 13). The words that follow are usually warnings or judgment, some of them against neighboring nations (as in Isaiah 13:1–23:18; Ezekiel 25–32; Amos 1; Nahum), but most of them against Israel and Judah.

early history, the Lord had been a warrior, winning battles for Israel. But beginning with Amos, the day of the Lord came to mean judgment and wrath to the prophets. God would turn warfare, normally directed at Israel's enemies, against Israel itself—including Judah and Jerusalem.

Around 620 B.C., Josiah, now in his twenties, began a religious reform (2 Kings 23). He renovated the Temple. In the process, the high priest Hilkiah found a portion of the Book of Deuteronomy, "the book of the law" (22:8). Josiah had the book read aloud and proceeded to enforce it. He purified the Temple, tore down the "high places," defiled the place of child sacrifice, and celebrated Passover throughout the kingdom. Zephaniah pleaded for massive repentance:

"Seek righteousness, seek humility;
perhaps you may be hidden
on the day of the LORD's wrath" (Zephaniah 2:3).

But Egypt's armies swept up the coast, met Judah's army at Megiddo in the rich valley of Esdraelon (also called Jezreel). Josiah was mortally wounded and died shortly after in Jerusalem (2 Kings 23:29; 2 Chronicles 35:20-24), resulting in Judah's becoming a vassal of Egypt. Josiah, high hope of Zephaniah (and Jeremiah), was dead. Biblical historians smile on his reign. "Before him there was no king like him, who turned to the LORD with all his heart, with all his soul, and with all his might" (2 Kings 23:25).

Zephaniah despaired. He realized the people's deep pride:

"It [Jerusalem] has listened to no voice;
it has accepted no correction.
It has not trusted in the LORD;
it has not drawn near to its God" (Zephaniah 3:2).

The prophet condemned four groups of people—princes who devour the poor, judges who steal, prophets who are frivolous windbags, and priests who ignore Torah. People are not even ashamed (3:3-5). The prophet's call for repentance has gone unheeded. The reform is superficial, not a real conversion of the heart.

Zephaniah's theme is the sin of human pride (3:11). People believe they can control the world and their own destiny without God and God's ways.

Do you remember the tower of Babel (Genesis 11:1-9) when prideful people couldn't understand one another because they spoke different languages? In the restoration after the day of the Lord, God will give pure speech, perfect unity so all people can understand one another. People can clearly "call on the name of the LORD" (Zephaniah 3:9). Pride will be replaced by humble, obedient faith. The faithful will recognize that God, not they, controls the world.

Like other prophets, Zephaniah holds out hope. Usually the prophets speak of people, after the punishment, coming back from the east and the west, the north and the south to Mount Zion. Zephaniah does that: "I will bring you home" (3:20).

NOTES, REFLECTIONS, AND QUESTIONS

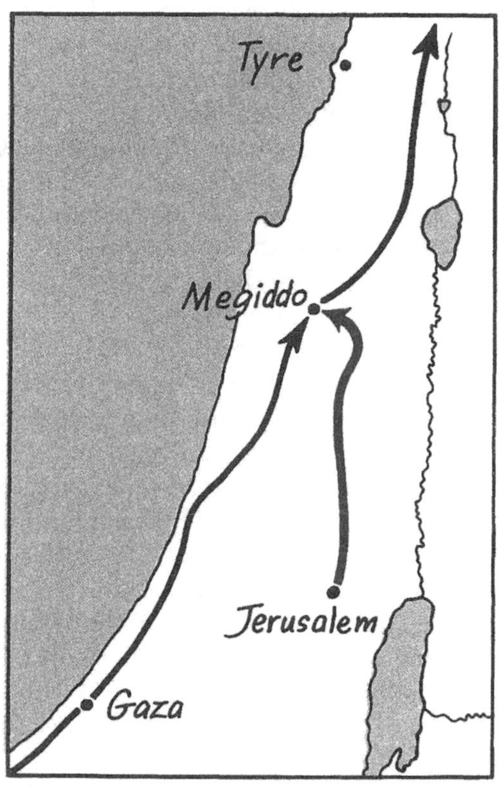

In 609 B.C. Pharaoh Neco of Egypt, then an ally of Assyria, went up the coast of Judah and Israel to help Assyria. King Josiah of Judah, rebelling against Assyrian control, marched to Megiddo to stop Neco's advance. He was mortally wounded in the battle (2 Kings 23:29-30; 2 Chronicles 35:20-24).

Nahum: Destruction of Nineveh

Nahum's two poems concentrate on a single message: God will bring judgment on Nineveh. In vivid detail, Nahum foretells the destruction of Nineveh.

The people of Judah were not alone in celebrating Assyria's collapse, but they were front and center among the cheerleaders. They had suffered much; so had the Medes, the Egyptians, the Scythians, and the Babylonians. All joined in the victory shout. No wonder Nahum closed his poem,

"All who hear the news about you
clap their hands over you.
For who has ever escaped
your endless cruelty?" (Nahum 3:19).

Remember this slice of history: Assyria's day in the sun was crowded with cruelty. Its fierce armies raged across the desert to burn, pillage, and rape. With the rise of Tiglath-pileser III in 744 B.C., Assyria became a major world power. Assyria ravaged Israel in 722 B.C. and in 663 B.C. torched Thebes in Egypt with its lovely gardens and precious libraries. Its powerful kings, Esar-haddon (680–669 B.C.), son of Sennacherib, and his son Ashurbanipal (668–627 B.C.), ruled the eastern Mediterranean world for over half a century. At the height of its power, Assyria ruled the area from the plateaus of northern Iran to the upper reaches of the Nile, an expanse of over a thousand miles.

The goddess Ishtar protected Nineveh, the capital of Assyria. Her warriors, on horseback and in chariots, went to great lengths to use terror as an instrument of public policy. They believed fear would melt opposition, that terror would bring about passive submission. Their custom was to inflict unnecessary pain. But these strategies had the reverse effect. Intense hatred burned in the hearts of subject peoples all over the empire. When Ashurbanipal died, there was a moment of silence, and then people all over the empire rebelled simultaneously. How Nahum mocked Nineveh's efforts to defend itself. He could almost hear the cry of the city's officers:

"Guard the ramparts;
watch the road;
gird your loins;
collect all your strength" (2:1).

In Nahum's vision,

"The chariots race madly through the streets,
they rush to and fro through the squares;
their appearance is like torches,
they dart like lightning" (2:4).

But it is too late. God will humiliate the goddess Ishtar:

"I am against you,
says the LORD of hosts" (3:5).

Notice that it is the Lord God Almighty who will destroy Nineveh (2:13; 3:5). That "city of bloodshed," that mighty evil empire, because of God's judgment, will be like a swarm of

NOTES, REFLECTIONS, AND QUESTIONS

A relief from the palace of Ashurbanipal at Nineveh shows a grapevine in the royal garden (about 640 B.C.).

locusts sitting on fences on a cold day. The sun comes up, and "they fly away; / no one knows where they have gone" (3:17).

The Word in Nahum

Can we discern word from the Lord in Nahum? Consider:

God allows all manner of human emotions to be expressed. The Bible contains raw humanness, flesh-and-blood reality. People who are angry say so. What could be more human than for Judah to celebrate freedom from the heavy yoke of oppression, to rejoice in the possibilities of peace once again?

God holds evil on a tether. God will not let wickedness run rampant forever. God gets weary of evil regimes and calls them to accountability. Notice that, amid his description of a powerful and angry God, Nahum declares,

"The LORD is good,
a stronghold in a day of trouble" (Nahum 1:7).

Most of the Hebrew prophets condemned the sins of Israel and Judah and foretold awful consequences. Nahum reminds us that all nations are under divine judgment, that evil will not go undisciplined forever. Just because Assyria served for a time as the instrument of God's wrath, that does not mean Assyria will go unpunished for its gross cruelties.

Nahum seems not to see the Babylonian invasion looming in the not-too-distant future. He fails to provide the call to repentance that might restore Judah to wholeness. Still he expresses a shout of victory, for God has acted.

Habakkuk: In God's Time

Little or nothing is known about the prophet Habakkuk, except that he prophesied in Judah toward the end of King Josiah's reign. He may have seen reform come to a halt with Josiah's death (609 B.C.). He may even have learned of the great battle when Egypt's upward reaches were smashed by Babylonia at Carchemish (605 B.C.). Judah's dreams of independence were shattered. Babylon would soon rule the world.

So Habakkuk began to question God. "O LORD, how long shall I cry for help . . . ?" (Habakkuk 1:2). Trouble continued. Strife and violence were everywhere. Justice did not prevail. Order was slipping into chaos (1:2-4).

Habakkuk's question is not, Is there a God? Nor is the question, Is God just? The question is about the providence of God. Is God really making any progress toward achieving God's ultimate plan of order, justice, and peace? God answers in effect, "I'm not asleep. Look, I'm doing great things." God is doing a work so mighty that Habakkuk wouldn't believe it even if he were told. Then God lets the prophet in on a terrible secret. God is "rousing the Chaldeans," the Babylonians (1:6). They are fierce and terrible. They will destroy the Assyrians who have cruelly ruled the world for more than two hundred years.

Habakkuk is bewildered, horrified. Lord, "your eyes are too

NOTES, REFLECTIONS, AND QUESTIONS

pure to behold evil" (1:13). The Babylonians are "treacherous." With their symbolic fishnets they will take captive many people. In their arrogance they will worship other gods, not you (1:15-16). Mystified, the prophet stands at a watchpost, not to fight or to protect, just to watch and wait for an answer (2:1).

God responds, in effect, "I'm going to explain the matter so clearly you can write it on a billboard. Write it so big that a person running by can read it at a glance" (2:2). The dream that chaos will become order—the vision that nation will not lift up sword against nation, the goal of a time of justice and peace—is not lost. God is ushering in the great day of harmony. "If it seems to tarry, wait for it" (2:3). Be patient. There is still a vision for the appointed time. As a person of faith, Habakkuk, you are living in the "not yet," in the "meanwhile" times of faith and trust. The righteous will live, quietly, humbly, trusting God in faithfulness (2:4).

God is at work. The proud are still being brought low. Arrogance and greed continue to destroy people. God will give evil its due. The mighty get puffed up. Their lives are crooked and bent (2:4-5). If wickedness is what you want, then you shall have it. A family or a government that gains power by robbing and deceiving will reap the results of its actions. A military power, ruthlessly lording it over its neighbors, will ultimately drink the same cup of wrath that it made its neighbors drink (2:15-17). God sets a limit on human wickedness. The proud challengers of God's rule cannot *rest* or *abide* or *live* (2:4-5). God is working out God's purpose.

> "The earth will be filled
> with the knowledge of the glory of the LORD,
> as the waters cover the sea" (2:14).

The dialogue between the Lord and the prophet in Chapters 1 and 2 has ended. Now in Chapter 3 a majestic hymn of praise surges forth. Notice how it praises the God of creation who is victorious over chaos. God is Lord of all the nations. God scatters the wicked but protects the poor.

Is there still a vision? As Habakkuk prays, he stands in awe (3:2), remembering God's power in the past and praying for God's activity in the present. Habakkuk is given a vision of God's ultimate purpose fulfilled. His vision comes directly from God. God's glory fills the heavens, bright as the sun (3:3-4). Pestilence and plague march along with God. The wickedness of nations is destroyed. God stands, calm amidst the tumult, sizing up everything and everyone. Even the mountains wither beneath God's gaze. God will come again to conquer the chaos just as at the time of Creation.

No more questions rise to the prophet's lips; no more anguish disturbs his peace. God is working out the vision. For us, in the interim, we are to live out the instruction, "the righteous live [now and forever] by their faith" (2:4).

Gratitude soars in the psalm's crescendo (3:17-19). Give thanks to God in all circumstances. Logical explanations will not help us understand evil; we will gain such knowledge

NOTES, REFLECTIONS, AND QUESTIONS

through trust in God. The faithful, in spite of sickness and sorrow, sin and evil, learn to sing with Habakkuk:

"Though the fig tree does not blossom,
and no fruit is on the vines; . . .
yet I will rejoice in the LORD;
I will exult in the God of my salvation" (3:17-18).

MARKS OF OBEDIENT COMMUNITY

The faith community is at home in the "meantime" because it remembers and is confident that God is at work in ways we can't imagine. In God's time we will see the working out of God's purposes. Toward that end we respond to God's call to repent.

Are you ever tempted to doubt that God is in control? If so, say why.

For what do we most need to repent—false gods? blending our gods with our God? indifference?

Within the fellowship, deep emotions can be expressed—anger, guilt, shame, frustration as well as joy, gratitude, and praise. Sometimes we can argue, struggle, complain, doubt. We know God is approachable even if we are confused, angry, or filled with questions.

How open is our faith community to listen to blasphemy, rage, wild questioning by others who are rebelling or who have been hurt?

What spiritual ingredients help people rejoice even when "the fig tree does not blossom"?

IF YOU WANT TO KNOW MORE

Israel and Judah were often forced to pay tribute to foreign nations. Look up *tribute* in a Bible dictionary.

See what you can discover about kings Esar-haddon, Ashurbanipal, Nabopolassar, and the city of Carchemish.

NOTES, REFLECTIONS, AND QUESTIONS

The obeying community remembers and is confident that God is working out God's purposes and repents of its actions that contradict God's purposes.

LAMENT

"O that my head were a spring of water,
  and my eyes a fountain of tears,
so that I might weep day and night
  for the slain of my poor people!"

—Jeremiah 9:1

8 God's Anguish

OUR HUMAN CONDITION

Why all the talk of spiritual and moral decline? Things are going nicely. Somehow we're special. We've always managed to escape the consequences of our actions. No need to change. It won't happen to us. In our false confidence we misread the signs.

ASSIGNMENT

Jeremiah's ministry is long, his prophetic work varied, his emotional life interwoven with Judah. Events in the book flow neither sequentially nor smoothly. Stop from time to time to ponder what you are dealing with. Notice how reluctantly, how painfully Jeremiah spoke. See how lonely he was. Savor his imagery.

Some material from Kings you have read earlier, but rereading it will provide context for Jeremiah's prophecy.

Day 1 Jeremiah 1–3 (Jeremiah's call, Israel's apostasy, call to repent)

Day 2 Jeremiah 4–6 (a doomed nation, invasion and desolation of Judah coming)

Day 3 Jeremiah 7–11 (Temple sermon, laments over Judah and Zion, broken covenant); 2 Kings 22:1–23:30 (Josiah's reform)

Day 4 Jeremiah 12–15 (linen loincloth, wine jar, exile and punishment, personal laments); 2 Kings 23:31-37; 2 Chronicles 36:1-10 (Jehoahaz and Jehoiakim)

Day 5 Jeremiah 16–20 (sin of Judah, the potter and the clay, sabbath, personal laments, the broken jug)

Day 6 Read and respond to "The Word of the Lord" and "Marks of Obedient Community."

Day 7 Rest

PRAYER

Pray daily before study:

"I have relied on you since the day I was born,
  and you have always been my God.
Do not stay away from me!
  Trouble is near,
  and there is no one to help" (Psalm 22:10-11, TEV).

Prayer concerns for this week:

LAMENT

Day 1 Jeremiah 1–3 (Jeremiah's call, Israel's apostasy, call to repent)

2 Samuel 12:13 I have sinned against the Lord.

Day 2 Jeremiah 4–6 (a doomed nation, invasion and desolation of Judah coming)

5:19 Just like you have served foreign gods in your own land, you will serve foreigners in a land not your own.

6:16 Stand at the crossroads & look; ask for the ancient paths.

Day 3 Jeremiah 7–11 (Temple sermon, laments over Judah and Zion, broken covenant); 2 Kings 22:1–23:30 (Josiah's reform)

7:6 oppress the alien, the fatherless, the widow, shed innocent blood, follow other gods.

7:23 Obey me, walk in all the way I command you,

9:24 I am the Lord who exercises kindness, justice & righteousness on earth, for in these I delight.

2 Kings 23:25 heart, soul, strength worshiped the Lord. Josiah.

Day 4 Jeremiah 12–15 (linen loincloth, wine jar, exile and punishment, personal laments); 2 Kings 23:31-37; 2 Chronicles 36:1-10 (Jehoahaz and Jehoiakim)

17:10 The Lord is spring of living water.

Day 5 Jeremiah 16–20 (sin of Judah, the potter and the clay, sabbath, personal laments, the broken jug)

Day 6 "The Word of the Lord" and "Marks of Obedient Community"

THE WORD OF THE LORD

NOTES, REFLECTIONS, AND QUESTIONS

Jeremiah was born shortly after the child Josiah was made king of Judah. Jeremiah's father and some of his family were priests in the village of Anathoth, situated a few miles northeast of Jerusalem. Perhaps Jeremiah was a descendant of Abiathar, the high priest banished to Anathoth by King Solomon for political reasons (1 Kings 2:26-27).

We can identify four phases in Jeremiah's ministry. His early ministry lasted from his call (626 B.C.) to the discovery of "the book of the law" (the scroll of Deuteronomy) (622 B.C.). The second phase was a time of pulling back from public life as the prophet anxiously watched the reform movement unfold. The third phase, during the reign of Jehoiakim (609–598 B.C.), was a time of spiritual crisis when Jeremiah became vigorously active again, much as Isaiah had done during the rule of Hezekiah. His final phase of ministry coincided with Zedekiah and the Exile (597–587 B.C.).

God's Call

No call is formed in a vacuum. Did Jeremiah's mother put drops of honey on the Torah scrolls when he was a child so he would love the Scriptures? Did his father, a village priest in Anathoth, take him by the hand when they walked from the village to the Temple, three or four miles away? How did the boy know that God loves an honest measure, hates a bribe, and cares for the poor? He must have learned it at home.

Jeremiah's call from God was overwhelming.

"Before I formed you in the womb I knew you,
and before you were born I consecrated you;
I appointed you a prophet to the nations" (Jeremiah 1:5).

How old was Jeremiah? Fifteen or sixteen? The Hebrew word translated "boy" (1:6) denotes a young man not yet independent or head of a household. Too young to be a prophet, Jeremiah felt ill-prepared before the Lord. Jeremiah protested vigorously against what God called him to do, but to no avail. The Lord said,

"Do not say, 'I am only a boy';
for you shall go to all to whom I send you,
and you shall speak whatever I command you.
Do not be afraid of them,
for I am with you to deliver you,
says the LORD" (1:7-8).

Then visions came—an almond branch (God will perform his word) and a boiling pot, tilted from the north (Babylon is coming). The message was the vision; the vision was the call; and the call, etched deeply in his mind, became a fire in his bones (20:9). Jeremiah prophesied in Judah for nearly half a century (626–580 B.C.) during his country's most frightening and tragic period of history. God prohibited him from marrying or having children. That imposed celibacy was to be a sign that many families were doomed (16:1-4). Jeremiah was destined to be a lonely man, often cut off from friends and relatives, often weeping over his beloved but troubled country.

"My anguish, my anguish! I writhe in pain!
Oh, the walls of my heart!
My heart is beating wildly;
I cannot keep silent;
for I hear the sound of the trumpet,
the alarm of war" (4:19).

Jeremiah weeps because God weeps. The prophet reveals the ache in the heart of God. Jeremiah's heart breaks for his beloved Jerusalem; but his voice, demanding holiness of heart, thunders on.

Jeremiah announced a message that ran contrary to his own natural inclinations. Deep inside, he would have preferred to have spoken differently. He cared enormously about his people but was driven against his nature by a holy word that had to be spoken.

Beginning Ministry

Much of Jeremiah's early work is recorded in Jeremiah 1–6. We can hear in his preaching the influence of earlier prophets. Like Amos and Micah, he denounced greed. Following Hosea, Jeremiah understood faith as a love relationship as well as obedience to the Law. Like Hosea, he used both the father-son and the husband-wife analogies to reflect the intimacy between the Lord and Israel. Just like Hosea, Jeremiah denounced the nation's spiritual harlotry.

"You have played the whore with many lovers;
and would you return to me?
says the LORD" (Jeremiah 3:1).

The betrayal is unbelievable. Can you imagine a bride forgetting her gown? "Yet my people have forgotten me" (2:32).

Jeremiah was filled with despair over the moral and spiritual decline he witnessed.

"The prophets prophesy falsely,
and the priests rule as the prophets direct;
my people love to have it so" (5:31).

Some prophets only chastised the leaders, but Jeremiah lambasted the entire population—rich and poor, high and low.

"From the least to the greatest of them,
everyone is greedy for unjust gain" (6:13).

More than any other prophet, Jeremiah cries out for repentance, for a radical return. " 'Return, faithless people,' declares the LORD, 'for I am your husband' " (3:14, NIV). It is the heart of the people that is evil. The heart must be changed. Circumcision, the ancient rite every male child received as a sign of identification with the covenant people, is not enough.

"Circumcise yourselves to the LORD,
remove the foreskin of your hearts" (4:4).

But as Jeremiah grew older, he, like Isaiah, realized the

NOTES, REFLECTIONS, AND QUESTIONS

people's ears were closed and their eyes were shut (5:21).

The problem of idolatry is pride, a pride that confuses the creation with the Creator, that sees this world as an end in itself. That pride links politics and economics into an oppressive form, fortified by a religion of false gods that are under official control. Jeremiah believed God was trying to get the people to grieve, to weep, to change before it was too late.

King Josiah's Reform

Josiah, even as a teenager, began to reverse the religious syncretism (mixing pagan gods with worship of Israel's one God) of his father Amon and his grandfather Manasseh. Perhaps he was tutored by priests and prophets zealous for the Lord. But he was also supported by nationalistic zealots who sensed the power vacuum in Mesopotamia as Assyria began to falter. So Josiah began to repair the Temple in Jerusalem. That act was perceived by Assyria as rebellion.

King Josiah had a twofold vision—religiously to purify Jewish ritual leading to Deuteronomic reform (2 Kings 23:21-24) and politically to reunite the divided kingdoms under one king of Davidic descent. Probably the single most important aspect of Josiah's reform was the centralization of worship in Jerusalem—one God, one people, one form of worship. Without doubt, every act of Josiah, religious or otherwise, was seen by Assyria as sedition and rebellion. Fortunately for Judah, Assyria was too weak to respond. Unfortunately for Judah, both Egypt and Babylon were moving into the power vacuum. The whole nation of Judah, religious leaders and national patriots, wept when Josiah was killed (609 B.C.). Jeremiah wrote a lament to express his own and the nation's grief (2 Chronicles 35:25).

Memory

Prophets lifted up the core memory:

"Thus says the LORD:
Stand at the crossroads, and look,
and ask for the ancient paths,
where the good way lies; and walk in it,
and find rest for your souls" (Jeremiah 6:16).

The prophets called for people to believe and practice what they already knew. "Hear, O Israel: The LORD is our God, the LORD alone. You shall love the LORD your God with all your heart, and with all your soul, and with all your might" (Deuteronomy 6:4-5). Judah tested her prophets by whether their foretelling actually came true. Jeremiah said often that after the destruction came, the people would know who were the false prophets and who the true prophets. Centuries later we read Jeremiah's words, and we soberly say, "It came to pass."

Jeremiah could hear, as it were, decibels above the others, the rumblings of far-off chariots, while kings and people stuck their fingers in their ears. He cried out for repentance:

NOTES, REFLECTIONS, AND QUESTIONS

When David established his capital in Jerusalem, he moved the ark of the covenant from Kiriath-jearim to the capital city. From that time on, Jerusalem became the only proper place to worship God through sacrifices—though festivals, offerings, and prayers continued in other places. When Solomon built the Temple, the ark was housed in the Holy of Holies, which came to be perceived as the throne of God and the permanent dwelling place of God. This understanding led the people to believe the ark and the Temple could not be corrupted or destroyed. When Josiah attempted to remove all worship of foreign gods, he also outlawed the use of other sites used for the worship of God, even those in what had been Israel, outlawing official worship at any place other than Jerusalem.

"Take warning, O Jerusalem,
  or I shall turn from you in disgust,
and make you a desolation" (Jeremiah 6:8).

Have you observed that the prophets wasted little time on externals? They scarcely mentioned Jewish food laws or carefully prescribed festival days. How little attention they gave to the exact time sabbath would begin or whether circumcision was performed. The washing pools outside the Temple were designed for ceremonial cleansing. But Jeremiah would plead for a much deeper cleansing than that.

During the reign of King Jehoiakim, Jeremiah denounced the people for their belief that God would protect the Temple and them. He walked boldly into the Temple courtyard on a holy festival day. Judeans were there from all over the world. Jeremiah shouted his sermon at the crowd: "Do not trust in these deceptive words: 'This is the temple of the LORD, the temple of the LORD, the temple of the LORD' " (7:4, 11).

Hadn't the prophet Nathan told David, "Your house [dynasty] and your kingdom shall be made sure forever before me; your throne shall be established forever" (2 Samuel 7:16)? After four hundred years of Davidic kings and a Temple unscathed, the Judeans were understandably confident.

Judah had been protected by the Lord repeatedly. Every school child learned about the Assyrian invasion of the Northern Kingdom and the destruction of Samaria. They knew that those same Assyrian armies swept up to the gates of Jerusalem and laid siege to the city. They quoted Isaiah's announcing to King Hezekiah, with armies surrounding Jerusalem, "Therefore thus says the LORD concerning the king of Assyria: He shall not come into this city, shoot an arrow there, come before it with a shield, or cast up a siege ramp against it. By the way that he came, by the same he shall return; he shall not come into this city, says the LORD. For I will defend this city to save it, for my own sake and for the sake of my servant David" (Isaiah 37:33-35). That prophecy proved true in 701 B.C., but the people thought it meant eternal protection.

They misunderstood the meaning of Shiloh, said Jeremiah. Shiloh, about sixteen miles north of Jerusalem, was the most important place of worship during the period of the judges. The ark of the covenant had rested there. Hannah, Samuel's mother, had prayed there. Eli taught young Samuel at Shiloh. It was Saul's favorite sanctuary, but the Philistines destroyed it. Now the people of Judah said, Aha, that meant God wanted the place of supreme worship to be in David's city, in the Temple in Jerusalem. God will protect his house forever.

Jeremiah said, You've got it all wrong. The same God who permitted Shiloh to be destroyed will allow Jerusalem to be destroyed also. You are violating Torah so badly, fracturing covenant so completely, that God will allow the Babylonians to ravage your Temple. (Remember this is Jeremiah, a son of a priest, who is talking.) You are putting your trust in the

NOTES, REFLECTIONS, AND QUESTIONS

The inscription on this fragment of a stela, found at Tel Dan in 1993, dating from the ninth century B.C., refers to both "the House of David" and "the King of Israel." This is thought to be the first time the name David has been found outside the Bible. The fragment lay beneath debris from Tiglath-pileser III's eighth-century conquest.

Temple, not in God. Worship for you has become mechanical. You practice wickedness; you worship as hypocrites. Then you boast that the holy God of Israel will protect you from all enemies. You are deceiving yourselves.

When Jeremiah denounced the Temple, the priests, the prophets, and even the people wanted to kill him. What saved him was the historic tradition that allowed unpopular prophets to speak. "Some of the elders of the land arose and said to all the assembled people, 'Micah of Moresheth, who prophesied during the days of King Hezekiah of Judah, said . . . Jerusalem shall become a heap of ruins' " (Jeremiah 26:17-18). Micah's prophecy and Judah's tolerance saved Jeremiah's life.

But Jeremiah became weary. Everyone was turning against him. He complained to God. God's answer was tough:

> "If you have raced with foot-runners and they have
> wearied you,
> how will you compete with horses?" (12:5).

Recall times when you thought you were spiritually exhausted, only to discover that more difficult challenges still lay ahead.

Sabbath

Concern for sabbath in Jeremiah catches us by surprise (Jeremiah 17:19-27). It has not been a major theme for the prophets. But notice that the details of sabbath observance are not there. Jeremiah's demand is as basic as the Decalogue itself. "Remember the sabbath day, and keep it holy" (Exodus 20:8). Sabbath is an identifying mark of the religious community. It honors God and declares that God can be trusted.

An earlier prophet complained that people spent their sabbaths planning their work days, eager for sabbath to be over (Amos 8:5). Today we tend to think of adultery and stealing as much more serious than sabbath-breaking, but the Decalogue of Moses puts it ahead of them. Why? When love of God breaks down, love of neighbor deteriorates. If we do not hand our lives back to God regularly, the world will have us in its grip and will destroy us.

How are you doing with keeping God's sabbath?

Don't miss the imagery of Jeremiah and the crashing earthenware jug (Jeremiah 19:1-13). He breaks it with great ceremony. Jerusalem would be so broken. That act put him in stocks where people could walk by, laugh at him, and spit in his face (20:2). The broken jug sermon and the punishment

NOTES, REFLECTIONS, AND QUESTIONS

that followed caused Jeremiah to reconsider his divine call. Had not God told him in that early teenage call,

"Do not be afraid of them,
for I am with you to deliver you,
says the LORD" (1:8)?

The prophet wished he had never been born (20:14), but the searing sense of call would not go away.

"Within me there is something like a burning fire
shut up in my bones" (20:9).

The reconsideration is over. The message is a part of him. Sometimes we have to do something because we think it right. No way to get out of it whatever the cost.

When, if ever, have you felt that way?

MARKS OF OBEDIENT COMMUNITY

Jeremiah is called "the weeping prophet"; he wept over Judah. Jesus wept over Jerusalem. The community of faith weeps over a broken world. The tears are holy tears. Weeping can be a sentimental escape from reality, but it can also bring involvement. Weeping can lead to repentance, a changed life, an entrance into the city of pain and compassion.

What is causing God anguish today?

Over what should we be weeping?

Over what sins or failures of our own should we be weeping?

Being the older brother

IF YOU WANT TO KNOW MORE

Jeremiah is one of the most accessible of the prophets. Begin writing a sketch of Jeremiah the man. Add to the sketch after Lesson 9.

Do some further reading on Shiloh.

NOTES, REFLECTIONS, AND QUESTIONS

The community of faith, moved by compassion, weeps over a broken, unheeding world.

NEW COVENANT

"I will set my eyes upon them for good, and I will bring them back to this land. I will build them up, and not tear them down; I will plant them, and not pluck them up. I will give them a heart to know that I am the LORD; and they shall be my people and I will be their God, for they shall return to me with their whole heart."

—Jeremiah 24:6-7

9 God Will Not Abandon

OUR HUMAN CONDITION

We prefer to hear positive things even if they are false. Though our families and our communities may be falling apart, we ignore the warning signs and reject the messages we don't like.

ASSIGNMENT

Read Jeremiah 22–26 before 21 to help you keep the kings in order. (Chapter 21 is out of sequence.) Why did the editors of the Jeremiah materials put the Jehoiakim scroll incident (Jeremiah 36) out of place and after much Zedekiah material? Because it graphically symbolizes Jeremiah's entire ministry and Judah's consistent response. Make notes as you read to keep straight in your mind who the various kings are and where they fit into history. Remember three—good Josiah, bad Jehoiakim, and weak Zedekiah.

Day 1 Jeremiah 22–26 (royal arrogance, Branch of David, false prophets, good and bad figs, captivity foretold, Temple sermon); 2 Kings 23:31–24:19 (Jehoahaz [Shallum], Jehoiakim, Jehoiachin, Zedekiah)

Day 2 Jeremiah 21; 27–29 (oracle against Jerusalem, the yoke, Hananiah opposes Jeremiah, letter to the exiles, Shemaiah); 2 Chronicles 36:11-21 (Zedekiah)

Day 3 Jeremiah 30–33 (promised return, a new covenant, Jeremiah buys a field, the righteous Branch)

Day 4 Jeremiah 34–36 (slaves freed, sign of the Rechabites, the scroll read and burned); 2 Kings 25 (siege of Jerusalem, Judah in captivity)

Day 5 Jeremiah 37–38 (Jeremiah imprisoned, consultations with Zedekiah); 42:7–44:14 ("Do not go to Egypt," Jeremiah taken to Egypt); 52 (destruction reviewed)

Day 6 Read and respond to "The Word of the Lord" and "Marks of Obedient Community."

Day 7 Rest

PRAYER

Pray daily before study:

"Remind me each morning of your constant love,
for I put my trust in you.
My prayers go up to you;
show me the way I should go" (Psalm 143:8, TEV).

Prayer concerns for this week:

NEW COVENANT

Day 1 Jeremiah 22–26 (royal arrogance, Branch of David, false prophets, good and bad figs, captivity foretold, Temple sermon); 2 Kings 23:31–24:19 (Jehoahaz [Shallum], Jehoiakim, Jehoiachin, Zedekiah)

Day 2 Jeremiah 21; 27–29 (oracle against Jerusalem, the yoke, Hananiah opposes Jeremiah, letter to the exiles, Shemaiah); 2 Chronicles 36:11-21 (Zedekiah)

Day 3 Jeremiah 30–33 (promised return, a new covenant, Jeremiah buys a field, the righteous Branch)

Day 4 Jeremiah 34–36 (slaves freed, sign of the Rechabites, the scroll read and burned); 2 Kings 25 (siege of Jerusalem, Judah in captivity)

Day 5 Jeremiah 37–38 (Jeremiah imprisoned, consultations with Zedekiah); 42:7–44:14 ("Do not go to Egypt," Jeremiah taken to Egypt); 52 (destruction reviewed)

Day 6 "The Word of the Lord" and "Marks of Obedient Community"

THE WORD OF THE LORD

NOTES, REFLECTIONS, AND QUESTIONS

Jeremiah was a voice to be reckoned with. No matter what the kings did or what the court prophets said, they looked at Jeremiah out of the corner of their eyes. He had access to the kings, and he constantly demanded justice. If the kings would turn and be faithful to their duty to do justice, the Davidic dynasty could continue; if not, other nations would wonder why the Lord punished Judah so severely.

Jehoiakim

Some leaders of Judah wished good King Josiah could return. They still mourned. Jeremiah said, Don't weep for him; weep for Jehoahaz (Shallum), who will never come back from Egypt (Jeremiah 22:10). Now comes the frontal attack on Jehoiakim. In Judah's most critical hour, the arrogant king remodeled his quarters. He used the most expensive materials, imported woods and furnishings. Lacking money, he conscripted poor working people, families off their plots of land, and made them work without pay (22:13-17).

What an act of *self-deception!* That beautiful mansion would soon smolder in ashes. What an example of *injustice!* Conscripted labor would cause families to go hungry, farmers to lose their crops, laborers to become slaves. What an illustration of *arrogance,* of pride, of trusting self! Remember, the prophet Micah had declared a king's job was to do justice and to provide equity (Micah 3:9-10). From the beginning, kings of Israel were to serve, not to be served.

Do you call yourself a king because you excel in remodeling? Don't miss the key word the prophet uses, *neighbors:* The king "makes his neighbors work for nothing" (Jeremiah 22:13). Jews in the covenant community were to eat manna together, to be free, to be neighbors, from the least to the greatest.

Jeremiah appealed to the memory of the king's father, Josiah, who "judged the cause of the poor and needy" (22:16). Then it was well in the land. But the appeal failed. Jeremiah forecast the lonely burial: No one will call Jehoiakim "brother"; no one will mourn, saying, "Alas, his majesty!" (22:18). He will be buried without fuss or bother, like a dead farm animal (22:19). Jehoiakim died when he was about thirty-six years of age, during the siege of Jerusalem. His son Jehoiachin, called "Coniah" in 22:24, would soon be carried to Babylon where he would die. Nothing could stop the inevitable. God would cast him away even if he were "the signet ring" on God's right hand (22:24). "Record this man as childless," said Jeremiah, for no descendant of Jehoiachin would sit on David's throne (22:30).

The prophet enlarged the concept of "shepherds" (23:1-4). Not only the king but the leaders of the nation, including priests and prophets, were supposed to be "shepherds." Instead, the leaders were destroying and scattering the sheep (23:1).

In our nation, in our towns, in our churches, how are our leaders self-serving? Or how are they shepherds?

Because the leaders have failed, God will step in personally after the "scattering" takes place to be shepherd for Israel, just as in the beginning (23:3). A glimmer of hope begins to shine in Jeremiah. Someday, after the destruction, after the Exile, God will bring the lost sheep of Israel back into the fold. A righteous king will rule (23:5). No longer will the people of Israel refer to the Lord as the one who brought them up out of the land of Egypt; after the ingathering they will say, the Lord who brought us back out of the lands of captivity (23:7-8).

Jeremiah blasts the court prophets, calling them adulterers (23:9-17). The term likely meant an "adulterous" relationship with other gods from foreign lands, thereby making them spiritually unfaithful. They were liars. They aided those in power who were destroying the country.

Without question the great prophets of Israel and Judah expected moral and spiritual leadership from those with political and religious authority. How much of that expectation do we still have? In what sense is it appropriate for us to expect a lot? How are our leaders measuring up?

The vision of the good figs and the bad figs (Jeremiah 24) carries a simple message. The good figs are those exiles carried into Babylon by the earlier invasion. The bad figs are those people remaining in Jerusalem, still resisting God's will. Once again Jeremiah runs at cross purposes with the court prophets. They were smugly saying that God had punished the wicked by removing them, that God had rewarded the righteous by allowing them to remain. Just the opposite, said Jeremiah. Those who are still rebellious will die (24:8-10); those who have been deported will return (24:5-7).

From a purely historical viewpoint, years later the Jews who came home to rebuild were those who had been disciplined by years in exile. They came rejoicing with new zeal and fresh spiritual insight. Most of the post-exilic writings, most of the theological editing of Deuteronomy, Kings, and Chronicles came from the pens of these Jews of the Diaspora.

Jeremiah is specific now (25). King Nebuchadrezzar is God's servant for a time, an agent of punishment for Judah and surrounding nations. His own punishment will come later, after a decade of sabbaths, about seventy years. God rules all the nations of the world.

NOTES, REFLECTIONS, AND QUESTIONS

Nebuchadnezzar (Jeremiah 27:6–29:3) and *Nebuchadrezzar* (other occurrences in Jeremiah) are the same person. The different spellings reflect different transliterations of the Babylonian form *Nabu-kudurru-usur*. In the NRSV, only Jeremiah and Ezekiel use the form with an *r*. All other parts of the Old Testament use an *n*. Some translations use *Nebuchadnezzar* exclusively.

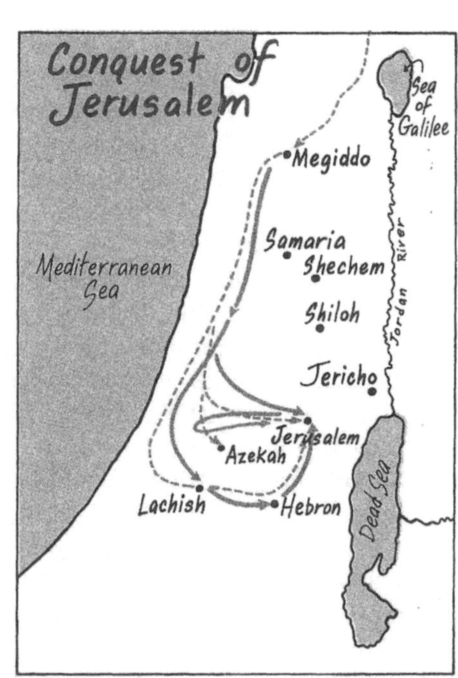

Nebuchadnezzar waged two campaigns against Jerusalem, one in 597 B.C. (broken arrow) and one in 587 B.C. (solid arrow).

Public Debate

Our sympathies go out to King Zedekiah. He was in a tough spot. True, the Babylonians had put him in power after their invasion of 598. But now Babylon was having troubles in other parts of the empire. Egypt offered to join Judah in armed rebellion. Many politicians and most of the prophets were saying, "Strike now; it is time to be free. God is with us." To think otherwise was to appear pro-Babylonian and traitorous to Temple and king.

King Zedekiah had already joined forces with Egypt in rebellion against Babylon before he called Jeremiah in for advice (Jeremiah 21:1-2). Perhaps the prophet would give consolation even as Isaiah had been able to do for Hezekiah a century before. But to no avail. Jeremiah's eye was single. The enemy was God, and Babylon at this moment was doing God's bidding. Stop the rebellion, yield to the Babylonians (Chaldeans). Those words during wartime smacked of cowardice and complicity. Zedekiah ignored them.

Symbolic Yoke

Jeremiah built a symbolic yoke of straps and wood, similar to the yoke used on oxen (Jeremiah 27:2). He put it on his shoulders and apparently wore it around town to send a message: God put the yoke of Babylon on Judah and other nations. Everyone, including the prophet Hananiah, was saying the exiles would soon be free and would bring the precious silver and gold Temple vessels back home (28:2-3). Watch carefully in Jeremiah 28:6-9; Jeremiah responds somewhat respectfully, in effect, "Amen; so be it." That would be wonderful. But those prophets who preceded you and me told of war and not of peace. If peace comes, you will be right. But it will not come. Hananiah tore off Jeremiah's yoke right in the Temple courtyard (28:10). He shouted that God would break the yoke that Babylon was forcing them to wear and the exiles would soon be home.

Jeremiah's vision was still crystal clear. He announced that a heavier yoke was coming, a yoke forged of iron bars. And he said Hananiah did not have the word of the Lord. In fact, within the year, Hananiah would be dead because he had "spoken rebellion against the LORD." Two months later, Hananiah died (28:16-17).

Correspondence moved back and forth between Jerusalem and the exiles from 598 to 590. Jeremiah wrote, "Take wives and have sons and daughters; take wives for your sons, and give your daughters in marriage, that they may bear sons and daughters; multiply there, and do not decrease. But seek the welfare of the city where I have sent you into exile, and pray to the LORD on its behalf, for in its welfare you will find your welfare" (29:6-7). Jeremiah saw the hand of God working out a slow but important providential design. The Jews in the Diaspora would learn that God is not just the God of favored

NOTES, REFLECTIONS, AND QUESTIONS

This letter, one of eighteen written in ink on pieces of broken pottery (ostraca) and found in a military outpost at Lachish, is from a Judean soldier to his commanding officer. It says, "we are watching for the signals [probably bonfires] of Lachish . . . for we cannot see Azekah." Probably Azekah had already fallen to Nebuchadnezzar's army (587 B.C.), and Lachish and Jerusalem would follow.

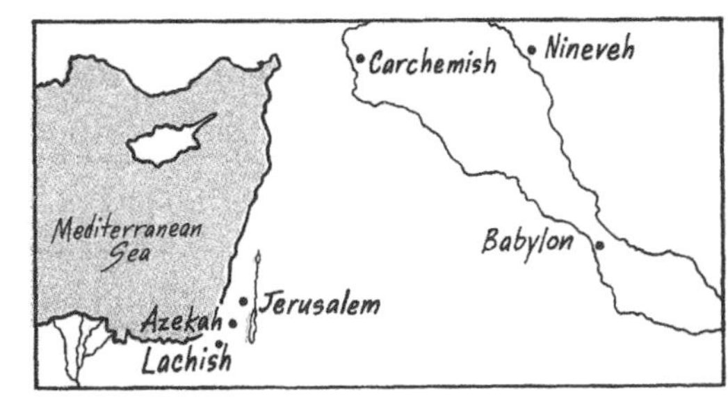

Israel but God of the nations, not limited to Jerusalem but living in all the world. Jeremiah also knew that, tempered and sobered, they would be the remnant people to whom God would give a new covenant (31:31-34).

Shemaiah, one of the false prophets, wrote an angry letter back asking the Temple authorities to shut Jeremiah up, for he was taking the heart out of the exiles (29:24-28). They thought their thin thread of hope lay in the salvation of the Temple and in quick return. Jeremiah knew their only hope lay in the God of the universe who would sustain them if they would trust.

Restoration sometimes takes a long time. That's why faith is essential. Contemplate a time of exile for you, your family, or your country when restoration was a long time coming. When you find it hard to wait on the Lord, what helps you?

How do you know when to act and when to wait?

A New Covenant

Mostly, Jeremiah is not apocalyptic in the sense of seeing a vision of end times, of a new world to come. Rather, he sees the exiles returning to the land of Judah, renewed in spirit. They will come back to the land of promise. The assurance is clear. The Babylonian yoke will one day be broken by the Lord (Jeremiah 30:8).

The entire experience of exile was an act of divine discipline. God punished Israel as a loving parent corrects a child. God not only will punish but will teach as well. The prophet warned Israel to "set up road markers" so they would learn from this experience (31:21). So their geographical return home would also be a return by way of Torah to faithfulness. Then came a theological breakthrough. We will spot it again in Ezekiel. People were saying, we're suffering because of our parents' sins (they ate sour grapes, so our teeth are set on edge). There was truth in that, of course. But a bold new truth was emerging. We don't have to suffer for the sins of our ancestors. We can be freed from that to wrestle with our own problems (31:29-30). In other words, we can't blame our parents; we are responsible for our own predicament.

God will make a new covenant with Israel (31:31-34) to replace their earlier covenant with God, broken through their disobedience. The renewed people in a new covenant will have faithful and obedient hearts for God.

NOTES, REFLECTIONS, AND QUESTIONS

NOTES, REFLECTIONS, AND QUESTIONS

Time for Hope

Jeremiah languished in prison, listening to the sounds of war. A cousin named Hanamel appeared, just as God had said he would, wanting to sell a family property in Anathoth, a few miles away in already-occupied territory (Jeremiah 32:6-15). The grapevines had been torn down, the booth arbors burned, and the destitute cousin wanted Jeremiah to buy the land so the family would not lose it. Since Jeremiah was next of kin, he had first right of purchase to protect the family inheritance (Leviticus 25:25-31).

Instead of laughing at the ludicrous proposal, Jeremiah knew God was speaking once again. While he sat in the court of the guard, wondering how to give hope to Judah, God sent him a cousin with a farm to sell! Jeremiah took infinite pains to make everything legal (and to dramatize the symbolic act). They transferred cash (the full value of the land in peacetime) and signed the deeds. Witnesses watched the transaction. Jeremiah instructed Baruch, his secretary, to make a public filing of the deeds and to deposit them where they would be safe (Jeremiah 32:14).

The word went out that Jeremiah believed God would bring the people home and one day people would farm the land again. The word has gone out across the centuries that in the moment of deepest despair God does not abandon God's people.

When have you experienced someone acting with hope in a moment of despair, giving encouragement to others?

Jeremiah Rejected

Picture the prophet, barred from the Temple and the palace, working with his scribe and friend Baruch, preparing a scroll of prophecy for the people of Judah and the king (36:1-8). Watch King Jehoiakim as Jehudi reads the message aloud in the king's private chamber. After hearing each portion, Jehoiakim, unaffected by what he has heard, takes his penknife, cuts off the passage from the scroll, and throws that piece into the fire (36:21-23). What a graphic portrayal of total rejection. Jeremiah learns about the incident, as does all of Judah. He and Baruch prepare a second scroll with much of the same material. The climax of the incident comes in 36:31: "I will punish him [Jehoiakim] and his offspring . . . I will bring . . . on the people of Judah, all the disasters with which I have threatened them—but they would not listen."

A *bulla* from a seal from Judah with an impression that reads "(Belonging) to Berekhyahu [Baruch] son of Neriyahu the scribe" may have belonged to the scribe of Jeremiah. A *bulla* is a small lump of clay impressed with a seal to seal a document.

Taken to Egypt

After the collapse of the city, the Babylonians offered to take care of Jeremiah in Babylon, but he chose to stay among the people in the land (Jeremiah 40:2-6). In response to an inquiry from the people, Jeremiah counseled them and their leaders not to seek haven in Egypt but to stay as a remnant in Judah. His counsel was rejected. Then some of his enemies took him and Baruch along with others and carried them to Egypt. What could be a more fitting symbol than to be taken unwillingly to Egypt? Jeremiah's last recorded words were of ruin for Egypt and of the consequences of the choice to leave Judah and, in effect, Judah's God and the covenant. Thus, Baruch and Jeremiah became Jews of the Diaspora.

Jeremiah never lost the fire in his bones, never lost faith that God is in ultimate control. He died in Egypt, still owning land in Judah where one day, as he had foretold, people would return, raise their children and their crops, and "know the LORD."

MARKS OF OBEDIENT COMMUNITY

We want to listen to the word of the Lord speaking to us today. What is tearing at the fabric of our homes? our communities? What can we do about it?

The prophets, no matter how hard the word, did not speak without hope. We are a community with a future, for God has given us a future. We do not lose hope, ever.

What is the underlying, unshakable basis for our hope?

How can a warning lead to hope?

How can pain produce change and foster hope?

IF YOU WANT TO KNOW MORE

Read the oracles against other nations in Jeremiah 46–51 for additional words of warning.

Complete the sketch of Jeremiah you began in Lesson 8.

Look up Nebuchadnezzar, Pharaoh Neco, and Babylon in a Bible dictionary.

NOTES, REFLECTIONS, AND QUESTIONS

The faith community knows that its hope springs from its willingness to hear the word of the Lord and to trust that God will not abandon God's people.

DOOM

"Your doom has come to you,
  O inhabitant of the land.
The time has come, the day is near—
  of tumult, not of reveling on the mountains. . . .
See, the day! See, it comes!
  Your doom has gone out."

—Ezekiel 7:7, 10

10 The Day of the Lord Has Come

OUR HUMAN CONDITION

With tears and pain we discover our own ways judge us. We can't buy our way out. We can't blame anyone else. We are accountable.

ASSIGNMENT

Many Bible students skip over Ezekiel. The visions are bizarre, the poetry obscure, the imagery symbolic. But don't be put off. The form may be complicated, but the message is simple. The instruction of the priestly prophet is profound and clear once we get inside the oracles.

We will omit the oracles against other nations; but we will not forget that Ezekiel, like the other prophets, wants us to know God judges and rules all the nations of the world. Look for the meaning, the main point, in the detailed imagery. Watch for the recurring phrase, "You will know that I am the LORD."

Day 1 Ezekiel 1–3 (visions of the chariot and the scroll, sentinel for Israel)
Day 2 Ezekiel 4–7 (symbols of the siege, the coming judgment)
Day 3 Ezekiel 8–11 (Temple visions, judgment and promise)
Day 4 Ezekiel 12–16 (symbols of Exile, false prophets and prophetesses, useless vine, unfaithful foundling, God's faithless bride)
Day 5 Ezekiel 17–18; 20; 24 (the two eagles and the vine, the cedar, individual responsibility, Israel continues to rebel, God promises restoration, the boiling pot, death of Ezekiel's wife)
Day 6 Read and respond to "The Word of the Lord" and "Marks of Obedient Community."
Day 7 Rest

PRAYER

Pray daily before study:
"Do not abandon me, O LORD;
  do not stay away, my God!
Help me now, O Lord my savior!" (Psalm 38:21-22, TEV).

Prayer concerns for this week:

Doom

Day 1 Ezekiel 1–3 (visions of the chariot and the scroll, sentinel for Israel)

Day 2 Ezekiel 4–7 (symbols of the siege, the coming judgment)

7:20 God gave silver & gold but they used it to make idols. The resources God gives should be used to do his work & carry out his will.

5:7 Israel behaved worse than the neighbouring nations.

Day 3 Ezekiel 8–11 (Temple visions, judgment and promise)

8:6 God held an open house in your life today, how comfortable would you be?

11:5 no secrets can be kept from God.

11:15-21 God will evaluate your life by your faith & obedience, not by your earthly success.

11:19-20: I will give them one heart & put a new spirit within them.

Day 4 Ezekiel 12–16 (symbols of Exile, false prophets and prophetesses, useless vine, unfaithful foundling, God's faithless bride)

13:2,3 God promises his followers health & material success (false prophets)

No one's beyond redemption.

Day 5 Ezekiel 17–18; 20; 24 (the two eagles and the vine, the cedar, individual responsibility, Israel continues to rebel, God promises restoration, the boiling pot, death of Ezekiel's wife)

17:23 – Mustard seed like. Mark 5:30-32

18:20 The soul who sins is the one who will die.

18:32 Repent & Live.

Individual responsibility.

Ex 34:6-7 ~~Ex 5:8-10~~ Deu 5:8-10

Lev:

Day 6 "The Word of the Lord" and "Marks of Obedient Community"

THE WORD OF THE LORD

Ezekiel, a contemporary of Jeremiah, was born during the reform of King Josiah. He and his wife, presumably in their early twenties, were carried off with King Jehoiachin and his royal entourage in the first deportation to Babylon (597 B.C.). Nebuchadnezzar placed Ezekiel in a settlement on the Chebar canal called "Tel-abib."

"By the rivers of Babylon—
there we sat down and there we wept
when we remembered Zion" (Psalm 137:1).

While Jeremiah prophesied in Jerusalem, Ezekiel prophesied and gave counsel to the exiles settled on the canal in Babylon.

God's Mobility

The "glory of the LORD" swooped down upon Ezekiel during the fifth year of his exile when he was about thirty years old. As you read the vision in Ezekiel 1, remember Ezekiel is experiencing God. He is trying to describe what words fail to describe. Notice how often he says "like" or "the likeness of." Ezekiel does not see God but only "the glory" enthroned above a blazing chariot of fire.

Here are a few tips: The number four is all encompassing, as in all four directions, or the four corners of the earth. God goes everywhere. The amber color, the jewels, the burnished bronze, the crystal—all point to the magnificent splendor of the throne of God. Four living creatures, servants of God, dart to and fro at God's bidding. Wherever the spirit goes, they go. The four faces—human, lion, ox, and eagle (Ezekiel 1:10)—have been given different interpretations. They hint of creation, humanity, the animal and the bird kingdom. They symbolize strength and power.

The wheels of the chariot are crucially important. Wheels within wheels represent freedom and mobility. God has been confined to Jerusalem, resident in the Temple, present at the altar of sacrifice. Ezekiel now learns God can go wherever God wants to go. When the wheels moved, "they moved in any of the four directions without veering" (1:17). God traveled to Babylon along with the exiles. They walked in fetters behind the creaking wheels of military chariots. God flew through the air in a chariot of fire. The people of God have moved; God has moved with them, not in a box like the ark of the covenant but high and lifted up, above all nations.

The rims of the wheels are full of eyes (1:18), eyes all over the place, moving with the wheels within the wheels. God can see anything; God sees everything. No use hiding or moving to another town. God sees and knows. God is with us.

When have you ever felt you moved away from God? When have you felt God's all-seeing presence?

NOTES, REFLECTIONS, AND QUESTIONS

The "river Chebar," a canal deep enough for navigation, flowed out of the Euphrates River close to what is today Baghdad, moved gently to the southeast through Nippur, and rejoined the river again. It was a part of the vast complex of irrigation canals that took the water from both the Tigris and the Euphrates rivers into the rich Mesopotamian flood plain, making the desert green.

In dramatic fashion, God asked Ezekiel to open his mouth and eat the scroll (3:1). God had written on it, front and back, lamentations and woes (2:9-10). No room for interpretations or additions. Take it straight. It contained everything he needed to say. The scroll tasted "as sweet as honey" (3:3).

God's words, spoken by the prophet, would be simple. Would the people back in Jerusalem listen? God tells Ezekiel that God doesn't know for sure whether they will repent. "Whether they hear or refuse to hear (for they are a rebellious house), they shall know that there has been a prophet among them" (2:5).

They are a hardheaded bunch, those people of Jerusalem, with stubborn hearts. So God gives them a prophet in Babylon as tough as they are (3:8-9). Never did a prophet appear with a harder "forehead" or a more stubborn will than the strange visionary by the Chebar. He was in a trance for seven days, but he came out speaking strong words (3:16-21). The uncompromising message was aimed at Judah, yet it still contained a hint of hope for repentance.

Siege on a Brick, the Shaved Head

Not even Isaiah or Jeremiah acted out oracles as dramatically as Ezekiel. No wonder the exiles at the Chebar gathered around the prophet each evening when the day's work was done. What would he do next?

We can imagine that in Jerusalem, during the lull between the two invasions, about 593 B.C., folks were saying, "The worst is over. God has come through for us once again. We are saved." And in Babylon, many exiles were whispering, "No use trying to adapt to this place. Soon we will be going home" (see Jeremiah 29:5-7).

So Ezekiel was tied up with ropes to symbolize slavery (Ezekiel 3:25; 4:8); didn't open his mouth (3:26); made a bread of tasteless grain and beans over dried cow dung (4:9, 15); measured bread and water in survival rations (4:10-11); drew a relief map of Jerusalem on a sun-dried brick and like a child at play built siegeworks against it (4:1-3); lay on his left side for 390 days as punishment for Israel, then on his right side forty days as punishment for Judah (4:4-8).

Do you get the picture? Long siege, terrible deprivation, total destruction. Nobody is going home for a while. In fact, more exiles will soon be joining those in Babylonia.

If that picture didn't penetrate the hard foreheads and stubborn hearts, the shaved head should. What is Ezekiel doing now? Come and see. Why, he's burning one third of his hair in the fire. You can smell it. He's chopping one third of his hair with a sword, fine as parsley. He's scattering the rest of his hair in the wind. No, wait, he's grabbing part of that and throwing it into the fire too, except for a few strands he's hiding in his robe. Only a meager remnant will even make it as exiles.

The prophet doesn't spell out the sins, only says Judah has

NOTES, REFLECTIONS, AND QUESTIONS

acted just like other nations. Actually, they behaved even worse (5:7). Later Ezekiel would express fiery wrath toward puppet king Zedekiah for breaking his oath to Nebuchadnezzar, thereby bearing false witness before God by joining forces of rebellion with Egypt (17:11-16).

How do you think religious people will be judged? In what sense might we be held more accountable because we have been given greater guidance?

Contrite heart & seeking Him always.

Sometimes it seems as if we have to break our promises. How do you feel about making commitments and then trying to keep them? How does God come into your making and keeping commitments?

Don't sin against God.

The Day of the Lord

For many of the prophets, doomsday was coming but was quite a way off. Now Ezekiel says the time of retribution has come. The awful "day of the Lord" foretold by Amos had arrived. "Your doom has come to you" (Ezekiel 7:7). God will "judge you according to your ways" (7:8). Often the judgment of God seems fair, consequences for actions. Those who tell lies become known as liars and cannot be trusted. Those who commit adultery violate their marriage, and their home disintegrates. Many who steal are caught and called thieves. Those who are greedy and selfish generally live lives of isolation from other people. Not always, but often judgment comes according to our ways.

"They shall fling their silver into the streets" (7:19). It doesn't do any good to throw money at most of our major life problems. It doesn't help to throw money at a rebellious child or at a disintegrating marriage. When a deadly disease or tragic accident comes, our gold and silver are impotent. We can't buy off God. When judgment comes, riches are "treated as unclean" (7:19).

Flight Over the Temple

Some people wonder how Ezekiel knew the intimate details of the Temple even though he was in Babylon. Keep in mind that priestly families owned no land; they were paid by tithes and offerings and earned their keep by presiding at the prayers and sacrifices. The office was hereditary. They were descendants of Aaron, the levitical priesthood. So Ezekiel, like Jeremiah, would have been taken to the Temple by his father, placed in training at an early age, and allowed to serve

NOTES, REFLECTIONS, AND QUESTIONS

as priest while still a young man. He knew the Temple like the back of his hand.

So when the spirit of the Lord grabbed him by the hair of his head, lifted him up in a vision, and transported him to Jerusalem (Ezekiel 8:2-3), the prophet knew where he was. The glory of the Lord was there (8:4); but, oh, the abominations were there too (8:6). He saw creeping things displayed as idols (8:10). And the seventy elders of Israel were waving incense pots over the idols in prayer (8:11). He knew at least one of these respected leaders by name.

But wait! It is worse than that. In their heart of hearts the elders believe that God has gone from Israel, that foreign gods will save them. Worst of all, they believe God does not know what they are thinking (8:12).

They have idols in their hearts (14:3, 7). Abomination! God says, "Repent and turn away from your idols; and turn away your faces from all your abominations" (14:6). The Almighty wants a people who have a heart for God.

At the north gate women were weeping in front of Tammuz, the Babylonian god of the life-death cycle (8:14). In the inner court, men, probably priests, sat facing the east, their backs to the Temple, bowing toward the daily birth of the sun god of Egypt (8:16). Idolatry and paganism had invaded the very house of God.

A sense of individual responsibility emerges in Ezekiel as in Jeremiah. When the Lord's scribe clothed in linen put a mark on the forehead of those who sighed and groaned over the abominations in the Temple, he differentiated between individual innocence and guilt (9:3-6).

Note the similarity of Chapter 10 to Chapter 1. Yes, here is the glory of the Lord, riding in the fiery chariot again—same wheels, same four directions, same cherubim, same eyes. Now the glory stopped at the east gate (10:19). What is happening in the Temple vision? The glory of the Lord is leaving the Temple! Are you certain? Yes, "these were the living creatures that I saw underneath the God of Israel by the river Chebar" (10:20). God has already been to Babylon, and now God is departing the Temple for good. Why did the glory of the Lord visit the east gate last? Because that's the main gate, the processional gate, the way God, the king, hundreds of priests, and thousands of worshipers entered the Temple on the great festival days. God is going out the way God came in! The people wanted the creeping things, the sun god, and Tammuz. Let those gods protect the Temple now.

Ezekiel wondered if any remnant would be left (11:13). Yes, because little settlements of Jews had been scattered among various countries. God says, "I have been a sanctuary to them for a little while in the countries where they have gone" (11:16). God will not abandon; God will not allow the remnant to perish. But more than that, God was doing a new thing. "I will give them one heart, and put a new spirit within them . . . so that they may follow my statutes and keep my

NOTES, REFLECTIONS, AND QUESTIONS

ordinances and obey them. Then they shall be my people, and I will be their God" (11:19-20).

Symbol of Exile

Because the people in Jerusalem would not see or hear, Ezekiel was instructed to act out for the people already in exile the going into exile and the king's attempted escape (Ezekiel 12:1-16). The prophet put a knapsack on a stick, dug a hole through the wall, and crawled out during the night. That's the way King Zedekiah would try to leave Jerusalem. But Zedekiah would be caught, blinded, and dragged off to Babylon (12:12-13).

Individual Responsibility

For centuries Israel's teachings included the idea that the sins of parents would bring suffering upon the children "to the third and the fourth generation" (Exodus 34:7) and quoted the proverb, "The parents have eaten sour grapes, and the children's teeth are set on edge" (Ezekiel 18:2). Now a flash of spiritual insight, no doubt grounded in the early covenant laws, blazes across the religious horizon. The one who sins is the one who is responsible—parent or child (18:3-4). You don't have to be responsible for the sins of your ancestors. Neither can you blame your ancestors for your sins. Turn. Return. Break loose through the power of God.

Are we holding this mystery in balance? What does this teaching have to say to us in our day?

Have compassion on people for the circumstances cannot be understood completely.

Ezekiel as a Sign

Ezekiel's wife died (Ezekiel 24:18). She was the delight of his eyes. In the morning she was alive; in the evening she was gone. The harsh instruction from God was that Ezekiel should not weep a tear, not permit a funeral, not allow mourners to wail the traditional laments, not eat the traditional burial meal with friends. When the elders asked why he acted so strangely, he was to say, "Thus says the Lord GOD: I will profane my sanctuary, the pride of your power, the delight of your eyes, and your heart's desire; and your sons and your daughters whom you left behind shall fall by the sword. And you shall do as I have done; you shall not cover your upper lip or eat the bread of mourners. Your turbans shall be on your heads and your sandals on your feet; you shall not mourn or weep, but you shall pine away in your iniquities and groan to one another" (24:21-23). The pain will be too deep for tears when the city dies.

NOTES, REFLECTIONS, AND QUESTIONS

MARKS OF OBEDIENT COMMUNITY

A thousand voices shout at us from all sides. Some are warnings; some are wooings. Some warnings come from God's Word; some come from human fears. On one hand, listening to every warning could make us cowards, afraid to get out of bed. Pity the Christian who is so timid as to refrain from the life God gives. Yet God gives deep moral and religious warnings that are built into the fabric of the universe. Those who betray these warnings will suffer.

What are some of these warnings built into the universe?

Wages of sin is death. As you sow so ye reap. They that wait upon the Lord shall fly up on wings like an eagle.

The faith community listens carefully to warnings but distinguishes between shouts that spring from human fears and the deep moral and religious warnings that come from God.

How can we distinguish fears that sap our courage from brave warnings that would save our souls?

Failing is a given. Spend time in the learning zone. Inner stance will help with outer stance.

How well are you able to move from one place to another, one period of time to another, and really believe God goes with you?

We moved continents.

When have you experienced "exile," perhaps after ignoring warnings?

College

When and how were you able to "go home again"?

Look for a job.

In what ways has hope come?

Getting right with the Lord.

IF YOU WANT TO KNOW MORE

Read the chapters we didn't have time to read, Ezekiel 19; 21-23.

NOTES, REFLECTIONS, AND QUESTIONS

The faith community heeds the deep moral and religious warnings built into the fabric of the universe.

PROMISE

" 'Mortal, can these bones live?' I answered, 'O Lord GOD, you know.' Then he said to me, 'Prophesy to these bones, and say to them: O dry bones, hear the word of the LORD. Thus says the Lord GOD to these bones: I will cause breath to enter you, and you shall live.' "

—Ezekiel 37:3-5

11 God Cleanses and Renews

OUR HUMAN CONDITION

How do we cope in exile? We didn't want to come. We don't feel at home. Sometimes we complain, sometimes repent. No sense putting down roots or making friends. We plan to go home soon.

ASSIGNMENT

Tough material! But don't let the obscure imagery, the harsh judgments, or the tedious detail of the Temple keep you from hearing Ezekiel's unique word from the Lord. Rejoice in the promise of Word and Spirit in the valley of dry bones. Relish the assurance of the river of grace flowing from the throne of the Temple.

Day 1 Ezekiel 33–34 (God's justice and mercy, fall of Jerusalem, shepherds of Israel, God the true shepherd)
Day 2 Ezekiel 35–36 (judgment against Edom, cleansing of Israel)
Day 3 Ezekiel 37 (valley of dry bones, Israel and Judah united)
Day 4 Ezekiel 40–45 (God's glory returns, levitical priests, holy district)
Day 5 Ezekiel 47–48 (river of mercy and healing, division of the land)
Day 6 Read and respond to "The Word of the Lord" and "Marks of Obedient Community."
Day 7 Rest

PRAYER

Pray daily before study:

"Remember your promise to me, your servant;
it has given me hope.
Even in my suffering I was comforted
because your promise gave me life"
(Psalm 119:49-50, TEV).

Prayer concerns for this week:

PROMISE

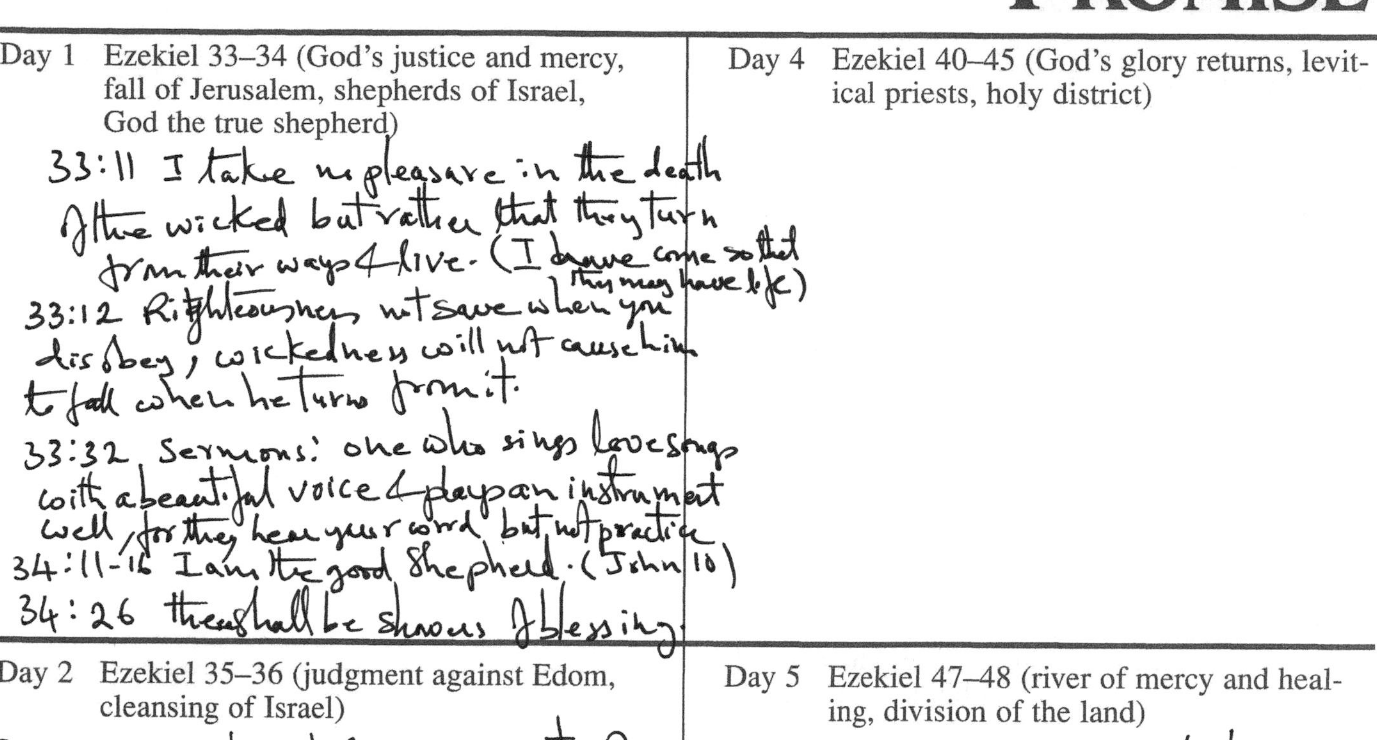

Day 1 Ezekiel 33–34 (God's justice and mercy, fall of Jerusalem, shepherds of Israel, God the true shepherd)

33:11 I take no pleasure in the death of the wicked but rather that they turn from their ways & live. (I have come so that they may have life)
33:12 Righteousness not save when you disobey, wickedness will not cause him to fall when he turns from it.
33:32 Sermons: one who sings love songs with a beautiful voice & plays an instrument well, for they hear your word but not practice
34:11-16 I am the good shepherd. (John 10)
34:26 there shall be showers of blessing.

Day 2 Ezekiel 35–36 (judgment against Edom, cleansing of Israel)

36:26 new heart & new spirit. Remove heart of stone & give you heart of flesh.

Day 3 Ezekiel 37 (valley of dry bones, Israel and Judah united)

Preach & leave the miracle of bring people alive to God.

Day 4 Ezekiel 40–45 (God's glory returns, levitical priests, holy district)

Day 5 Ezekiel 47–48 (river of mercy and healing, division of the land)

Allocation of land to tribes. Joseph two portion Manessa, Ephraim.

Day 6 "The Word of the Lord" and "Marks of Obedient Community"

DISCIPLE

THE WORD OF THE LORD

Let's pause and ask what really happened to the Judeans after 587 B.C. We have a good amount of historical data in Babylonian records. The able-bodied, the young men and women, the artisans, the scholars, the professionals, and priests—those who were not killed by war, famine, or disease—were marched off to Babylon. Unlike the Assyrians, the Babylonians did not replace the exiles with foreigners. Instead, they simply left behind in Judah a scattering of poor, rural people who worked the ravaged land and a handful of scavengers making do in the rubble of Jerusalem. The worst scenarios of the prophets were realized.

Babylonia

The Babylonians treated the exiles with restraint and permitted many to become prosperous across the years. The artisans worked at their specialties. The scholars and teachers joined faculties at schools and libraries. The former king of Judah, Jehoiachin, no longer capable of any kind of insurrection, dined at the table of the king (2 Kings 25:27-30).

Many exiled Jews maintained the irrigation canals and worked in the fields. They were allowed to live in settlements, to marry and have families, to enjoy freedom of conversation and prayer. Rebellion was out of the question.

Once Jerusalem was sacked, reality set in. Many Judean exiles followed the advice of Jeremiah and Ezekiel to build houses, work, and become a part of the economic community (Jeremiah 29:5-7).

The Jewish community in Babylon adapted its religious practices, its culture, even its language, leaving a legacy still felt today. Sacrifices could no longer be offered in the Temple, so Jewish traditions in the Torah were discussed. The prayers of the people substituted for the sacrifices of burnt offering. They no longer needed priests for the Temple, so teachers called rabbis emerged. These lay teachers taught the children and instructed the people in the ways of Torah. They began to reinterpret God's providential care to make sense of the Exile. They talked about return to Jerusalem and met regularly in small groups for prayer and study. They sang the ancient hymns, composed new ones, remembered the traditions of the ancestors, discussed the Exodus deliverance, and pondered the warnings of the prophets. Jewish settlements in other parts of the Diaspora developed similar clusters for study and prayer.

Fall of Jerusalem

Talk about understatement! The prophets, for a century and a half, had been doing everything they knew to dramatize the potential havoc. Now the announcement of Jerusalem's ruin is made in a single statement. A lonely, bedraggled escapee

NOTES, REFLECTIONS, AND QUESTIONS

From a secular viewpoint, the Babylonian Empire gleamed like a jewel in the ancient sun. It rested on great historical foundations, dating back as early as the sixth millennium B.C. and coming to its greatest power after 2000 B.C. When Abram and Sarai left this area, they left cities of high culture, music and art, mathematics and engineering, delicate foods and fine clothing. Babylonian scientists were famous for studying the stars for both astronomical and astrological interests, as noted by Isaiah (Isaiah 47:13). Under the famous Code of Hammurabi, laws were compiled during the eighteenth century B.C. that influenced the entire known world. Like the Torah, the code took people out of the spirit of revenge and tribal warfare, demanding instead only exact retribution, "eye for eye." (Torah often softened it, however; see Exodus 21:26-27.)

Nebuchadnezzar II (605–562 B.C.) embarked on an empire-building plan based on fertile farming, tribute from vassal countries, and trade throughout the known world. His canals, using the waters of the Tigris and Euphrates rivers, created an agricultural oasis of barley and wheat fields, palm groves and lush gardens. Gold and silver, fine fabrics, and ornamental gifts flowed in from captured territories. Traders from India and Egypt, from Macedonia and Syria bustled through the capital, hawking their wares and paying transport taxes. Travelers from all over the Mediterranean stood amazed at the palaces and temples in Babylon. The renowned hanging gardens were one of the wonders of the ancient world. Peace and prosperity reigned, at least in the heart of the empire, for over half a century.

comes to Ezekiel and says simply, "The city has fallen" (Ezekiel 33:21). That's it—no emotion, no embellishment.

God's Word is amazing. It is silent where we would be loud, loud where we would be silent. For some time Ezekiel has been unable to speak, except for prophecies of destruction (3:26-27). Now his tongue is loosened, and a fresh word is on his lips (33:22). In this time of lament, the prophet gives words of interpretation, meaning, and hope.

When we grieve, we often deny reality, express anger, blame God and others. Healing requires accepting reality. Health demands persons take responsibility for their own actions. We need not continue living as we do. God never closes the door to turning. We can redirect our lives. When have you consciously redirected your life?

Do you need to now?

The prophet had been faithful in sounding the warning trumpet. Had he not, he would have been derelict in his duties and would have been guilty too. But some people were claiming that God is not just (33:17, 20). The prophet insists that they accept culpability. It is their ways that are unjust; God's righteous justice is precisely what they have been up against.

Shepherds of Israel

Who were "the shepherds of Israel" (Ezekiel 34:2)? The kings to be sure, for they were God-ordained to look after the people's welfare. But in Ezekiel 34, the shepherds include the leaders, the royalty, the priests connected to the Temple, and the false prophets who looked after their own interests.

God will now take over the job personally. God will gather the wounded, the abandoned, the weak. God will search for the lost. Notice that the prophet makes a distinction between the fat sheep and the lean (34:16, 20). No longer does God judge the entire society as a single entity; Ezekiel allows for personal guilt and innocence. Part of the new message from Ezekiel is individual accountability within the community.

God, the true shepherd, will still need a servant leader. It will be "my servant David" (34:23-24). Will God restore the dynasty of David? Or is this a vision of someone greater than David, a messianic prince who will rule over a "covenant of peace" (34:25)? The people in exile must now listen to fresh prophetic words—acceptance of punishment, acknowledgment of personal responsibility, and assurance that God will look after their future.

All who wail the songs of lament, all who weep from tragedy or chastisement, now hold fast to this promise: God

NOTES, REFLECTIONS, AND QUESTIONS

will be your true shepherd, will heal your wounds and bring you home again. God's redemptive purpose can be delayed but not defeated.

Judgment Against Edom

Prophecies against Edom seem like an interruption. Amos, Obadiah, and Isaiah had spoken oracles against these desert kinfolk. We know that Edom helped Babylonian soldiers round up Jews fleeing Judah. To Edom God says, "I will deal with you according to the anger and envy that you showed because of your hatred against them" (Ezekiel 35:11). The oracle intends to show that Israel's land will one day be restored and that even the Edomites will be pushed aside. Don't forget that the Lord judges all the nations, not just Israel.

Cleansing the Spirit of Israel

For the deportees, the theological problem was this: Evidently their God had let them down. Foreigners ridiculed them. Were the gods of Babylon stronger? Had they won? The ancients believed wars were fought between the gods—the stronger ones winning, the weaker ones losing. People were saying that it was a sad day for the God of Israel. The "eternal Temple" was in a heap. In fact, the destruction was so complete that the God of the Jews was humiliated, perhaps destroyed. Think how many people today, when tragedy strikes, wonder why God did not prevent the disaster. They often experience God as absent. They question the power of God.

When have you wondered if God had any power?

9/11

Ezekiel argued that the power of God was seen precisely in the punishment (36:16-21). God did not lose; God used Babylon, even with all its false idols, to punish a wicked people. But now, with the land covered with blood, God will show power again. God will purify the remnant people and take them back to their land (36:24-25). The purpose is not merely to save Israel; it is to glorify the power of God. "It is not for your sake, O house of Israel, that I am about to act, but for the sake of my holy name" (36:22).

How will God do this mighty deed? By cleansing their hearts and ushering them home. By washing Israel. Symbolic purification was prescribed for ceremonial uncleanness. Repentance and obedience were called for, of course, for the ritual is not magic. But God says, "I will sprinkle clean water upon you, and you shall be clean from all your uncleannesses, and from all your idols I will cleanse you" (36:25). The land and the people will be washed clean by the grace of God. Why will God perform this mighty work? Ezekiel says it is to show that God is God.

Describe a testimony you have heard when someone told of

NOTES, REFLECTIONS, AND QUESTIONS

the amazing power God has to cleanse a heart. What was said about the power of God to forgive, to cleanse, and to restore?

NOTES, REFLECTIONS, AND QUESTIONS

Valley of Dry Bones

When despair is heaviest, God gives the strongest encouragement. God asked, "Can these bones live?" (Ezekiel 37:3). That was the question every Jew was asking: Can this bedraggled, scattered nation, which is no longer a nation, ever live again? The answer? "Prophesy to these bones, and say to them: O dry bones, hear the word of the LORD" (37:4). Suddenly the Creation story in Genesis became the framework for restoration. Life begins with the word of God. Ezekiel must speak the word of God to a dead Israel. But just as created man and woman were not living souls until God breathed into them the spirit of life, so the dry bones began to rattle but were not yet alive.

The breath, the wind, the *rûah,* the spirit of God, would give Israel life, individually and collectively (37:9-10). "I will put my spirit within you, and you shall live, and I will place you on your own soil; then you shall know that I, the LORD, have spoken and will act, says the LORD" (37:14). God's Holy Spirit can re-birth a person and give new life to a church. *Word* and *Spirit,* God's twofold plan for a people of God to be reborn.

The Holy Temple

Ezekiel's oracles are often bizarre but seldom boring. Abruptly, in Ezekiel 40, he begins to describe the new Temple. Keep in mind this description is a vision, not a blueprint. Ezekiel is still in Babylon (40:1). What is happening here? The oracle motivates as well as predicts. Prophets energize with visions of hope.

God becomes guide and shows Ezekiel every nook and cranny of the new Temple in Jerusalem. Ezekiel reports in meticulous detail. The date? About 570 B.C., more than a dozen years after the destruction, when the Jews are depressed in spirit, totally destitute of resources. The place of the vision? Babylon—hundreds of miles and seeming light years away from Israel. The prophet, who for years proclaimed doom, dramatically changes his message to one of hope and resurrection.

But this Temple is different, taller and wider to emphasize the holiness of God. It will not be adjacent to the royal palace but will be entirely separate. The kings have sinned and have let the people down. God will rule the people again. Let the prince be separate and be a servant.

Notice the emphasis on purity of worship. The faithful

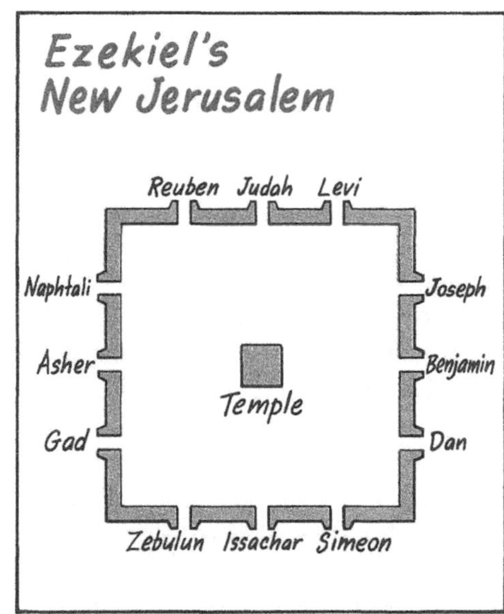

After twenty-five years in exile, Ezekiel had a detailed vision of the restored city of Jerusalem (Ezekiel 48:30-35) and the Temple (40–44), which he believed would be rebuilt after the exiles returned to Judah.

priests, descendants of Zadok, will be privileged to offer the sacrifice (40:46; 44:15). The other levitical priests, who participated in Israel's apostasy, will be relegated to doing chores in the Temple (44:10-14). This new priesthood symbolizes a new beginning of holy worship. Now the priests will help the people abandon their sins. The rituals of worship will be done properly because they will come straight from new hearts. In this new era, the people's lives will reflect covenant and justice.

The River of Mercy and Healing

Did you notice? The "glory of the LORD" appeared to Ezekiel by the waters of the river Chebar (Ezekiel 1:28). That same "glory of the LORD," whose scribe took coals of fire from the altar and scattered them over the city, stopped at the east gate, rose up, and departed the Temple before the destruction (10:1-19; 11:22-25). Now, in the vision, the glory of the Lord will return to God's Temple (43:1-5).

God's salvation will not be confined to the Temple but rather will pour out of it like a mighty river of healing grace (47:1-12). Instead of being deepest in the Temple, it's but a trickle there. The water of salvation comes from the throne of grace, out the south side, then east. The water is ankle-deep, then knee-deep, then waist-deep, then so deep and wide it could not be crossed (47:3-5).

It will enter the great Jordan rift—the longest rift on the earth's crust— and go to the Dead Sea—the lowest and saltiest sea on the earth's surface (Ezekiel 47:8). The water will make the Dead Sea clean; even fish will swim in its fresh waters (47:9). Israel (and we) learned a lesson: God is free to be God. God's healing compassion will once again flow from the mercy seat. It will flow to the lost, to those who live in a spiritual desert, to those who are dead like the saline waters of the Dead Sea. Healing and health shall pour from God and from God alone.

Trees will line the river with fruit for nourishment and leaves for healing (47:7, 12). They flourish all year long. The vision of the Temple now bursts into a messianic dream of wholeness and health for the whole world.

The land must be divided among the people as in the first distribution. This time, all twelve tribes will receive equal distribution. (Notice the symbolism of justice, for in actuality all the tribes are thoroughly mixed up.) No Samaria or Judah but one Hebrew people, like before. Each family will be given its inheritance. As the prophet Micah envisioned,

> "They shall all sit under their own vines and under
> their own fig trees,
> and no one shall make them afraid;
> for the mouth of the LORD of hosts has spoken"
> (Micah 4:4).

The hope for the future now reaches beyond specific measurements. Ezekiel's geography is no longer exact. In pic-

NOTES, REFLECTIONS, AND QUESTIONS

Zadok was a descendant of Eleazer, the older son of Aaron who inherited the high priesthood when Aaron died (Numbers 20:22-29). In the conflict over who would become king after David, the priest Abiathar, also a descendant of Aaron, supported Adonijah. Zadok supported Solomon. With the prophet Nathan, he anointed Solomon king. Zadok became sole high priest under Solomon. Descendants of Zadok controlled the Temple from the time it was built until it was destroyed, and only priests from the line of Zadok were allowed to serve in the restored Temple after the Exile (Ezekiel 40:46).

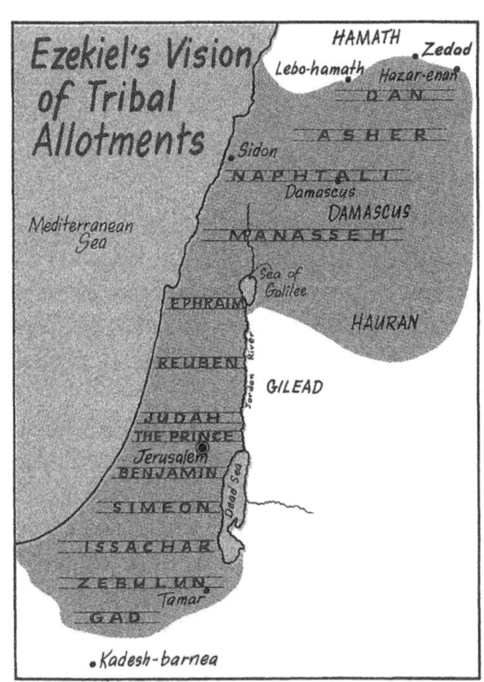

Ezekiel's vision of the future allotment of land in Israel (Ezekiel 45:1-8; 47:13–48:29) included twelve areas for the twelve tribes plus a central area, a holy district around the Temple reserved for "the prince," priests, and Levites. As in the original tribal allotment of territories, the tribe of Levi had no assigned land of its own.

ture language the area is roughly the size of Solomon's kingdom (Ezekiel 48). Ezekiel's mind is so filled with God's Spirit that he sees God's ultimate vision. The resurrection of the covenant people will be glorious.

MARKS OF OBEDIENT COMMUNITY

We live in an uprooted society. Some of us have been located in new places; all of us have been transported into new life experiences. We cannot go home; we are exiles. What in our faith gives us moorings?

unchanging God. Good Shepherd.

We do have a home! We are not without roots. We have a memory. We have an identity. Exiles we may be, but we have a future homeland and a planned homecoming.

In our society we are surrounded by people who feel like exiles, cut off forever from a home. What can we do to help these exiles feel at home? feel at home in God?

Outreach

The healing, forgiving river of grace flows even to the Dead Sea. What can we do to help spiritually dead people feel the health and restorative power of that grace?

Be filled with His grace.

When have you felt the restoring power of grace?

Dubai, Aust., US

IF YOU WANT TO KNOW MORE

Do some research on the Babylonian Empire. See what you can discover about Nebuchadnezzar's famous hanging gardens.

Ezekiel 25–32 and 38–39 were not included in daily assignments. Read them if time permits.

NOTES, REFLECTIONS, AND QUESTIONS

Obedient community turns exile into remembering. We rehearse our traditions. We claim our identity. We declare the God to whom we belong.

REDEEMER

"Those who wait for the LORD shall renew their strength,
they shall mount up with wings like eagles,
they shall run and not be weary,
they shall walk and not faint."

—Isaiah 40:31

Risen
Young Messiah.

12 God Will Save

OUR HUMAN CONDITION

We've lost everything. We're suffering. No one seems to care. What is there to wait for? How can we trust that our circumstances will change?

ASSIGNMENT

Read Isaiah 40:28-31 aloud each day until you know it by heart.

The first word in Isaiah 40–55 is "comfort," for these messages come after the destruction of Jerusalem. Sometimes called "Isaiah of the Exile," these Scriptures have inspired great music and art and have given comfort to millions of people. They include the great servant passages. Read like a thirsty person searching for water or like a watcher scanning the sky for the first light of dawn.

Day 1 Isaiah 40–42 (comfort, trial of the nations, servant of the Lord)
Day 2 Isaiah 43–45 (restoration and blessing, absurdity of idol worship, the Lord's anointed)
Day 3 Isaiah 46–48 (humiliation of Babylon, redemption)
Day 4 Isaiah 49:1–52:12 (the servant's mission, Zion restored, the servant's humiliation, deliverance)
Day 5 Isaiah 52:13–55:13 (the suffering servant, assurance, eternal covenant of peace)
Day 6 Read and respond to "The Word of the Lord" and "Marks of Obedient Community."
Day 7 Rest

PRAYER

Pray daily before study:
"I will always put my hope in you;
I will praise you more and more.
I will tell of your goodness;
all day long I will speak of your salvation,
though it is more than I can understand.
I will go in the strength of the LORD God;
I will proclaim your goodness, yours alone"
(Psalm 71:14-16, TEV).

Prayer concerns for this week:

- Bob's sister Robin
- Janet & Luka travel mercies
- Shooting victims
-

REDEEMER

Day 1 Isaiah 40–42 (comfort, trial of the nations, servant of the Lord)

40:11 Caring shepherd
42:1-4 Jesus' attributes

Day 2 Isaiah 43–45 (restoration and blessing, absurdity of idol worship, the Lord's anointed)

44:28 Cyrus mentioned by name years ahead.

Day 3 Isaiah 46–48 (humiliation of Babylon, redemption)

God is reasoning & wanting to be close & understood.
48:16-19

Day 4 Isaiah 49:1–52:12 (the servant's mission, Zion restored, the servant's humiliation, deliverance)

50:5-9 Servant's obedience
52:7 how beautiful on the mountains are the feet of those who bring good News

Day 5 Isaiah 52:13–55:13 (the suffering servant, assurance, eternal covenant of peace)

53:1-12 most famous passage about messiah.

Day 6 "The Word of the Lord" and "Marks of Obedient Community"

THE WORD OF THE LORD

NOTES, REFLECTIONS, AND QUESTIONS

The historical context of the great book of Isaiah covers nearly two centuries. Some scholars argue for one prophet with editing and later additions; others suggest a school of Isaiah prophets who revered their teacher. But all agree to the unusual spiritual power of this monumental book. Like a mountain range with towering peaks, this magnificent book includes the writings of perhaps three prophets: Isaiah son of Amoz, or "Isaiah of Jerusalem" (Isaiah 1–39); Second Isaiah, also called "Isaiah of the Exile" or "Isaiah of Babylon" (40–55); and Third Isaiah, or "Isaiah after the Exile" (56–66). We have separated the three parts of Isaiah to keep our sense of history clear. Judaism kept them together to give, in one great book, the full sweep of the Exile experience.

As we open Isaiah 40, promises of hope replace the warnings of doom we read in Isaiah 1–39.

"Comfort, O comfort my people,
says your God" (40:1).

Judgment, shocking and devastating, has been accomplished; God is now ready to save. Isaiah of Babylon sees the discouraged faces of his fellow exiles, but his heart is filled with joy. The people don't know it, but God is going to set them free. In language reminiscent of previous prophets, especially Isaiah of Jerusalem, he presents the great affirmations about God in a fresh way.

Isaiah's Call

We join Isaiah, sitting in the great council hall of heaven. Voices are speaking from the throne of God. Isaiah of Babylon, like all the prophets, receives a call. His call is simple: "Cry out!" With the normal prophetic hesitancy, Isaiah cautiously asks, "What shall I cry?" (Isaiah 40:6). He heard the exact message he was to declare:

"The grass withers, the flower fades;
but the word of our God will stand forever" (40:8).

All else is transitory. God's word will accomplish God's purpose, for God's word and God's purpose are one.

Mighty Babylon, with all her pomp and power, is like the grass of the desert. When the hot wind, the breath of God's Spirit, blows over it, it will wither and die. The word of God will govern.

In Isaiah 40:9, Zion is the bearer of the good news to Judah that God is returning with the exiles: Tell the towns of Judah (that is, the people who used to live in Judah) that God is coming. They have suffered long enough; they have been punished more than necessary.

Now Isaiah's voice is like the voice of God. "Comfort, O comfort" (40:1). Why? Because God's way will go right through the desert. It will not go in roundabout ways. It will go straight as the crow flies. It will be smooth, without precipitous heights or dangerous valleys (40:3-4). It will be free of enemies. Even in the great stretches of desert God will feed and water the people like a shepherd who knows the way and cares for his flock (40:11).

"When the poor and needy seek water,
and there is none,
and their tongue is parched with thirst,
I the LORD will answer them. . . .
I will make the wilderness a pool of water,
and the dry land springs of water" (41:17-18).

God will travel the highway with them; in fact, God will lead the way just as the fire and cloud led Moses through the wilderness. Isaiah announces a new Exodus! The "glory of the LORD" will walk the highway to freedom with the exiles, and everybody in the world will see it (40:5).

God Will Do a New Thing

What are the exiles to do? Wait. Trust and be ready. The God who names each star in the sky and who lifts up and brings down vast empires, who determines the course of history, is ready to do a new thing (Isaiah 41:4; 42:5-9). God has already called Cyrus of Persia to march so fast his feet will scarcely touch the ground. Though the exiles feared God had forgotten them or did not have enough power to save them, Isaiah of Babylon assures them God is strong to give them a new beginning (43:1-21).

Biblical faith brought into the world a new concept, the idea of *hesed,* a Hebrew word that means "constant covenant love." The covenant love of God shows constant compassion and righteousness. God would use the people of faith to teach the nations of the world how to live in just and compassionate community.

"I have given you as a covenant to the people,
a light to the nations" (42:6).

God never cancels the plan; *hesed* is forever. The message of Isaiah now sings with assurance and hope:

"See, the former things have come to pass,
and new things I now declare;
before they spring forth,
I tell you of them" (42:9).

Life is not fate or happenstance. Life is certainly not influenced by figurines in the house or by the stars in the sky (47:13). If you will wait, if you will trust, God has a plan for you and will soon bring it to pass (46:10-13).

The Almighty is coming to save you. Are you tired? Are you discouraged? Have you lost heart? Don't be afraid, for

"those who wait for the LORD shall renew their strength,
they shall mount up with wings like eagles,
they shall run and not be weary,
they shall walk and not faint" (40:31).

The exiles, with images of the rubble of Jerusalem in their minds, don't believe it. The words of hope bounce off their

NOTES, REFLECTIONS, AND QUESTIONS

ears the same way the prophecies of doom had years before. It is understandable. Babylon seems firmly in control. Judah is no more. God seems indifferent and far away. In fact, the people murmur the same way the Hebrews murmured in the wilderness. God is oblivious to our troubles, they thought. God doesn't know and worse, doesn't care (40:27). But God "never grows tired or weary" (40:28, TEV).

Have you noticed a double layer of spiritual instruction? On one hand, Isaiah speaks specifically about Babylon, Cyrus, and the return to Jerusalem. On the other hand, every reader, regardless of time or place, receives hope and encouragement. Easily we identify our own bondage. Quickly we spot our own fears. How hard it is for us to trust that God will lead us on safe ways through life's desert. How difficult for us to see a distant Cyrus hurrying to help us. How desperately we need God's encouragement to sing praise when we are still in trouble.

"Sing a new song to the LORD;
sing his praise, all the world! . . .
Sing, distant lands and all who live there! . . .
shout for joy from the tops of the mountains!"
(42:10-11, TEV).

The songs of praise announce the victory before it comes.

A Powerful Communicator

Few messengers have been able to convey the message of God so forcefully as Isaiah. In the courtroom scene in Isaiah 41:1-4, 21-29, God is merciless and relentless against the false gods: Who is breaking the Babylonian yoke? Not the false gods. Who has done it? "I, the LORD." God brings all the puny gods into the docket, demanding they tell about their exploits. Remember Tiglath-pileser III (Pul) and his fierce Assyrian gods? Where are they now? What about Nebuchadnezzar and the gods of Babylon? Speak up so "we may know that you are gods" (41:23). Silence. Other prophets laughed at the weakness of foreign gods; Isaiah goes further: They are totally powerless.

"They are all a delusion;
their works are nothing;
their images are empty wind" (41:29).

When Israel stands before the court, we hear a tone more gentle than in previous prophetic trials. Earlier prophets pronounced Israel guilty and sentenced him to punishment. Isaiah softens the verdict. In 42:18-25, Israel is charged with being blind and deaf to the ways of God. He didn't understand his sins when they were pointed out to him. He thought he was being misused by God when in fact he was being punished. Now he cannot hear or see the salvation God has in store for him. Isaiah becomes one with the exiles and says,

"We never knew what was happening;
we learned nothing at all from it" (42:25, TEV).

NOTES, REFLECTIONS, AND QUESTIONS

Describe an experience when you actually listened and learned from the action of God.

Jesus looked for figs out of season.
Mark 11:12

Oracles of Salvation

We are familiar with past oracles or visions of destruction. Now Isaiah uses oracles of salvation. God proclaims the freeing word:

"Do not fear, for I am with you,
do not be afraid, for I am your God;
I will strengthen you, I will help you,
I will uphold you with my victorious right hand"
(Isaiah 41:10).

God announced ahead of time he was going to do a great thing. Now in a long poem (44:24–45:13), Isaiah declares specifically that King Cyrus will be God's instrument. God calls Cyrus "his anointed" (45:1-3). Babylonian magicians and astrologers who say Babylon will rule forever are wrong. Cyrus will be shepherd king for a while because God says so (44:28).

What do we know from secular history? From Babylonian and Persian records we discover that Babylon grew weaker after mighty King Nebuchadnezzar. In 553 B.C. King Nabonidus simply left Babylon and lived in the Arabian desert for ten years. His son Belshazzar (Daniel 5:1-2) ruled as co-regent during his absence.

Meanwhile, a man of remarkable ability named Cyrus rose to power. His father was a Persian king, his mother a Median princess. His grandfather was King Astyages of Media. In 550 B.C., Cyrus overthrew his grandfather and moved his forces through present-day Turkey to the Aegean Sea. His contact with the Greek city states Athens and Sparta led to two centuries of conflict between Persia and Greece.

Even before Cyrus turned his forces toward Babylon, his reputation as a fair and generous man preceded him. History records that he rode into Babylon without unsheathing his sword. The gates were thrown open, and not a drop of blood was shed. His edict of 539 B.C. allowed Jewish exiles who wanted to return to Judah to go (Ezra 1:1-3). So the Jews would know God's hand was in it, Isaiah announced it well ahead of time.

Bel (Isaiah 46:1) is short for Bel-Marduk, god of war and well-being for Babylon. Nebo (Nabu) is his son. Isaiah says the gods will be loaded on donkeys like stacks of firewood (46:1-2). God is still in the saving business. God carried Israel from birth and will not abandon her. Israel, stubborn as she is, will be saved for the sake of God's own name (48:9).

"I am the LORD your God,
who teaches you for your own good,
who leads you in the way you should go" (48:17).

NOTES, REFLECTIONS, AND QUESTIONS

The Ishtar Gate in Babylon, the entrance through which processionals to the temple area passed, was decorated with over two hundred animal figures like this bull on walls of blue and red glazed tiles.

If you had kept my commandments, you wouldn't have to go through all this. Now, says God, I have to split the rock, just as I did for Moses (Exodus 17:6), so the water will gush out and my people can make it through the wilderness (Isaiah 48:21).

Servant Songs

A new form and a new message emerge. A compassionate servant will serve as an instrument of God in the saving task. This person is not King Cyrus, who will serve as a political and military agent for freedom. Rather, the servant in four different "servant songs" brings spiritual healing. In the first song (Isaiah 42:1-4), a chosen servant is commissioned to implement justice. The other three songs are 49:1-6; 50:4-9, and the great suffering servant passage in 52:13–53:12.

Across the years, scholars have argued, and people have wondered, about the identity of the servant in these four passages. Sometimes the servant is understood as the nation Israel, sometimes as a righteous remnant within Israel, sometimes as a single righteous individual, and sometimes as a composite figure—both a group and an individual.

Whatever the identity of the servant, the servant image certainly carries within it the concept of Israel's role in God's purpose. Traditionally Jews have understood Israel to be the suffering servant, sensing the agony not only of the Exile but also of the persecution Jews have experienced across the centuries.

Isaiah sensed that redemption comes when the innocent suffer on behalf of others. Running as a quiet undercurrent through this section of Isaiah is the feeling that God suffers great anguish over the evil in the world. Christians immediately see the passion of Christ portrayed in this prophecy.

> "He was wounded for our transgressions,
> crushed for our iniquities;
> upon him was the punishment that made us whole,
> and by his bruises we are healed" (53:5).

For Christians the crucifixion of Jesus Christ is prophetically defined more than five centuries before Calvary. Within the Christian community is the assurance that Christ's wounds bring healing, forgiveness, and peace with God.

Whether Isaiah specifically foresaw the Savior we do not know; but we do know that he understood the eternal truth that God suffers for God's people, that innocent suffering brings vicarious healing to others, and that one day there will be righteousness and justice.

Grace and Peace

Those who say the Old Testament pictures only a God of wrath cannot have read Isaiah 54–55. Listen to the shout of victory and salvation; listen to the declaration of covenant faithfulness:

NOTES, REFLECTIONS, AND QUESTIONS

"For the mountains may depart
and the hills be removed,
but my steadfast love shall not depart from you,
and my covenant of peace shall not be removed,
says the LORD, who has compassion on you" (54:10).

Isaiah sounds a note of salvation for everyone. The water of mercy, the milk and wine of grace are available to all—and without price (55:1). The tragedy is that so many of us spend our money "for that which is not bread" (55:2). Where do you see yourself in these words?

How would you describe the experience of laboring for that which does not satisfy?

Realization teaches us humility to learn from word. Horseriding.

The prophet concludes with a picture of the new and joyful Exodus:

"You shall go out in joy,
and be led back in peace;
the mountains and the hills before you
shall burst into song,
and all the trees of the field shall clap their hands"
(55:12).

MARKS OF OBEDIENT COMMUNITY

The faith community acknowledges pain, hurt, even punishment, but allows itself to be comforted. We listen for God's messengers to bring us succor and signs of hope. We keep our eyes open, trusting, waiting for God's new possibilities.

When have you been part of a faith community that needed comfort?

Let down by church leaders' scandles

"Those who wait for the LORD shall renew their strength" (Isaiah 40:31). What does that promise mean to you?

Eagerly waiting & preparing for the Lord's time.

IF YOU WANT TO KNOW MORE

Look up Cyrus II of Persia and three fairly unfamiliar kings who have interesting connections: Nabonidus, Belshazzar, and Astyages.

NOTES, REFLECTIONS, AND QUESTIONS

The obeying community finds comfort in knowing God is never without new possibilities and trusts even while waiting for those possibilities.

VISION

"And the foreigners who join themselves to the LORD,
to minister to him, to love the name of the LORD,
and to be his servants,
all who keep the sabbath, and do not profane it,
and hold fast my covenant—
these I will bring to my holy mountain,
and make them joyful in my house of prayer."

—Isaiah 56:6-7

13 God's Vision for a New World

OUR HUMAN CONDITION

When reality falls short of our expectations and our dreams are shattered by disappointment, we lose our balance and fall victim to despair.

ASSIGNMENT

Compare other translations as you read these visions of end times. You may also want to compare these visions with those of earlier prophets. Note the universality of the vision, the inclusion of the foreigner and the eunuch at the holy mountain.

Day 1 Isaiah 56–57 (covenant extended to the obedient, Israel's futile idolatry)
Day 2 Isaiah 58–59 (true fasting, kindness and justice, the people's transgressions, need for repentance)
Day 3 Isaiah 60–61 (restoration of Jerusalem, mission to Zion, an everlasting covenant)
Day 4 Isaiah 62–64 (salvation of Zion, God's mercy for the penitent)
Day 5 Isaiah 65–66 (God's righteous judgment, future hope, reign of God)
Day 6 Read and respond to "The Word of the Lord" and "Marks of Obedient Community."
Day 7 Rest

PRAYER

Pray daily before study:
"Everything you do, O God, is holy.
No god is as great as you.
You are the God who works miracles;
you showed your might among the nations"
(Psalm 77:13-14, TEV).

Prayer concerns for this week:

- Houston + Florida (Matt's Family)
- Jeremy - Resignation
  - Nicholas - court stuff guidance
- Phil - pray for wife for employment - guidance
- Wayne - had a mini-stroke, blood pressure issue
  - Breaks out in hives in June
  - alphagal - tick borne illness
  - healthy → prevent systems
- Wayne - son
  - daughter-in-law has kept kids away from Wayne & his daughter
  - pray for strength

VISION

Day 1 Isaiah 56–57 (covenant extended to the obedient, Israel's futile idolatry)

Day 2 Isaiah 58–59 (true fasting, kindness and justice, the people's transgressions, need for repentance)

Day 3 Isaiah 60–61 (restoration of Jerusalem, mission to Zion, an everlasting covenant)

Day 4 Isaiah 62–64 (salvation of Zion, God's mercy for the penitent)

Day 5 Isaiah 65–66 (God's righteous judgment, future hope, reign of God)

Day 6 "The Word of the Lord" and "Marks of Obedient Community"

THE WORD OF THE LORD

At the beginning of Isaiah 56, the mood has changed. Many of the Israelites have walked the highway of the Lord back to Jerusalem. Not all the exiles returned, of course. Like Jews of the Diaspora everywhere, some had put down roots, gained property, raised children, and learned the ways of the people among whom they lived. Under the tolerant Persians, some, like Nehemiah, even helped in the king's court.

Those Jews who were fueled by the visions of Ezekiel's Temple or Isaiah's highway through the desert walked to Judah with their possessions on their backs or in a pushcart but with light steps and happy hearts. They came from Babylon, where many had been forced to live since the destruction of Jerusalem. The Persian victory over Babylon in 539 B.C. established Persian control across the two thousand miles from India to Greece, the largest Mediterranean empire to date. With the edict of Cyrus (538 B.C.), children and grandchildren of the exiles made their way home.

But ask yourself, What would it be like to return to a war-ravaged land after fifty or more years? And for many, to a city of rubble where you had never lived? These people are free at last, thank God, but free in a tough land where landmarks have been removed, where strangers live, where the social and religious structure has totally collapsed. The people who had been left behind had set up their own organization and had occupied the property that was abandoned. So friction was inevitable. Isaiah's prophecies of freedom and restoration came true; but the streets were not lined with trees, and justice and peace did not govern the land (Isaiah 55:12).

Isaiah 55–66 was written in Jerusalem during the post-exilic period, probably after the rebuilding of the Temple but well before the rebuilding of the walls by Nehemiah. We need to read this Scripture on at least three distinct levels:

- Listen to the messenger deal with the *specific problems* of his immediate time and place. As we listen to pronouncements that were conditioned by the experiences of the returned exiles, we can learn lessons to apply to our lives.
- The messenger gives deep *spiritual insight.* His oracles give profound godly guidance for faithful living to people of all generations.
- The God-inspired dreams pull us into eternity. The oracles sometimes start out local and concrete, then expand into *end-time visions* of peace and justice for all humankind.

The new religious community must keep the old faith—right living and sabbath observance (56:1-2). They need to rebuild on the old foundations, spiritual as well as physical (58:12). But the doors of faith need to be flung open to others as well. The prophet widens Israel's arms of inclusiveness.

"A foreigner who has joined the LORD's people should not say, 'The LORD will not let me worship with his people.'

NOTES, REFLECTIONS, AND QUESTIONS

"A man who has been castrated should never think that because he cannot have children, he can never be part of God's people" (56:3, TEV). This teaching contrasts with an earlier law that barred such people from the assembly of the Lord (Deuteronomy 23:1). Foreigners as well as Jews who love the Holy One will be welcomed in worship on the holy mountain (Isaiah 56:6-7).

The faithful were expecting a spiritual utopia with cleansed, dedicated leaders. Instead, both civic and religious leaders sadly neglected their duties. Like watch dogs that wouldn't bark, they failed to warn people of the dangers of wickedness. They were lazy, greedy, and self-indulgent. They drank too much wine and yearned for more. If such leadership continues, shouted the prophet, other peoples will come like wild animals to devour them (56:9-12).

No one since Amos had chastised people so ferociously for their sexual immorality and idolatry as this prophet. Pagan worship with high places, fertility rites, and child sacrifice was not a thing of the past. The prophet condemned those who fornicated on the hillsides where the old Canaanite cults of prostitution had been. New freedoms broke down old prohibitions. Rebellion against God persisted. People dedicated themselves to fancy clothes, expensive perfumes, and continual sexual escapades until they nearly wore themselves out (57:3-10).

God says they do not fear, do not even "remember me / or give me a thought" (57:11). Healing is offered, mercy extended to the sorrowful (57:18-19). But to those who continue in their idolatry and wickedness? The spiritual leaders have been silent; so the prophet simply explains the Lord's judgment by saying, "I will denounce your conduct" (57:12, *The New English Bible*), and then adds,

> "The wicked are like the tossing sea
> that cannot keep still;
> its waters toss up mire and mud.
> There is no peace, says my God, for the wicked"
> (57:20-21).

A Holy Fast

Many of the homecomers tried to be religious. They did not use their foreign statuettes or idolatrous figurines. They were more careful about sabbath prayers. Some serious Jews prayed in public, put on rough sackcloth, and fasted. But in fierce prophetic tradition, Isaiah insists that religious exercises designed to impress God are worthless. What kind of a fast would please God? You guessed it: Remove injustice and oppression, save food to share with the hungry, take the homeless into your house, or at least help them find a place to sleep, provide clothing for the destitute, and look after your kinfolk. Oh, yes, be sure to keep sabbath in your hearts and in your actions (Isaiah 58:6-7, 13-14). Someday everyone will

NOTES, REFLECTIONS, AND QUESTIONS

recognize sabbath as a healthful practice and make regular sabbath pilgrimages to the Lord (66:23).

Care for one's relatives received continual emphasis so that it became a distinguishable Jewish trait. Grounded in the culture of the ancient Near East, such caring was fortified with the fifth commandment: "Honor your father and your mother, so that your days may be long in the land that the LORD your God is giving you" (Exodus 20:12). It was further strengthened by the commandment "You shall not commit adultery" (20:14) and by intense stress on teaching moral values and religious tradition to one's children (Deuteronomy 6:6-7, 20-25). It became a proverb in Israel:

"Listen to your father who begot you,
and do not despise your mother when she is old"
(Proverbs 23:22).

Within the Christian community, this Jewish truth is so fundamental that it is scandalous to think otherwise. "Whoever does not provide for relatives, and especially for family members, has denied the faith and is worse than an unbeliever" (1 Timothy 5:8). How are you doing in this area of your life?

What is the reward for a godly fast? God will lift your gloom. The Lord will guide your thoughts and decisions. You will be healthy and feel like a well-watered garden (Isaiah 58:10-11). But wait, something more important: You will be part of the rebuilding of the city. You will build on the old foundations of justice. You will be known as a builder, one of the righteous persons who keep a city alive.

"Your ancient ruins shall be rebuilt;
you shall raise up the foundations of many generations;
you shall be called the repairer of the breach,
the restorer of streets to live in" (58:12).

As you think about the deteriorating cities of our world, as you ponder your own area, town, or city, what are some ways you could be a "restorer of streets"?

Like Isaiah of Jerusalem nearly two centuries before, the prophet pleads for people to refrain from sin, to repent, to live holy lives. But the influence of Jeremiah and Ezekiel causes him to be more personal, more individual. Notice: God will forgive and save "all of you that turn from your sins" (59:20, TEV). The community, tight as it is, is seen no longer only as a single entity. God distinguishes between the behavior of individuals and judges accordingly.

NOTES, REFLECTIONS, AND QUESTIONS

The sins are as public as today's newscast—lying, violence, murder. People hurt people and then lie in court. Innocent people are destroyed; no one is safe (59:3-8). A heart-broken litany of lament follows a list of sins. It shows the way back into mercy and godly living (59:9-15).

But in the face of such sin, God will act.

"He put on righteousness like a breastplate,
and a helmet of salvation on his head;
he put on garments of vengeance for clothing,
and wrapped himself in fury as in a mantle"
(Isaiah 59:17).

A Bright Future

Discouragement clouded the lives of the returned exiles. So much work to be done, such limited resources. Against this grim background, the prophet projects a vision of divine help. "The glory of the LORD" will bring light to their gloom, and material resources as well (Isaiah 60:1-3). Other exiles will come to help them, some by ship (60:4-5). And they did. Traders will pass through with goods from far-off lands (60:6). They did, for under Persian peace the fertile crescent was alive again. Money will come from unexpected sources. Cyrus, and later King Darius, had actually sent aid to rebuild the Temple. God will bring in foreigners to help repair the city (60:10). The message was clear. The picture was not so bleak as they thought; God would bring resources to their aid if they would work hard and keep the faith.

But wait a minute. The vision is too good to be true. God's glory will be so bright, so glorious, that Jerusalem will need neither sun nor moon (60:19-20). Violence will come to an end. Rulers will be just. Everyone will do exactly the right thing. God will name a new overseer for the city of Zion whose name will be *Peace* (60:17). God will appoint a new chief administrator whose title will be *Righteousness*. *Salvation* will be the strong walls, and *Praise* will be the gates (60:18). Everyone will be wearing new clothes, beautiful as a bride ready for her wedding; but the gorgeous gown will not be made of cloth but of the saving love and righteousness of God (61:10).

It has happened again: The prophet got close to God. God elevated hope to a higher level, transformed a good future into a heavenly vision. Once again the prophet sees the far horizon.

Go to Work!

When Jesus stood up in his hometown synagogue, the elders handed him the Isaiah scroll. Jesus chose a servant passage and took on his shoulders the mission of Israel:

"The spirit of the Lord GOD is upon me,
because the LORD has anointed me" (Isaiah 61:1).

Israel was called to be a nation of priests, a holy people driven to teach God's word of salvation to all the world. And

NOTES, REFLECTIONS, AND QUESTIONS

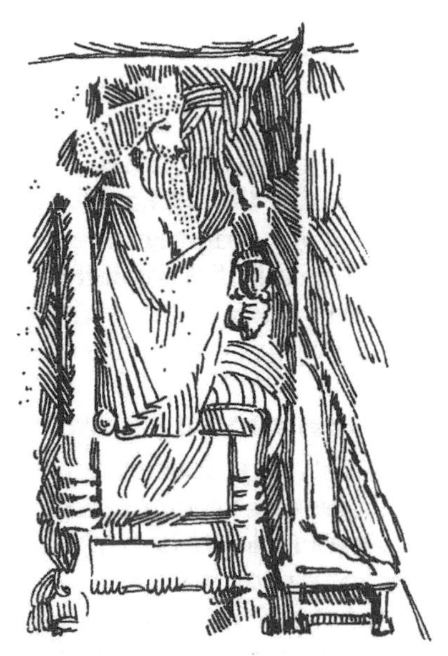

A wall relief from Persepolis, Iran, shows Darius I sitting on his throne, perhaps receiving annual tribute from the empire's subject peoples.

in their doing it, God will continually bless and strengthen.

Don't be discouraged. You are defeated now, "Forsaken," living in a place named "Desolate." I will give you and your place a new name, Beulah Land, which means "Married to the Lord." "Desolate" will become "Delight" (62:4). Trust God, and don't lose hope. Good prophets will stand at the sentinel posts. They will bark warnings. They will not be the false prophets of old who cried, "Peace, peace," when there was no peace (Jeremiah 6:14; 8:11; Ezekiel 13:10).

Now, go to work! Pick up the rubble. Clear the old stones. Prepare the highway so worshipers may come. Construct the gates, the walls. You are no longer a city forsaken. You are God's city. Build up! Build up! (Isaiah 62:10).

Why are God's robes stained with red? Because God has been busy stomping God's opponents in the wine press of judgment.

"I trampled down peoples in my anger,
I crushed them in my wrath" (63:6).

Thoughts of judgment overwhelm the prophet. He intercedes on behalf of the people. O God, please come down now (64:1). Don't delay. You are the Holy One. We have sinned. "We are the clay, and you are our potter" (64:8). Save us.

New Heavens and New Earth

God is about to create new heavens and a new earth (Isaiah 65:17). There is no room in the new creation for a rebellious people who follow their own devices. The new era calls for a new people, people who rejoice in God. Again a vision of the new earth, of a world transformed: No babies will die; people will live to be a hundred; no one will weep. Those who build their houses will live in them. Those who plant vineyards will not have the fruit stolen from them; they will be able to enjoy the fruit of their labors (65:19-23). All nature will be in harmony. Compare 65:25, the wolf and the lamb, the lion and the ox, to the vision in 11:6-9. All nature has been disturbed by sin; therefore all nature will be healed by grace. Once again God's final purpose fills the prophet's mind with vision.

Don't be impatient. "Shall a land be born in one day?" (66:8). God has opened the womb and will deliver (66:9).

"As a mother comforts her child,
so I will comfort you. . . .
You shall see, and your heart shall rejoice" (66:13-14).

The prophet brings his message to a climax by underlining the essential truths: God will usher in new heavens and a new earth, and everyone—people from all nations, "all flesh"—will come to worship before the Lord (66:22-23).

MARKS OF OBEDIENT COMMUNITY

Like the prophet, the community of faith looks to the far horizon, holds on to a guiding vision.

Can you envision a new future, a godly future for yourself,

NOTES, REFLECTIONS, AND QUESTIONS

The obedient community, fueled by vision and sustained by hope, keeps the long view in mind but is faithful in the present.

your group, your church, your community? What would be required? Prayer? reconciliation? hard work?

If your dreams are in tune with God's dreams, how can God help you? What resources do you have? What resources do you need?

We believe God is at work, breaking down the walls of hostility, wiping away the tears of sorrow, and ushering in peace. We believe one day God will create a new heaven and a new earth where justice, goodwill, and joy will prevail. We live in that expectancy and strive toward it.

How does this vision affect your daily life?

How does it influence your faith community?

How can you work for it while you wait?

When the heart harbors hope, the human spirit can achieve great things. When did you believe in God so much, believe in yourself and in your future so much that you worked tirelessly to achieve something good?

IF YOU WANT TO KNOW MORE

Read Revelation 21:1-4, 22-26 and 22:5 and ponder the similar imagery of the kingdom of God's righteousness and peace.

NOTES, REFLECTIONS, AND QUESTIONS

COURAGE

"My people, why should you be living in well-built houses while my Temple lies in ruins? Don't you see what is happening to you? . . . Now go up into the hills, get lumber, and rebuild the Temple; then I will be pleased and will be worshiped as I should be."

—Haggai 1:4-5, 8, TEV

14 God's City of Peace

OUR HUMAN CONDITION

Faced with competing priorities, we tend to hedge: Times are not good. We have our own responsibilities. This is not the time to do for others. But the right word from the right leader might get our cooperation.

ASSIGNMENT

The Ezra material gives helpful historical background for Haggai and Zechariah. Don't get bogged down in the imagery in the visions of Zechariah. You may find Today's English Version helpful. Watch for hints that both Haggai and Zechariah look toward the coming messianic age.

Day 1 Haggai 1; Ezra 1–3 (time to rebuild the Temple, exiles return, foundation laid)
Day 2 Haggai 2; Ezra 4–6 (promises and blessings, opposition to rebuilding, Passover)
Day 3 Zechariah 1–3 (call to repentance, visions in the night)
Day 4 Zechariah 4–6 (visions of the restored community)
Day 5 Zechariah 7–8 (kindness and mercy, not fasting; God's promises to Jerusalem and Judah)
Day 6 Read and respond to "The Word of the Lord" and "Marks of Obedient Community."
Day 7 Rest

PRAYER

Pray daily before study:
"Pray for the peace of Jerusalem:
'May they prosper who love you.
Peace be within your walls,
and security within your towers.' . . .
I will say, 'Peace be within you.'
For the sake of the house of the LORD our God,
I will seek your good" (Psalm 122:6-9).

Prayer concerns for this week:

COURAGE

Day 1 Haggai 1; Ezra 1–3 (time to rebuild the Temple, exiles return, foundation laid)

Day 2 Haggai 2; Ezra 4–6 (promises and blessings, opposition to rebuilding, Passover)

Day 3 Zechariah 1–3 (call to repentance, visions in the night)

Day 4 Zechariah 4–6 (visions of the restored community)

Day 5 Zechariah 7–8 (kindness and mercy, not fasting; God's promises to Jerusalem and Judah)

7:8-10 true justice; mercy & compassion; don't oppress the widow, fatherless, alien, poor; think evil of each other.
8:19 love truth & peace

Day 6 "The Word of the Lord" and "Marks of Obedient Community"

THE WORD OF THE LORD

NOTES, REFLECTIONS, AND QUESTIONS

Haggai and Zechariah lived under new attitudes toward governing (Ezra 6:14). The Assyrians had ruthlessly mixed and exchanged populations to weaken social fabric. The Babylonians had reduced the Temple to ruins and had taken away as exiles the brightest and the best. But the brilliant politician Cyrus put together the Medes, the Persians, and the Babylonians into a vast empire that was more tolerant of differences in its people. Cyrus, in one of his first acts after conquering Babylon, permitted exiled peoples to return to their homes, carrying with them their sacred vessels for use in worship (Ezra 6:3-5). His theory was to encourage cooperation from the subject peoples throughout the Persian Empire.

Cyrus allowed the first wave of exiles to return to Jerusalem in 538 B.C. (1:1-4; 6:14). Under Cyrus's orders, Sheshbazzar, a "prince of Judah," led nearly fifty thousand people (2:64) to return to a pile of rubble. A homeless, rootless, exiled people need more than words. They need things they can touch, things that remind them of who they are. That is why they brought the holy vessels. That is why they began to rebuild the Temple. Within two years (536 B.C.), even while they were trying to build houses and eke out an existence, they cleared the site and laid the foundation of the Temple (3:8-11). But suddenly the work stopped; no further Temple construction took place for sixteen years.

The returnees faced huge obstacles. Residents voiced objections. Local Persian authorities believed the effort to be seditious. Old and new landowners argued over property rights. Intermarried Israelites and non-Israelites, probably including Samaritans, had counterproposals. And they ran out of money and material. Even the king called a halt to the project (4:21). However, when King Darius the Great came to power in 521 B.C., he allowed more exiles to return, bridled his Persian officials, and supported the rebuilding of the Temple (6:6-12). He appointed a new political agent, Zerubbabel, grandson of the Davidic king Jehoiachin, to lead the effort.

This silver coin from the Persian Period (sixth to fourth centuries B.C.) bears the letters YHD, pronounced "Yehud," the Aramaic name for the Persian province of Judah. An eagle is on one side and a lily, the symbol of Judah, on the other.

Haggai and Zechariah

Haggai and Zechariah, two minor prophets, loom large in the rebuilding of Jerusalem (Ezra 5:1-2). They stimulated the restoration of religious and political life for the returning exiles. These two cheerleader prophets challenged the returnees to organize their religious community, work together, and rebuild the Temple.

Haggai and Zechariah succeeded where others had failed. Called by some "the fathers of Judaism," these prophets did more than encourage the rebuilding of Solomon's Temple, great task though that was. They fortified the governor's political position and elevated the high priest to religious authority. They began a reshaping of theology that would continue for five centuries, until the time of Jesus Christ. And they gave spiritual courage to the Jews to move forward in reconstruction of the country.

Haggai prophesied for only four months, as far as we know, from August to December of 520 B.C. He saw that the people lacked resources, and they lacked resolve. Everybody said, "It's not the right time." Times *were* tough, of course—little rain, poor crops; money ran right through their pockets.

Can't you see why this has happened? Haggai said. God is not blessing us because you are living in paneled houses while God's house (the Temple) lies in ruins (Haggai 1:4). No wonder things are going badly.

Like earlier prophets, Haggai stirred up things with a powerful speech. Zerubbabel, governor of a disorganized city, listened. Joshua, high priest without a Temple, listened. Haggai gave a rousing proclamation on the twenty-ninth of August, 520 B.C. By the middle of September the people were hard at work. The right leader at the right time who hears the whispers of God can excite a whole people to action.

Memory Becomes Vision

"Who is left among you that saw this house in its former glory?" asked Haggai (Haggai 2:3). Few raised their hands. Maybe a handful of elderly. Probably not Haggai. Certainly not Zerubbabel, grandson of Jehoiachin. But the prophet held up the memory of Solomon's Temple as a vision to inspire the people. Men and women, young and old, will have to put their shoulders to the wheel to make things happen. But if they can visualize it, they can build it. "Take courage . . . take courage . . . take courage," he shouted (2:4-5). God is with us; don't be afraid.

What assurances did Haggai give? First, if God could bring them out of Egypt (out of Babylon too), God would help them build a Temple (2:5). Moreover, God is going to shake the whole world for more resources. God is never short of gold and silver (2:7-8).

The problem is always one of distribution. God needed to shake some pockets. Sure enough, other refugees returned, some with gold in their pockets and a love for the Temple in their hearts. King Darius sent money. Gifts of lumber and stone plus offers of labor came from unexpected sources. The Temple was completed in 515 B.C., requiring about five years for construction. Haggai put great hopes in Governor Zerubbabel. In his final prophecy Haggai called Zerubbabel God's servant, and again, an expression Jeremiah used, God's "signet ring" (2:23; see Jeremiah 22:24).

Describe a time when you were involved in a church or community project and strangers and outsiders offered unexpected help.

NOTES, REFLECTIONS, AND QUESTIONS

The First Temple, built by Solomon about 960 B.C., was destroyed when the Babylonians conquered Jerusalem in 587 B.C.

The Second Temple, built by the returned exiles under Zerubbabel (520–515 B.C.), was desecrated and damaged by the Greeks in 325 B.C. and desecrated again by the Seleucid Antiochus IV in 167 B.C.

In 20/19 B.C. Herod the Great began to restore and refurbish what was left of the Second Temple and to construct a complex of buildings around it. The renovation continued after his death and was not completed until shortly before this Temple was destroyed by the Romans in A.D. 70.

Visions in the Night

Zechariah heard the call from God a couple of months after Haggai heard his. His visions came in the night—wild, bewildering oracles full of strange prophetic imagery. The four different-colored horses, for example, simply represent messengers going to the four corners of the earth, on patrol, to scout for God (Zechariah 1:7-17). With two thousand miles of Mediterranean territory ruled by the Persians, they report, "Lo, the whole earth remains at peace" (1:11). But God is not happy (and neither is the prophet), because Jerusalem lies in ruins while the nations are at ease (1:15). The four horns (1:18) depict the powerful nations of the world who have conquered the people of Israel and Judah and held them in exile (1:19). God will "strike down" the horns (1:21), and scattered Jews can return home.

In another night vision a man is measuring Jerusalem (2:1-2). Surveyors and engineers are at work. That's good. But some are already anxious about the immense distance and cost involved in rebuilding the walls. Don't worry about that now, says the prophet. God will protect the city, as "a wall of fire all around it" and a presence within it (2:5). Meanwhile, those of you still remaining in Babylon, come on home. You are "the apple of my eye," says the Lord (2:8).

In 3:1-2, the word *Satan* would be better translated "the Adversary," for its meaning is different from that in the New Testament. The Adversary's job is to accuse, to point a finger of guilt, this time at the high priest Joshua. Joshua, symbolizing all of Judah, is cleansed and renewed; for God says, "I will remove the guilt of this land in a single day" (3:9). God is slow to punish, quick to forgive. The mournful lamentations are over; it is time to rebuild.

Dreaming God's Dream

In the vision of Zechariah 4, *seven* represents God. Seven lamps with seven wicks in each lamp show God full of light, able to see everything, everywhere (4:2, 10). Two olive trees, Zerubbabel and Joshua, stand beside the lamps (4:3). Remember, governor and high priest, the task of rebuilding the Temple will not require slave labor or military conscription as Solomon used to build his ostentatious palaces. God's Spirit will do it. "Not by might, nor by power, but by my spirit, says the LORD of hosts" (4:6).

In Chapter 8, Zechariah dreams God's dream—a faithful city where the "glory" dwells. The streets will be safe again, peaceful for little children and the elderly, even late in the evening. People from all over the world will hear about the peace of Jerusalem and be drawn to it, just as they once were driven from it. "They shall be my people and I will be their God, in faithfulness and in righteousness" (8:8). Once again the vision hints of a joyful end time of peace (*shalom*). Then back to earth: Don't be afraid to go forward with your work.

NOTES, REFLECTIONS, AND QUESTIONS

Four great migrations from Babylon took place:

- under Cyrus (about 538 B.C.) led by Sheshbazzar
- under Darius I (521 B.C.) led by Zerubbabel and Joshua
- under Artaxerxes I (464–423 B.C.) led by Ezra
- under Artaxerxes II (404–358 B.C.) led twice by Nehemiah

"Let your hands be strong," for "I will save you" says the Lord (8:13).

How we need a faithful city of peace where God's glory dwells today. What could we do to improve the quality of life for the elderly?

What could we do right now so boys and girls could play in our streets safely?

MARKS OF OBEDIENT COMMUNITY

The faithful community knows our time is now. This is our time to see and hear the plan of God. We neither daydream about yesterday's opportunities nor fantasize over tomorrow's possibilities. We accept today's task God gives us as our immediate faith response. Haggai said, "Take courage." Zechariah said, "Be strong."

What do you see God calling your DISCIPLE group to do right now?

Your church?

Where is the "iron hot" for Christian work, witness, or service?

IF YOU WANT TO KNOW MORE

Do some research on the different Temples. Compare this Temple to Solomon's Temple. Find out how Herod's Temple, where Jesus taught, relates to this Temple.

Use a Bible dictionary to learn more about Darius the Great, Ahasuerus, Media, and Persia.

NOTES, REFLECTIONS, AND QUESTIONS

The obedient faith community accepts the task God gives us for today as our immediate faith response.

RESTORATION

"See, I am sending my messenger to prepare the way before me, and the Lord whom you seek will suddenly come to his temple. The messenger of the covenant in whom you delight—indeed, he is coming."

—Malachi 3:1

15 God Will Restore Zion

OUR HUMAN CONDITION

We often lose hope when everything and everyone seem to be going against us. It is easy to become depressed and believe we have been forgotten.

ASSIGNMENT

Take each prophet at face value, separate and distinct. Listen to the unique message, even if it is limited as in Obadiah or heavily eschatological as in Zechariah. Watch Obadiah's poetic word play on "rock," the high places, Mount Esau, eagles' soaring, and their nest among the stars (3-4). Joel's promise (Joel 2:28-32) lays the foundation for Peter's Pentecost sermon (Acts 2:14-42). Malachi states God's promise in the tithe. Zechariah's images of the Prince of Peace and the Good Shepherd are familiar to us as later descriptions of Jesus Christ.

Day 1 Obadiah; Amos 1:11-12; Ezekiel 35 (woe to Edom, the day of the Lord)
Day 2 Joel 1–2 (plague of locusts, call to repentance, outpouring of the Spirit)
Day 3 Joel 3 (judgment on the nations, future blessings on Judah)
Day 4 Malachi 1–4 (corrupt priesthood, the coming messenger, the great day of the Lord)
Day 5 Zechariah 9–14 (the coming king, Jerusalem's strength, the scattered flock, future warfare and victory)
Day 6 Read and respond to "The Word of the Lord" and "Marks of Obedient Community."
Day 7 Rest

PRAYER

Pray daily before study:
"Send your light and your truth;
may they lead me
and bring me back to Zion, your sacred hill,
and to your Temple, where you live.
Then I will go to your altar, O God;
you are the source of my happiness.
I will play my harp and sing praise to you,
O God, my God" (Psalm 43:3-4, TEV).

Prayer concerns for this week:

RESTORATION

Day 1 Obadiah; Amos 1:11-12; Ezekiel 35 (woe to Edom, the day of the Lord)

Day 2 Joel 1–2 (plague of locusts, call to repentance, outpouring of the Spirit)

2:13 Rend your heart & not your garments. Lord is gracious & compassionate, slow to anger & abounding in love.

Day 3 Joel 3 (judgment on the nations, future blessings on Judah)

Day 4 Malachi 1–4 (corrupt priesthood, the coming messenger, the great day of the Lord)

3:9-12 Tithe

Day 5 Zechariah 9–14 (the coming king, Jerusalem's strength, the scattered flock, future warfare and victory)

9:9 Jesus' humble entry

13:7 Christ's death

Day 6 "The Word of the Lord" and "Marks of Obedient Community"

THE WORD OF THE LORD

Obadiah, like a hot desert wind, blasts the people of Edom with one brief, vitriolic message.
"Thus says the Lord GOD concerning Edom: . . .
I will surely make you least among the nations;
you shall be utterly despised" (Obadiah 1-2).

Who were the Edomites? Notice Obadiah often names them "Esau." Remember Esau, the ruddy-complected, hairy twin brother of Jacob, son of Rebekah and Isaac (Genesis 25:23-28)? The Edomites are Esau's descendants (36:1), making their home in the rocky hills southeast of the Dead Sea and on the western edge of the Arabian desert. Their fortress capital, nestled high in the hills, was Teman (Tema), which means "rock," near today's Petra (rock) in southern Jordan. Teman (Obadiah 9), a caravan oasis, was on the "incense road," linking Damascus and India to Egypt and the Mediterranean.

What was Edom's sin? Uncaring toward kin in time of trouble! Even though the kinship was strained across the centuries, still, they shouldn't have pounced on Judah when invaders from the north ravaged Jerusalem (10-12). Worse, they gloated over Judah's misfortune, joined in the looting, even captured some runaways and gave them over to the enemy (13-14). Damnable behavior for blood relatives, claimed Obadiah, deserving the wrath of God. Where did this prophet get his understanding of blood responsibility and fair play?

When have you been guilty of uncaring attitudes toward relatives in time of trouble?

The prophecy borders on being a nationalistic diatribe against one of Judah's enemies. But it is broadened by a sense of justice, "You'll get what's coming to you," and by the sure knowledge that God judges all the nations of the world, not just Judah.

What difference does it make to you in your faith to know that every nation stands under the judgment of God?

A Time to Turn

Joel had the heart of a farmer, the soul of a poet, and the spiritual sensitivities of a priest. A person who loves the soil grieves when "the seed shrivels under the clods" (Joel 1:17-18). As the locusts devour the vegetation, he weeps:
"Before them the land is like the garden of Eden,
but after them a desolate wilderness" (2:3).

NOTES, REFLECTIONS, AND QUESTIONS

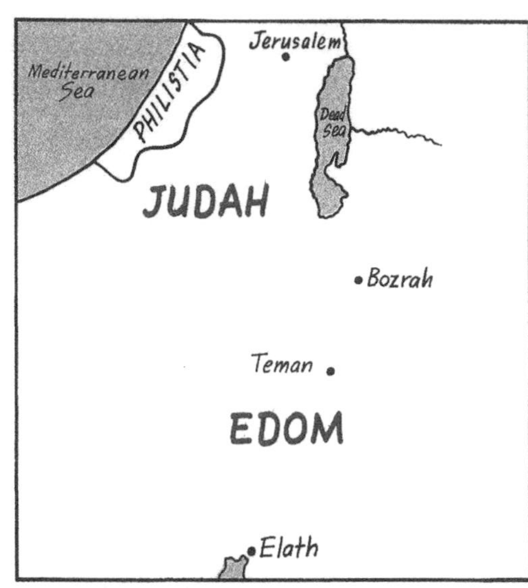

The enmity between Judah and Edom stretched from the time of Saul (before 1000 B.C.) through the Exile. Edom was sometimes under the control of Judah, sometimes an independent state with a king of its own. Obadiah's oracle indicts Edom for pride and for rejoicing over the ruin of Judah.

Joel sings like a poet. Read aloud his description of the locusts attacking like a foreign army (1:4; 2:4-11).

"Like warriors they charge,
like soldiers they scale the wall" (2:7).

Joel's spiritual perceptions have helped people of faith in all ages.

"Rend your hearts and not your clothing.
Return to the LORD, your God,
for he is gracious and merciful,
slow to anger, and abounding in steadfast love" (2:13).

The vision of a man ripping his clothes in repentance drives the spiritual point home. The prophets were not so interested in outward forms as they were in inner attitudes.

What response or action is called for by the phrase "rend your hearts" (Joel 2:13)?

Notice that Joel includes female and male, old and young, slave and free in his prophecy of the day of the Lord, a remarkable early insight into the universality of the Spirit of God: "I will pour out my spirit on all flesh" (2:28-29).

Joel connected the destruction wrought by the locusts to the coming day of the Lord, and he used the plague of locusts as a call for repentance. But even then, when people saw the hand of God in all natural phenomena, they were inclined to pray for rescue rather than for forgiveness.

Do we not today, in times of sickness, tragic natural disorders, and impending death, pray for rescue? What would it mean for us today to hear Joel's cry to mend our ways in the face of natural calamity?

Even amid the swarming locusts, Joel promises a better day (2:21-24). But he goes deeper:

"I will repay you for the years
that the swarming locust has eaten" (2:25-27).

People of faith have been blessed by the promise that God will bring a blessing out of tragedy.

Describe a personal experience when God has restored for you "the years the locusts have eaten."

God Will Restore

Joel lived probably during the time of the great Persian Empire (539–331 B.C.) when relative peace pervaded the land. The frightful foretelling of the great Assyrian and Babylonian

NOTES, REFLECTIONS, AND QUESTIONS

Joel interpreted the plague of locusts as God's judgment.

invasions was all in the past. Now Joel, perhaps a prophet of the Temple, has liturgical interests. He wants the people to love God and not lose hope in the future. Little Judah languishes in the backwaters of history. Joel envisions the day when God will "restore the fortunes of Judah and Jerusalem" (Joel 3:1). He hints at preparation for war and judgment, but his emphasis is on renewed strength and vitality. Everyone will know that "the LORD is a refuge for his people" (3:16).

The locusts will be gone, the enemies vanquished. Joel faithfully promises the final victory of God in earthly terms. He even uses military terms to underline God's power of judgment. "Prepare war, / stir up the warriors" (3:9).

The judgment will take place in "the valley of Jehoshaphat" (3:2, 12), "the valley of decision" (3:14), probably a symbolic name for some place around Jerusalem. Readers are surprised to see Micah's vision of peace—"they shall beat their swords into plowshares" (Micah 4:3)—turned upside down by Joel:

"Beat your plowshares into swords,
and your pruning hooks into spears" (Joel 3:10).

But what seems to be a call to holy war becomes instead a time of God's judging all the nations.

The Great Day of the Lord

The word of the Lord to Malachi demands serious and sincere worship. The Temple has been rebuilt. The priests are in place. The city has a governor under Persian authority. Malachi wants worship to be done properly.

The law of Moses demanded only perfect animals for sacrifice. Would people actually cheat God by giving inferior gifts—blind, sick, or lame animals? Such practices were forbidden by the Law. "When anyone offers a sacrifice of well-being to the LORD, in fulfillment of a vow or as a freewill offering, from the herd or from the flock, to be acceptable it must be perfect; there shall be no blemish in it" (Leviticus 22:17-21).

How might we be tempted to cheat when we give gifts to God today?

Attitude, forgiving brother before bringing the gift,

Even when giving is voluntary, when we don't have to donate at all, how do we find ways to give less than we pretend?

Just enough

What are some ways God might show rejection of our offerings? Or are we unable to consider such an idea?

Point out opportunity to mend our ways

NOTES, REFLECTIONS, AND QUESTIONS

Malachi is severe on the priests, insisting that they practice integrity and that their lips guard knowledge. If they do not speak the truths of the covenant, they cause others to stumble (Malachi 2:4-9). Similarly, in what ways might those of us who teach and preach be judged more strictly than others?

Personal integrity. Personal & Private life matching Public life

Divorce is not often mentioned by the prophets, but God says through Malachi, "I hate divorce. . . . So take heed to yourselves and do not be faithless" (2:16). The call to faithfulness permeates Malachi's prophecy—faithfulness to the covenant God, to the covenant community, and to the covenant of marriage. We know divorce often does harm to the couple, to children, to families, and to the church. What is being done in your congregation to strengthen marriages?

Bringing the Word of the Lord in renewed ways. Keep the whole family involved in His ministry

A messenger will prepare the way of the Lord (3:1). Often the messenger is symbolized by Elijah. In Malachi, the messenger will cleanse the priesthood first. He will be like "a refiner's fire," purifying the community in preparation for the Lord (3:1-3).

Malachi is a part of the prophetic tradition demanding that people return to the Lord. True worship, key to that return, includes not robbing God. "But you say, 'How are we robbing you?' " (3:8). The answer: by failing to bring the full tithe into the Lord's storehouse. Seldom in Scripture does God ask to be put to the test in keeping the Law (and the tithe, like all the rest, was part of the covenant). But look at the challenge: "Put me to the test . . . ; see if I will not open the windows of heaven for you and pour down for you an overflowing blessing" (3:10).

When have you put God to this test? What were the results?

Pray vs Wish

Malachi concludes his prophecy by announcing that Elijah will come "before the great and terrible day of the LORD" and "will turn the hearts of [you would expect him to say of people to God, but no] *parents to their children and the hearts of children to their parents,* so that I [God] will not come and strike the land with a curse" (4:6, italics added; see Deuteronomy 5:16). Such are the ways of God!

NOTES, REFLECTIONS, AND QUESTIONS

NOTES, REFLECTIONS, AND QUESTIONS

Zechariah 9–14

Zechariah 9–14, probably written by disciples of Zechariah, is composed of oracles, remembrances, and visions to fortify or balance Zechariah 1–8. We understand these passages best if we think symbolically. For example, the list of traditional enemies means all the enemies of God.

Zechariah 1–8 speaks of God's victory in concrete terms—the return of Israel to Jerusalem, the victory of God in praise on Mount Zion. But that didn't happen. People were becoming discouraged; they did not see signs of God's ultimate kingdom. So Zechariah begins to see "end times." God is the Great Warrior who will redeem Israel (9:13-14). Enemies of God will be destroyed (9:1-6). Some Gentiles who love the Lord will be saved (9:7). God, who has fought against Israel because of its sins, now turns to fight for Israel (9:16). God will powerfully win the final victory. This oracle makes Israel "prisoners of hope" (9:12).

The Messiah King

In this bewildering maze of prophecy stands a glorious messianic passage. Rejoice! Rejoice!

> "Lo, your king comes to you;
> triumphant and victorious is he" (Zechariah 9:9).

We are ready to hear that. The prophets have been honoring kings and princes; Judah is on the rise; the governor is praised as the "signet ring" of God (Haggai 2:23). But wait. What is this strange, upside-down phenomenon? He comes "humble and riding on a donkey" (Zechariah 9:9). The messianic oracle shows a peaceful king, not like the greedy, haughty rulers of an earlier Judah. Now the peace of God will come as a servant king, a shepherd king so humble that he rides the lowliest beast of burden, his feet nearly touching the ground. How the ways of the world are reversed by the ways of God. God, mighty warrior, will conquer with a Messiah servant, humble and just. Jesus, in a calculated effort to interpret his servant kingship, lived out this prophecy by riding into Jerusalem on a donkey. What a picture of messianic humility in Zechariah! What an act of messianic humility in Jesus Christ!

Blood of My Covenant

God or the representative of God will be pierced (Zechariah 12:10). Blood will flow. The house of David will mourn. All Israel will mourn. Blood, for the Jews, meant life, the sanctity of life, life linked to the Lifegiver. Zechariah refers to "the blood of my covenant with you" (9:11). It will "set your prisoners free." A sacrifice of blood on the altar as a guilt offering was life crying out to the Lifegiver for peace of soul. Such was the experience on the Day of Atonement (Leviticus 16). The great Suffering Servant passage in Isaiah 53 declares that innocent suffering is an expiation for the sins of others (Isaiah 53:5, 12).

NOTES, REFLECTIONS, AND QUESTIONS

Early Christians saw the messianic king riding on a donkey when Jesus entered Jerusalem. They also understood "the blood of my covenant" declared by Zechariah, which would "set . . . prisoners free" as the blood of the crucified Christ poured out to free men and women from their sins. For Christians, Jesus on the cross fulfills the innocent blood sacrifice of Isaiah 53:5, ushers in the new covenant of Jeremiah 31:31, and pours forth a river of grace to the depths of the earth's need (Ezekiel 47:1-12).

Will the messianic shepherd be well received? No! The flock will not follow. The shepherd breaks his staffs into pieces (Zechariah 11:7-14). The wage they offer him—thirty shekels of silver—was the price of a slave (11:12-13).

What is Zechariah saying? Sin is deeper than imagined; it has a near stranglehold on the world. Why has the kingdom of righteousness not come? Because of incomprehensible human resistance. So these latter chapters of Zechariah respond to earlier dreams that had dissipated. Do not abandon hope. God is mightier even than sin. God will finally triumph.

MARKS OF OBEDIENT COMMUNITY

A faith community is a hope-filled community. The Spirit has come down so that our young see visions and our old dream dreams. Both daughters and sons give testimony of God's love and power. We praise God, not because life is easy but because God is faithful.

Obedient community lives hope-filled, Spirit-filled, vision-guided because God is faithful.

Despair is everywhere. Many young people sing songs of death, take drugs, commit suicide. Some people have lost purpose; some see only closed doors. Many people have lost all hope.

What about our fellowship keeps us from this sadness?

Group worship & meditation on His Word

How can we effectively offer the source of our hope to others?

Small ways

IF YOU WANT TO KNOW MORE

Trace the tithe through the Scriptures. Notice its spiritual and material elements.

Use the maps in your Bible to locate the Negeb and the Shephelah. See what you can learn about them in a Bible atlas or dictionary.

"Get up, go to Nineveh, that great city, and proclaim to it the message that I tell you."

—Jonah 3:2

16 God's Mission for Israel

OUR HUMAN CONDITION

It's hard to think kindly of those who have treated us cruelly, caused us misery. And to be asked to be bearer of a message that will result in their forgiveness—unthinkable. We don't want to go.

ASSIGNMENT

Skim the book of Jonah as a total story. Then reread slowly, thoughtfully, a chapter a day, pondering the symbolism. After reading "The Word of the Lord," read the story again in its entirety with that information to stimulate new insights.

Day 1 Jonah 1–4
Day 2 Jonah 1 (running from God's call)
Day 3 Jonah 2 (Jonah's hymn of deliverance)
Day 4 Jonah 3 (Nineveh repents)
Day 5 Jonah 4 (Jonah's anger, God's compassion)
Day 6 Read and respond to "The Word of the Lord" and "Marks of Obedient Community."
Day 7 Rest

PRAYER

Pray daily before study:
"I wait eagerly for the LORD's help,
and in his word I trust.
I wait for the Lord
more eagerly than watchmen wait for the dawn—
than watchmen wait for the dawn" (Psalm 130:5-6, TEV).

Prayer concerns for this week:

Correction not punishment

WITNESS

Day 1 Jonah 1–4

God has many ways to get our attension
- He sends storms into your life
- He touches someone near you
- He sends someone to you
- He exposes your disobedience
- He touches you physically

Day 4 Jonah 3 (Nineveh repents)

God of second chances
Adam, Moses murder, Elijah complained, Peter denied, Authentic revival impacts both the individual & the culture.
I A sovereign work of God to forgive & change
II Spiritual work of God to correct error.
- must speak the truth in love
- we offer the truth to all people
- we obey the truth whole-heartedly
III A sudden work of God on an unexpected people
IV A saving work of God on an undeserving people
V Sanctifying work of God in the culture.
Nehemiah, Ezra: Honor God & share God's blessings with neighbor

Day 2 Jonah 1 (running from God's call)

God desires to awaken our spirit
- God desires for us to ack His presence
- God desires for us to ack our sin.
- God desires for us to submit to His will

God require genuine repentance
of 1000 steps God will take 999 & leave the last one for you. Repentance
1996 Olympic flames went out.
It was lighted by the "mother flame"
Holy Spirit is the "mother flame".

Day 5 Jonah 4 (Jonah's anger, God's compassion)

Romans 3:10–12
Jonah thinks grace is earned & God is obligated to give grace to those who merit it.
Is it right for you to be angry?
Jonah knowing, Nineveh unknowing
Is it right for you to be angry about the plant?
We are angry with God when we are self-righteous
Prodigal Son example.
Jonah more concerned about a plant than the people of Nineveh.

Day 3 Jonah 2 (Jonah's hymn of deliverance)

Day 6 "The Word of the Lord" and "Marks of Obedient Community"

THE WORD OF THE LORD

Imagine you were a prophet in Judah during the period after the Exile. Haggai and Zechariah had encouraged the rebuilding of the Temple (Haggai 1:7-8; Zechariah 8:9). Ezra and Nehemiah had come along later to rebuild and strengthen the city walls and to bring reform through return to the law of Moses (Nehemiah 2:17; 8–9). The returned exiles, living under the relaxed policies of Persia, were trying to keep the Law. They had learned much from their experience in exile. Their social injustices, their mixing their religious practices with pagan gods, and their flirting with foreign alliances had cost them dearly. Through suffering, they learned that God's righteousness judges the nations, even Israel and Judah. They also learned God travels with the chariots; God was present even in Babylon. Pressed into their experience was the certain truth that God's constant compassion would never abandon them. Just as God had rescued Israel from Egypt, so God, with a second Exodus, had made a highway in the desert (Isaiah 40:3) to bring them home.

Not only had they rebuilt the Temple; they were trying to keep it ceremonially clean. No pagan gods were present. Only carefully prescribed rituals of sacrifice were offered. Tithes and offerings were brought to the Temple (Malachi 3:10).

Now they knew they were called to be a distinct people, a holy nation. But that presented real problems, for they lived among all sorts of peoples from all over the Near East. The Judeans who had survived the slaughter and stayed in Judah had intermarried and developed local customs. The Jews who returned from Babylon had to share the soil and participate in the economic and social life with people whose allegiance to Israel's God was at least compromised by other commitments. How could they live a holy life in a polluted world without getting contaminated?

Ezra's answer was to focus on being a separated people. The laws of Exodus, Leviticus, Numbers, and Deuteronomy were read regularly, maintained, even expanded. Jews would be pure Jews.

Israel as Witness

Now suppose you, as a prophet, sensed Israel was missing a key component from its spiritual commission. Suppose God had laid on you as heavy an oracle as God had laid on Amos or Jeremiah. You remembered the divine word to Abraham and Sarah. Through them "all the families of the earth shall be blessed" (Genesis 12:3). As you recalled or read the great prophecies of Isaiah of Babylon, you knew that God is God of all the nations.

> "I am God, and there is no other;
> I am God, and there is no one like me" (Isaiah 46:9).

NOTES, REFLECTIONS, AND QUESTIONS

The term *Jew* undoubtedly derived from Judah, the tribe of Judah, the name of the Southern Kingdom before the Exile. The subjects of the Persian province of Judah after the Exile were called Jews, and the term referred to participants in the covenant and heirs to belief in the one God, separate and distinct from other people because of their way of life. The term *Judaism* describes the religion of these Judeans (Jews). Because the Exile began a totally different phase in Israel's faith, the terms *Jew* and *Judaism* should be reserved for referring to believers and their religion after that important point in history.

False idols are a laugh. Had not Amos and Jeremiah, Obadiah, even Nahum, shown that God would judge all the nations?

If the nations are recipients of God's judgment, are they not also recipients of God's salvation? Isaiah had said the rulers of all the nations would see the works of the Lord (49:7). God was performing a new Exodus; everyone would watch.

"Then the glory of the LORD shall be revealed,
and all people shall see it together" (40:5).

Israel was not only called to be God's saved people; Israel was called to be the agent of God's salvation for the whole world. Israel was called to be a witness, a missionary. Isaiah had shouted it:

"You are my witnesses, says the LORD,
and my servant whom I have chosen,
so that you may know and believe me
and understand that I am he.
Before me no god was formed,
nor shall there be any after me" (43:10).

It would have been easy for God simply to rescue Israel from captivity. But God had a much bigger plan in mind.

"I have a greater task for you, my servant.
Not only will you restore to greatness
the people of Israel who have survived,
but I will also make you a light to the nations—
so that all the world may be saved" (49:6, TEV).

God, with infinite compassion, *hesed* (steadfast love), will not be satisfied until the whole world is saved (45:22-23).

The Prophet Jonah

Now pretend you, as a prophet, know that the religious establishment thinks of the God of Israel in exclusive terms. What would you do to proclaim your message of salvation to the whole world? You might tell a story so poignant it could penetrate closed ears. Or you could begin writing about a prophet named Jonah.

There had been a prophet named Jonah who lived in the Northern Kingdom during the time of King Jeroboam II. The writer's selecting this earlier prophet as the central figure in the book of Jonah was a great choice because of the meaning of his name. Jonah means "dove." A dove is a messenger. Remember when Noah sent a dove out of the ark (Genesis 8:8-12)?

Jonah's father's name was Amittai. Amittai means "truth." Sometimes *son of* means "child of," but sometimes it means "with the spirit of." Dove is filled with the spirit of truth. Jonah would have liked to have stayed in Israel. But he was called to go to another nation—to the city of Nineveh, of all places, the symbol of Israel's most vicious enemies, a prototype for paganism. God did not deny that they were full of "wickedness" (Jonah 1:2).

NOTES, REFLECTIONS, AND QUESTIONS

Jonah, the "dove," flew with truth in his wings—not to the east (Nineveh) but to the west. Tarshish, if ancient Tartessus, was located on the western shores of the Iberian peninsula, on the far side of the Strait of Gibraltar, just before you fall off the edge of the then-known world. Jonah was running in the opposite direction of God's call, intending to go as far as he could go.

Once Jonah was on ship, God sent a storm. Jonah fell asleep. Why? Did he think he had escaped God? Did he think the storm was not for him? The sailors, all Gentiles, were warm-hearted men who prayed to their gods for help. They didn't want to throw Jonah into the sea. But the storm raged on. So at Jonah's insistence, they threw him overboard; and right away he was swallowed by "a large fish" (1:17). Had Jonah outrun God? No. Psalm 104 reminds us that God made the fish.

"LORD, you have made so many things!
How wisely you made them all! . . .
There is the ocean, large and wide,
where countless creatures live,
large and small alike. . . .
which you made" (Psalm 104:24-26, TEV).

Jonah is still under the umbrella of God's power. Jonah, in the bottom of the sea, was as far from Mount Zion, the Temple, and Jerusalem as he could get; yet God was with him.

How long in the belly of the deep? Long enough to sing one of the great liturgical psalms of Israel (Jonah 2:2-9). The last line is the clincher: "Deliverance belongs to the LORD!" (2:9). Other great psalms sound the same triumphant note:

"If it had not been the LORD who was on our side . . .
then the flood would have swept us away" (Psalm 124:1, 4).
"Out of the depths I cry to you, O LORD. . . .
If you, O LORD, should mark iniquities,
Lord, who could stand?
But there is forgiveness with you,
so that you may be revered" (Psalm 130:1-4).

Nineveh the Gentile World

We are beginning to realize that Nineveh represents the whole Gentile world, all the foreign nations. Archaeologists measure the distance between the walls of ancient Nineveh to be two to three miles. For Jonah, it is "an exceedingly large city, a three days' walk across" (Jonah 3:3). A mission to the Gentiles would be a huge task.

When Jonah preached in Nineveh, everyone put on sackcloth and repented (3:5). In the Near East, in Arab and Jewish communities, when the people fast, they do not feed their animals. Imagine the bleating of the hungry sheep and the bellowing of the cows while the people mourned for mercy. Even the king repented. It was a miracle.

NOTES, REFLECTIONS, AND QUESTIONS

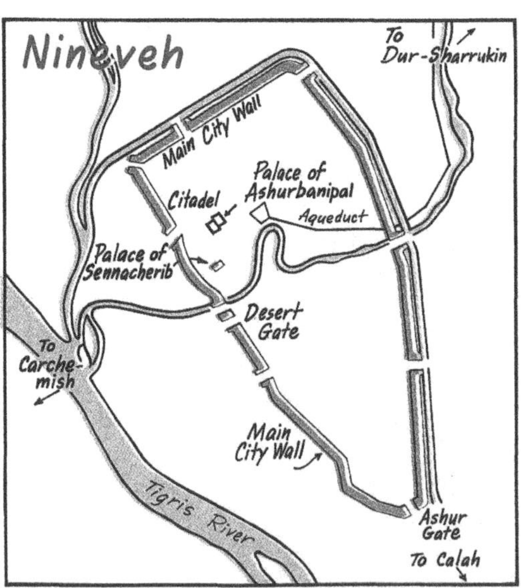

Based on archaeological evidence, this representation of Nineveh, "that great city" (Jonah 4:11), shows how it might have appeared before Ashurbanipal's death in 633 B.C.

But Jonah was angry over Nineveh's repenting. Because God had done what Jonah knew from the beginning God would do—show mercy and not punish Nineveh. What is the prophet saying? God wants not only to judge but to save.

Jonah sulks: " O LORD, please take my life from me, for it is better for me to die than to live" (4:3). God isn't moved. Instead, in another act of compassion—for that's the kind of God he is—God provides a bush to shade the angry Jonah. When the bush dies, Jonah feels sorry. Now the point: "Then the LORD said, 'You are concerned about the bush. . . . should I not be concerned about Nineveh . . . ?' " (4:10-11). In other words, God will be who God is—gracious and forgiving.

God wanted Israel, the messenger of truth and righteousness, to be "a light to the nations" (Isaiah 49:6). Why? In "Nineveh, that great city, . . . there are more than a hundred and twenty thousand persons who do not know their right hand from their left" (Jonah 4:11). In the Gentile world, often so foreign and sometimes so alien and hostile, God was at work. The dove of truth, the messenger of covenant love and law, Israel, must go to the Ninevehs of this world. Why? "That my salvation may reach to the end of the earth" (Isaiah 49:6).

If you had been a prophet in Israel around 400 B.C., you could have put this amazing story into the minds of the people, keeping Israel's mission and God's ultimate purpose alive.

MARKS OF OBEDIENT COMMUNITY

Our fellowship acknowledges the human tendency to become "closed," to withdraw from people who are different, from people whose ways we don't understand, from people who have hurt us.

Study your church. What images project "walls" to those outside?

How can it be that we who have experienced God's forgiveness might not want others to know the compassionate forgiveness of God?

What images project compassion and model the forgiveness of God?

NOTES, REFLECTIONS, AND QUESTIONS

This wall relief from the palace of Sennacherib in Nineveh shows a woman giving a drink to a child from an animal-skin container. Here are two ordinary people of the "more than a hundred and twenty thousand persons who do not know their right hand from their left" (Jonah 4:11).

The obeying community offers the compassionate, forgiving love of God to all persons, and leaves the judging to God.

Study your church life. What programs or ministries effectively reach out to include "outsiders"?

If you were Jonah and went to the "Nineveh" within a twenty-minute drive from your church building, where would you go?

IF YOU WANT TO KNOW MORE

See what you can discover about Nineveh, "that great city." Locate it on a map.

Reread Jonah 1 to see how the Gentile sailors came to have respect for Jonah's God. Some Gentiles were attracted to Judaism. Look up *God-fearers* (Acts 10:2; 13:16). Look up *Court of the Gentiles* at the Temple or *proselyte*.

The book of Ruth, recalling an ancient ancestry, was circulated the same time as Jonah to protest narrow nationalism. Read Ruth 1. In end times, all nations will come to God. See Isaiah 2:2-4; 66:18-21.

NOTES, REFLECTIONS, AND QUESTIONS

DISCIPLE

THE LETTERS OF PAUL

APOSTLE

"When God, who had set me apart before I was born and called me through his grace, was pleased to reveal his Son to me, so that I might proclaim him among the Gentiles, I did not confer with any human being."

—Galatians 1:15-16

17 Called Through God's Grace

OUR HUMAN CONDITION

When someone comes along to challenge what we believe and what we do, we often respond by becoming more zealous for our views and ways.

ASSIGNMENT

We quickly review Paul's life, noting his passions, his strategies, his controversies, because his letters flow out of his life and mission. Notice bits of autobiography in the letters.

Day 1 Acts 7:51–8:3; 9:1-31; Galatians 1:11-24 (stoning of Stephen, Saul's conversion)
Day 2 Acts 11:19-30; 12:24–14:28 (Paul and Barnabas in Asia Minor, preaching in Antioch of Pisidia, ministry in Iconium region)
Day 3 Acts 15–19; Galatians 2:1-10 (Jerusalem Council, Paul and Silas leave for Syria and Cilicia, Timothy, through Asia Minor to Troas, Macedonian call, Philippi, Thessalonica, Beroea, Athens, Corinth, Ephesus)
Day 4 2 Corinthians 11:21-33; Acts 20–23 (suffering as an apostle, Greece, Ephesian elders, visit to Jerusalem, assaulted in the Temple, on trial in Jerusalem)
Day 5 Acts 24–28 (on trial in Caesarea, defense before Agrippa, sailing to Rome, storm and shipwreck, Malta and Rome)
Day 6 Read and respond to "The Word of the Lord" and "Marks of Obedient Community."
Day 7 Rest

PRAYER

Pray daily before study:

"Teach me, Lord, what you want me to do,
and lead me along a safe path,
because I have so many enemies" (Psalm 27:11, TEV).

Prayer concerns for this week:

APOSTLE

Day 1 Acts 7:51–8:3; 9:1-31; Galatians 1:11-24 (stoning of Stephen, Saul's conversion)

Day 2 Acts 11:19-30; 12:24–14:28 (Paul and Barnabas in Asia Minor, preaching in Antioch of Pisidia, ministry in Iconium region)

Day 3 Acts 15–19; Galatians 2:1-10 (Jerusalem Council, Paul and Silas leave for Syria and Cilicia, Timothy, through Asia Minor to Troas, Macedonian call, Philippi, Thessalonica, Beroea, Athens, Corinth, Ephesus)

15 Gentiles: abstain from food polluted by idols; from blood; meat of strangled animals; sexual immorality.
Paul & Silas; Barnabas & John/Mark
16: Jailer's conversion; Lydia's generosity;
17: To an unknown God

Day 4 2 Corinthians 11:21-33; Acts 20–23 (suffering as an apostle, Greece, Ephesian elders, visit to Jerusalem, assaulted in the Temple, on trial in Jerusalem)

20: heals man who fell from third floor
Paul's farewell to Ephesian Elders.

Day 5 Acts 24–28 (on trial in Caesarea, defense before Agrippa, sailing to Rome, storm and shipwreck, Malta and Rome)

Paul's snake bite: murderer vs god.

Day 6 "The Word of the Lord" and "Marks of Obedient Community"

THE WORD OF THE LORD

He always used his Roman name, Paul. On the Damascus road, Jesus Christ spoke his Jewish name, Saul. This strange and marvelous man was both Jew and Roman. Paul was born in Tarsus of devout Jewish parents who were Roman citizens. They were Jews of the Diaspora, a part of the several million Greek-speaking Jews scattered in major cities all around the Mediterranean.

More than five hundred years had passed since the rebuilding of the Temple in Jerusalem. Alexander's armies had reshaped the world. So had Caesar's. Now under Roman peace, the seas were secure from pirate ships and the roads were safe for travel. Jews as merchants, artisans, teachers, workers, and traders now lived all over the western world.

Antioch had a population of half a million people with about fifty thousand Jews. Alexandria, second in size only to Rome at its zenith, had a million people with a huge Jewish population, including such distinguished scholars as Philo and Aristobulus. Rome's Jewish quarter contained at least nine synagogues.

Paul's Early Life

Tarsus was "an important city" (Acts 21:39); in fact, during its golden age in the reign of Augustus (27 B.C. to A.D. 14), it excelled as an intellectual city. Located on the fertile eastern plain, ten miles north of the Mediterranean on the southeastern coast of Asia Minor, Tarsus became the capital of the Roman province of Cilicia. Schools, theater, and sports flourished in this commercial, educational, and administrative center. Stoic philosophers taught in Tarsus, including Zeno, the traditional founder of Stoicism.

So Paul grew up speaking Greek as his first language, studying the Septuagint—the Greek translation of the Hebrew Scriptures—in his synagogue. (The Septuagint had been translated from Hebrew into Greek by Jewish scholars in Alexandria two centuries earlier.)

Paul learned a trade from his family, an important reality among Jewish families who generally had no land and were often required to move. He probably worked with leather, making tents for soldiers and shepherds. Paul took pride in his craft, pleased he could support himself while he taught and preached (1 Thessalonians 2:9).

Synagogues were all over Palestine, but the Temple was the focus of the national religion. Jews in the Diaspora studied Torah and prayed in synagogues. Different cultures produced different traditions; rabbis gave a variety of interpretations of Torah. In Jerusalem lived Sadducees, Pharisees, priests, and zealots, though the zealots were not necessarily centered there. The Essenes, of Dead Sea Scroll fame, lived in seclusion, untouched by the world.

Paul was a young man when he went to Jerusalem to study

NOTES, REFLECTIONS, AND QUESTIONS

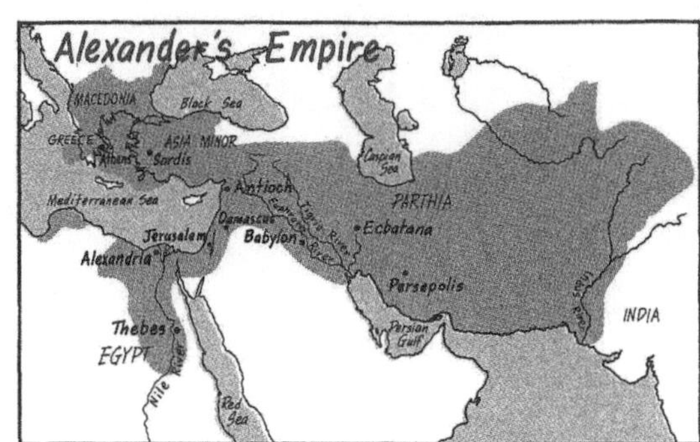

At the time of Alexander the Great's death in 323 B.C., his empire was the greatest expanse of empire that the world had ever known. Greek (Hellenistic) influence, introduced by his armies, continued to dominate culture, social structures, and economic systems through New Testament times.

(Acts 22:3), a fact that points both to dedication and to means. His teacher was the renowned Gamaliel, known within Judaism as a great scholar and statesman. He emphasized the graciousness of God, compassion for the poor, and hope for peace. Paul, under Gamaliel, would have studied in Hebrew using the Hebrew text. They would have spoken Aramaic. He became a Pharisee, a lay scholar determined to keep Torah teachings in daily life as a constantly obedient and faithful Jew.

Why Paul held the coats of the angry Jewish leaders who stoned Stephen we do not know. Nor do we know exactly why Paul sought to root out the Christian movement. In any event, he offered to travel for the priestly authorities (9:1-2), looking for Jewish Christians in Damascus.

Paul's Mission

Christians often speak of Paul's Damascus road experience as a conversion, and of course it was—a conversion of outlook, theological orientation, and focus, but not a conversion to another religion. Acts describes what happened; Paul does not. Paul wrote of it as a call, much like the call God gave to Isaiah or Jeremiah (Galatians 1:17-18). In the Christian church we focus on Paul's encounter with Jesus the Lord; but Paul, in both Luke's account in Acts and in his own letters, always emphasizes his call by Christ to be a missionary of the "good news."

Paul was hurrying to search out Jewish "believers" when Jesus Christ spoke to him. The force came from outside. "The gospel that was proclaimed by me is not of human origin; for I did not receive it from a human source, nor was I taught it, but I received it through a revelation of Jesus Christ" (1:11-12).

Paul says God set him apart from his mother's womb (1:15). Isaiah of Babylon wrote,

> "The LORD called me before I was born,
> while I was in my mother's womb he named me"
> (Isaiah 49:1).

When "the word of the LORD" came to Jeremiah, God said,

> "Before I formed you in the womb I knew you,
> and before you were born I consecrated you"
> (Jeremiah 1:5).

The blinding light (Acts 9:3; 26:13) reminds us of Isaiah's experience in the Temple, surrounded by the brilliant holiness of God (Isaiah 6:1-4). Ezekiel saw "a great cloud with brightness around it and fire flashing forth continually" (Ezekiel 1:4).

After being struck down and reprimanded by the Lord Jesus for persecuting him, Paul is told to "get up and stand on your feet" (Acts 26:16). God had told Ezekiel, in effect, it was time to be God's courageous messenger, to "stand up on your feet." Actually, God set him on his feet (Ezekiel 2:1-3).

What was happening? Each man was called to be a messenger, a spokesperson. Paul was called to be an "apostle," literally "one who is sent." Paul insists he was sent by Christ,

NOTES, REFLECTIONS, AND QUESTIONS

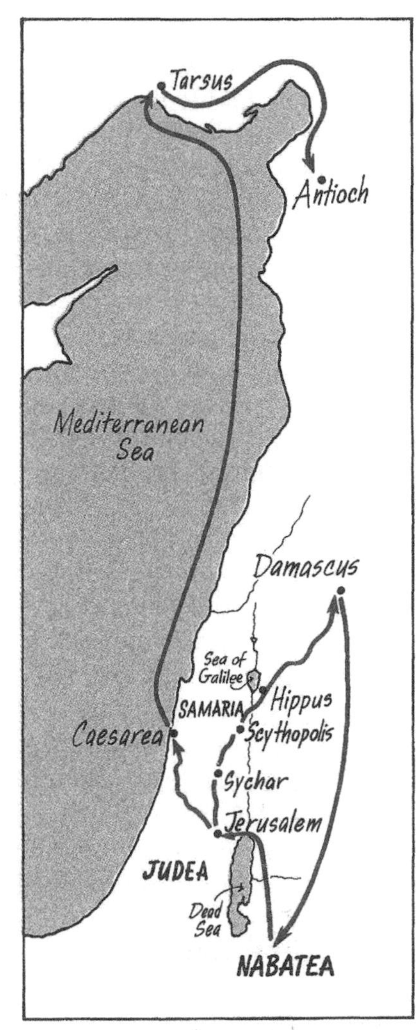

After the stoning of Stephen (Acts 7), Paul headed for Damascus, searching out Christians. Before he reached Damascus, he had an experience of the risen Christ. He was led into Damascus blind and was baptized there (9:1-9). He went off into the desert for a time and then came home to Tarsus, where Barnabas found him and brought him to the church in Antioch of Syria to begin a year of ministry there (11:19-26).

not by a church, though in Acts 13:1-3, in response to the Spirit, he is authorized by the church.

Apostle

Jesus used the Hebrew name Saul. He did not change Saul's name, as he had Peter's. Rather Jesus created an apostle. God "called me through his grace . . . so that I might proclaim him among the Gentiles" (Galatians 1:15-16). Yes, Paul became a "slave" of Jesus Christ; yes, Paul experienced forgiveness and cleansing; yes, Paul received power and blessing of the Holy Spirit, and in that sense, was converted. But Paul always understood that what mattered most was that he was given a message; he was given a mission. He began almost every letter saying who he was. Consider Romans 1:1-2: "Paul, a servant [slave] of Jesus Christ, called to be an apostle, set apart for the gospel of God, which he promised beforehand through his prophets in the holy scriptures."

Paul's entire ministry was surrounded by a swirl of controversy. Was he surprised at the conflict he caused? Grieved. Disappointed. Wounded. Yes. But probably not surprised. He himself had persecuted Jewish Christians. Right after his baptism by Ananias in Damascus, he began to proclaim Jesus, saying, "He is the Son of God" (Acts 9:20). Some Damascus Jews, unable to refute his message, plotted to kill him. But Paul's disciples lowered him in a basket through the Damascus wall to safety (9:25). Thus began a life of ministry filled with ridicule, beatings, imprisonments, narrow escapes, and finally martyrdom. Sometimes the Jews who refused the gospel got all the blame, but Paul's work offended nearly everyone.

In the Power of the Spirit

In Acts, Luke wants to make clear that Paul's mission had divine power. Many of the incidents he reports are intended to make that point. Paul's temporarily blinding a magician in Paphos on Cyprus (Acts 13:6-11) is one example. Watch for others.

Sailing to Asia Minor, Paul went into the interior to Antioch of Pisidia. Immediately he preached in the synagogue. His sermon (13:16-43) traced the saving work of God in Judaism, lifted up the crucifixion and resurrection of Jesus as the fulfillment of prophecy, and quoted Psalm 2:7, Isaiah 55:3, Psalm 16:10, and Habakkuk 1:5 for authority. Acts uses this sermon as an example of Paul's preaching to the Jews. For Acts the similarity between this sermon and Peter's preaching shows that Paul was in agreement with the Jerusalem church, not an innovator or a free-lance preacher of a different gospel.

Conservative Jewish Christians came to Antioch in Syria from Jerusalem to insist that all new Gentile converts must be circumcised (Acts 15:1). After much debate and dissension, the church sent a delegation, including Paul, to Jerusalem.

NOTES, REFLECTIONS, AND QUESTIONS

James the brother of Jesus made the definitive decision. James's decision, supported by the apostles and elders, was that the mission to the Gentiles should continue; but rudiments of bedrock Jewish teachings should be maintained: Gentiles should not eat meat sacrificed to idols, should not eat strangled animals or blood, and should abstain from sexual immorality (15:20). (Read Galatians 2:1-10; it tells the story somewhat differently. According to 2:10, they should remember the poor believers in Jerusalem, perhaps made poor by persecution.) Paul was ecstatic. With this mandate, he continued his ministry, never deviating from these guidelines. But the issue of circumcision and Jewish laws plagued him all his ministry and provided the focus for much of his correspondence.

Timothy Joins Paul

In Asia Minor, Paul found a young Christian named Timothy and asked him to help. Timothy's mother was Jewish; his father was Greek. He had not been circumcised. Whereas Paul insisted that Gentiles did not require circumcision after conversion, Timothy, a Jew, was different. He and Paul would offend the Jews even before they opened their mouths. Paul, trying to avoid needless controversy, had Timothy circumcised.

At Troas, on the coast near where ancient Troy had been, Paul had a vision of a man pleading with him to go to Greece. "Come over to Macedonia and help us" (Acts 16:9). Paul's decision to go would take Christianity to Europe (the west) and delay Christianity's going to northern Asia (the east) for nearly one thousand years. Apparently Luke the physician joined the group going to Macedonia, for he used the word *we* in reporting the journey.

Acts uses the Athens sermon (17:22-31) as an example of Paul's preaching to the Gentile world. It is the counterpart of his preaching to the Jews in Acts 13. Paul held the philosophers' attention, referring to an altar to an unknown god, quoting Greek poets, and recalling Israel's history. Later at Corinth Paul said he did not come there with worldly wisdom, but in Athens he gave it all he had. The audience would have stayed with him if he had taught the immortality of the soul; but when he proclaimed that God had raised Jesus from the dead, they shook their heads and left (17:32). Few were converted.

Paul started churches in the vital trade city of Corinth, south of Athens, and in the Greco-Roman seaport of Ephesus on the west coast of Asia Minor. The plan was always the same—to teach first in the synagogue. He was rewarded by some conversions, much dissension, and persecution. Paul in his letters reminded people how hard he had tried to carry out the mission and how much opposition he had encountered. Traveling teachers called Paul and his gospel into question, creating problems in his churches after he has gone elsewhere.

Paul's greatest concern was for the fledgling churches he

NOTES, REFLECTIONS, AND QUESTIONS

had founded. "I am under daily pressure because of my anxiety for all the churches" (2 Corinthians 11:28). But Paul went to Jerusalem in his later years rather than going back to Corinth, Philippi, or Ephesus to strengthen the churches there. He had collected an offering for the poor of Judea as agreed upon in Acts 11:27-30. For Paul personally to fulfill that holy promise, rather than to send a courier, must have been terribly important. It meant completing a sacred trust, even though he was not sure the offering would be accepted (Romans 15:28-32). Acceptance of the collection would symbolize the unity of the church. For Paul, as we shall see from his letters, that unity meant everything.

Last Trip to Jerusalem

When Paul arrived in Jerusalem, James and the elders heard his report of how God was working among the Gentiles, and they all praised God. But there was a problem: Jewish Christians said Paul was teaching Gentiles to forsake Moses and the Ten Commandments, to ridicule circumcision and Jewish traditions. So, at the leaders' suggestion, Paul agreed to pay the costs and participate in the Temple ritual with four pious Christian Jews who were completing a vow. That act would be a most holy, most pious Jewish act. Paul did it, but to no avail. Someone falsely accused him of taking an uncircumcised Gentile into the holy purification room in the Temple, and a riot broke loose.

Paul was arrested. He gave a powerful sermon in Hebrew to the crowd (Acts 22:1-21). He told a tribune of his Roman citizenship, was saved by a nephew (son of Paul's sister), and when forty men vowed not to eat or drink until they had killed him (23:12-22), the tribune surrounded Paul with nearly five hundred Roman soldiers and marched him to Caesarea. There he was in prison for over two years, on trial before Felix, then King Agrippa and Festus.

In Romans 15, Paul had indicated a desire to preach as far as Spain, symbol of the geographical limits of the world. He had always hoped to go to Rome, strengthen the church there, and then move on to Spain (15:23-28). Whether Paul used his appeal to Caesar to escape certain death, or whether he used it as a way to get to Rome, we do not know. We do know God used this final trip to allow Paul at least two years of teaching in the heart of the empire, the opportunity to encourage innumerable Christian missionaries and travelers, and the final act of "witness"—to be a martyr for his Savior in Rome, probably under Emperor Nero.

MARKS OF OBEDIENT COMMUNITY

As members of a called community, we are propelled by an inner assurance that God has put new life in us. We've been put right side up. We're not afraid. Our gift of grace thrusts us outward to tell others, even when we experience sacrifice or

NOTES, REFLECTIONS, AND QUESTIONS

Built by Herod the Great, this aqueduct at Caesarea carried water into the city from Mount Carmel.

The faithful community embraces its life-giving message with passion and hurries to take it to others.

resistance. Occasionally a "Paul" emerges from our fellowship who burns with unusual passion.

What causes our fellowship to sometimes become complacent?

having contributed some, we might feel it's others turn.

Why are new-found joy and fresh spiritual excitement sometimes a threat to other people?

New is a small start. History, failings, etc. are seen by self & other. We need His Grace.

Why do many people resist grace, forgiveness, new life in Christ?

It is not intuitive & sounds simple.

How can we make our life in Jesus visible to others?

Staying in the word. Personal life first & then in public.

If we say we believe Jesus is the Lord, even in a loving way, we create some conflict. People label us. Many people think our views narrow, intolerant. If we believe our lives are being made healthy and free through faith in Christ, how can we witness without appearing judgmental or condescending?

Remember we are forgiven servants.

How can we respect other religions and still offer Christ?

Unity in essentials; Liberty in non-essentials; In all things charity. Philip Melanchthon (Martin Luther's collaborator

IF YOU WANT TO KNOW MORE

Read about Paul in a Bible dictionary.

Each lesson on Paul will carry here a suggestion for writing a letter, not necessarily to be sent, though it may be. The idea for each letter grows out of the week's study and offers a way for putting your thoughts and reflections into words.

Letter: Write a letter to yourself reviewing your own call and reminding yourself of how the power of God has been at work in your life.

NOTES, REFLECTIONS, AND QUESTIONS

CORRESPONDENCE

"For I wrote you out of much distress and anguish of heart and with many tears, not to cause you pain, but to let you know the abundant love that I have for you."

—2 Corinthians 2:4

18 The Letters of Paul

OUR HUMAN CONDITION

We need connections. We do not survive well when isolated or out of touch with others. Any word received lets us know that someone knows we are here.

ASSIGNMENT

The readings this week are unusual. Concentrate on the *elements* of Paul's letters rather than on the content. We will turn from one letter to another, looking at comparable parts. Paul took the form of a standard letter and adapted it to a missional message.

Day 1 *Salutation:* Romans 1:1-7; 1 Corinthians 1:1-3; 2 Corinthians 1:1-2; Galatians 1:1-5; Philippians 1:1-2; 1 Thessalonians 1:1; Philemon 1-3

Day 2 *Thanksgiving:* Romans 1:8-15; 1 Corinthians 1:4-9; 2 Corinthians 1:3-11; Philippians 1:3-11; 1 Thessalonians 1:2-10

Day 3 *The body of the letter:* 1 Corinthians 1:10–4:21 (Christ the power and wisdom of God, divisions in the church)

Day 4 *Ethical instruction and exhortation:* 1 Thessalonians 4:1–5:22; Philippians 4:1-6 (rejoice in the Lord)

Day 5 *Conclusion:* Romans 15:33–16:27; 1 Corinthians 16:19-24; 2 Corinthians 13:11-13; Galatians 6:16-18; Philippians 4:7-9, 21-23; 1 Thessalonians 5:23-28

Day 6 Read and respond to "The Word of the Lord" and "Marks of Obedient Community."

Day 7 Rest

PRAYER

Pray daily before study:

"I will always thank you, God, for what you have done;
in the presence of your people
I will proclaim that you are good" (Psalm 52:9, TEV).

Prayer concerns for this week:

Bryce Brain Tamar
Elba "

CORRESPONDENCE

Day 1 *Salutation:* Romans 1:1-7; 1 Corinthians 1:1-3; 2 Corinthians 1:1-2; Galatians 1:1-5; Philippians 1:1-2; 1 Thessalonians 1:1; Philemon 1-3

Grace & peace

Day 2 *Thanksgiving:* Romans 1:8-15; 1 Corinthians 1:4-9; 2 Corinthians 1:3-11; Philippians 1:3-11; 1 Thessalonians 1:2-10

Day 3 *The body of the letter:* 1 Corinthians 1:10–4:21 (Christ the power and wisdom of God, divisions in the church)

I Corn 4:7
~~what~~ who makes you different from anyone else? What do you have that you didn't receive? If you did receive it why do you boast as though you didn't?

Day 4 *Ethical instruction and exhortation:* 1 Thessalonians 4:1–5:22; Philippians 4:1-6 (rejoice in the Lord)

I Thes 5:12-18 Be joyful always; pray continually; give thanks in all circumstances for this is God's will for you in Christ Jesus
21: Test everything. Hold onto the good.
Philip 4:4 Rejoice in the Lord always. I will say it again: Rejoice!

Day 5 *Conclusion:* Romans 15:33–16:27; 1 Corinthians 16:19-24; 2 Corinthians 13:11-13; Galatians 6:16-18; Philippians 4:7-9, 21-23; 1 Thessalonians 5:23-28

Phil 4:13 I can do everything through him who gives me strength.

Day 6 "The Word of the Lord" and "Marks of Obedient Community"

THE WORD OF THE LORD

Paul wrote his letters to the churches before any other New Testament documents were written. His letters were written mostly to churches he had started. They addressed real situations in these congregations and were filled with emotion as well as reason.

In a day before telephones and other modern forms of communication, the letter was the main way of sending information other than person-to-person contact. Lots of ancient papyrus letters have been discovered, preserved by the dry climate of Egypt. They help us understand the structure and form of letters during the time of the Roman Empire. Paul took the standard form and adapted it for his missional purposes. Remember, Paul was not writing essays or tracts to be published. He poured out his heart to people who were trying to live the Christian faith. Even the long and powerful Letter to the Romans is in letter form, although addressed to a church he had not yet visited.

House Churches

It might be more accurate to say Paul wrote to *churches* in Corinth or Rome because the clusters of Christians generally met in homes as house churches (Romans 16:3-5). The house church addressed in Philemon was in Colossae (Philemon 2). As yet, they had no buildings or facilities. Paul includes these clusters in the greetings of the letters by saying, "To all God's beloved in Rome" (Romans 1:7) and "To the church of God that is in Corinth, including all the saints throughout Achaia" (2 Corinthians 1:1). His letter to the region called Galatia included half a dozen cities. He also reinforces the message by giving greetings at the end of some letters from and to the house churches: "The churches of Asia send greetings. Aquila and Prisca, together with the church in their house, greet you warmly in the Lord" (1 Corinthians 16:19).

Paul's letters were not dashed off haphazardly. They were carefully crafted yet intensely relevant. The letters were intended to be read aloud. A letter from Paul was like hearing him speak. That's why we should read the letters aloud, to get the rhythm and feel of Paul's language. Picture in your mind Timothy or Silas arriving at someone's home on sabbath or on Sunday, in time for worship, then reading a letter from Paul for all to hear, with comment, interpretation, and personal emphasis.

Holding the Listener's Attention

Paul used all sorts of rhetorical devices to hold the listeners' attention. Sometimes, like the Stoics, he put a question on the lips of a would-be questioner: "Should we continue in sin in order that grace may abound?" (Romans 6:1). Then after capturing the listeners' attention, Paul gave an answer:

NOTES, REFLECTIONS, AND QUESTIONS

Scribes like the one to whom Paul dictated his letters carried pens and inkpots with them at all times. This pen and inkpot, found in the Tiber River, date from Paul's time.

"By no means!" (6:2). He used allegory, picturing Sarah and Hagar (Galatians 4:21–5:1) to symbolize a deeper truth of freedom from slavery to the Law. He quoted familiar passages of Scripture, especially from Psalms and the prophets. Paul alluded to the prophets more than fifty times, twenty-seven times in Romans. Such references help the listener track the argument.

From the rabbis, Paul learned ways of interpreting Scripture. He referred to Jewish traditions. He used one Scripture to interpret another. And like rabbis, he used much freedom in interpreting Scripture. For example, when the word *offspring* (singular) was used of Abraham's offspring (Genesis 22:18), Paul interpreted that "offspring" as Christ (Galatians 3:16).

Paul ducks no subject. He deals with taxes, sex, diet, lawsuits, marriage, circumcision, ecstatic speech, and intramural squabbles. He alludes to sports (1 Corinthians 9:24-27), to farming (2 Corinthians 9:9-11), and to soldiering (10:3-6).

He writes autobiographically, often to prove his call to be an apostle or to authenticate his witness, but also to hold listener attention (his testimony in Galatians 1:13-17, his list of sufferings in 2 Corinthians 11:21-29). People are interested in people. Paul sprinkles his letters with personal references. For example, Romans 16 mentions more than thirty people. Paul refers to himself largely to defend his gospel and its authority.

In his correspondence, Paul responds to problems; but more important, he proclaims his faith. In the process of preaching the good news of the crucifixion and resurrection of Jesus, Paul encounters issues of faith and deals with them. Everything Paul wrote came out of his overflowing sense of salvation. His rhythm is this: God has acted in Jesus Christ; here's what that means in our situation.

Most ancient personal letters were short. Paul extended the form and used it for his missional strategy.

Salutation

The *salutation,* the opening element in ancient personal letters, mentions both sender and receiver, and includes a greeting. But Paul bends it in several ways. He changes "greetings" to "grace." Instead of a typical "Hope you are well," Paul uses the word *peace,* asking for peace of mind and spiritual tranquillity. Notice, to Philemon, regarding a runaway slave, Paul immediately gives testimony to the fact that he too is a prisoner, "a prisoner of Christ Jesus" (see Philemon 1).

Paul's long salutation in Romans 1:1-7 establishes the genuineness of his gospel for a skeptical audience that does not know him personally, and authenticates his apostleship for those who consider him one who goes his own way.

In Galatians, Paul leaps right in. He knew the Galatians

NOTES, REFLECTIONS, AND QUESTIONS

well and was eager to get to the point—whether they trusted his gospel or believed the Judaizers who insisted on circumcision. So, to establish his authority at the start, he writes, "Paul, an apostle—sent neither by human commission nor from human authorities, but through Jesus Christ." Then he addresses "the churches of Galatia" and gives a strong testimony to the power of Christ, all in the salutation (Galatians 1:1-5).

Thanksgiving

The *thanksgiving,* the second element of the letter, was in ancient correspondence gratitude to the gods that everybody was well. Paul adapted again, offering thanksgiving for the Christians to whom he was writing and hinting at the issues in the body of the letter. Often his prayers of thanksgiving expressed gratitude for the listeners' faithfulness, yet also indicated the purpose of the letter.

Notice in Romans how carefully Paul avoided being overly confident with an unknown congregation: "I am longing to see you so that I may share with you some spiritual gift to strengthen you—or rather so that we may be mutually encouraged by each other's faith, both yours and mine" (Romans 1:11-12).

Only to the Galatians did Paul neglect a thanksgiving, so well did he know them and so heated was he over their turning away from their Christian freedom. He is not grateful for what has happened there. Often in the "thanksgiving" Paul takes notice of the local situation and its problems.

The Body

The *body* of the letter can be as simple as Philemon or as complex as Romans. Using conversational form, Paul tried to do by letter what he would have liked to do as an apostle in person. His tone varies greatly. He could threaten his small house churches—"Am I to come to you with a stick?" (1 Corinthians 4:21). He could be sarcastic—"I wish those who unsettle you would castrate themselves!" (Galatians 5:12) or emotional—"Had it been possible, you would have torn out your eyes and given them to me" (4:15). He could plead "like a father with his children" (1 Thessalonians 2:11) or suggest that he is "gentle . . . like a nurse" (2:7).

Always Paul witnessed to the salvation that had broken into the world with Christ. Always he tried to strengthen and build up the church.

He employed repeating patterns. The "I appeal to you" or "I urge you" pattern is one, and the "I want you to know" or "I do not want you to be unaware (uninformed)" is another. He begins with these, repeats them, and ends with his travel plans and future intentions.

Paul's references to himself or his situation fit closely with

NOTES, REFLECTIONS, AND QUESTIONS

the theological argument he is making, and he relates his situation to that of his readers.

When we study each letter, we will look carefully at the body of that letter. Look now at the simplest, most specific letter, Paul's appeal to his friend Philemon. Even in this intimate, personal matter, Paul expects the letter to be read "to the church in your house" (Philemon 2). The issues surrounding slavery would apply to everyone. Twenty percent of the population of the Roman Empire consisted of slaves, perhaps half the population in trade centers like Rome and Ephesus. Roman legions brought thousands of captives back after every military campaign. When a family came on hard times, they often sold themselves into slavery to get out of debt.

The body of the letter (verses 8-20) consists of a discussion of the return of Onesimus the slave.

Verses 8-10: Paul could command Philemon to do his duty, but he appeals in love for Onesimus, to whom he has become like a father.

Verse 11: Paul plays on the name Onesimus, which means "useful." The man has been useful to Paul, will be useful again to Philemon.

Verses 12-14: Paul is sending Onesimus (Paul's own heart) back, though he would prefer him to stay. But he wants Philemon's response to be voluntary, not forced.

Verses 15-16: "Separated" means ran away, which gives Philemon an opportunity to be magnanimous and accept Onesimus back as a brother in Christ.

Verses 17-20: Paul offers to repay anything Onesimus owes, but reminds Philemon that he himself owes Paul a lot more. Paul ends with a reminder that he expects "obedience."

Closing Commands

Paul closes his letters with *ethical instruction and exhortation.* Sometimes he lists a series of moral admonitions: "Let love be genuine; hate what is evil, hold fast to what is good; love one another with mutual affection; outdo one another in showing honor. Do not lag in zeal, be ardent in spirit, serve the Lord. Rejoice in hope, be patient in suffering, persevere in prayer. Contribute to the needs of the saints; extend hospitality to strangers" (Romans 12:9-13).

Often Paul moves into instruction or exhortation with the word *therefore*. Notice that the instructions usually focus on issues discussed in the body. Almost always, Paul expresses his future hopes or travel plans. He wants the churches to know he would like to be present with them. He also wants them informed about his mission work, and he pleads that they will undergird his plans with prayer.

NOTES, REFLECTIONS, AND QUESTIONS

Standards such as this were displayed in public buildings and streets as symbols of Roman authority in provinces and occupied territories throughout the empire and carried at the head of marching troops.

Conclusion

At the *conclusion* of a typical personal letter, the Greeks would simply say "good-bye"; the Jews would close with "peace." But Paul added more. Just as he began with "grace," so he closes with "grace." Both "grace" and "peace" are present but also projected into the future. "Live in peace; and the God of love and peace will be with you" (2 Corinthians 13:11). Sometimes Paul even picks up again an idea or two from the body of the letter. To Thessalonica, since some were worried about their bodies, some about their souls, Paul writes, "May the God of peace himself sanctify you entirely; and may your spirit and soul and body be kept sound and blameless at the coming of our Lord Jesus Christ" (1 Thessalonians 5:23).

First Thessalonians, besides asking for prayer, closes with a request that the believers greet everyone with a holy kiss and that they read the letter to all the company. Notice that Paul's final word, as his opening word, witnesses to Jesus Christ, in love: "The grace of our Lord Jesus Christ be with you" (5:25-28).

Probably all of Paul's letters were dictated to a scribe, though only in Romans do we have the scribe's name (Romans 16:22). It was customary for the sender to add a paragraph in the sender's own hand (1 Corinthians 16:21-24; Galatians 6:11-18; Philemon 19).

What sense do you get of the man Paul from the way he crafted his letters?

Extremly thoughtful, well versed, sensitive, spirit filled, ever aware of his acts & the grace he received.

About the Letters

For forty to fifty years, the letters circulated among the churches. Copies were made; some material was lost; some additions were made. One Corinthian letter, referred to by scholars as "the severe letter," is lost. Ancient manuscripts show minor variances. But the church saw so much spiritual power in these letters that they were collected and considered to have authority for the church by about A.D. 100–125.

Scholars agree that seven of the letters are truly from Paul: Romans, First and Second Corinthians, Galatians, Philippians, First Thessalonians, and Philemon. Then, because different ideas are introduced, different grammatical and theological constructions used, and most important, later church developments discussed, scholarly debate continues over whether the other letters that claim Paul as the author were really written by him or by his followers in his name. In antiquity, such practice was common and was regarded more as a tribute than as deceit. So in this study we are assuming that Ephesians, Colossians, Second Thessalonians, First and Second Timothy,

NOTES, REFLECTIONS, AND QUESTIONS

and Titus probably were written after Paul's death by his disciples.

MARKS OF OBEDIENT COMMUNITY

The faithful community reaches out to invite, support, counsel, persuade. Letters of insight, power, and goodwill flow in and out of the fellowship of faith. A church newsletter can call people to pray for the sick, to encourage a mission project, or to read the Scripture for the next Sunday's sermon. A letter from a DISCIPLE group can strengthen a missionary, encourage a pastor, lift the spirits of someone moving away. A note may assuage grief, drain hostility, invite a stranger.

What elements make a strong spiritual letter?

When the sender is seen as grace filled. Concer, counsil, love, grace filled letters

If your DISCIPLE group would write one letter, to whom would you write?

volunteer in any capacity. working for the love of God.

Decide what you would say in the salutation, thanksgiving, body of the letter, instruction or exhortation, and the closing.

Jot down your ideas to contribute to the group discussion and preparation of the letter.

IF YOU WANT TO KNOW MORE

Letter: Write a letter to someone you love using the same five elements in a letter written in Paul's day.

Choose two or three of your favorite passages from Paul's letters and read them aloud, concentrating on the rhythm and feel of Paul's language. In what sense do they appeal to the ear?

NOTES, REFLECTIONS, AND QUESTIONS

The faithful community reaches out in love to invite, support, counsel, and persuade.

ENCOURAGE

"For the Lord himself, with a cry of command, with the archangel's call and with the sound of God's trumpet, will descend from heaven, and the dead in Christ will rise first. Then we who are alive, who are left, will be caught up in the clouds together with them to meet the Lord in the air; and so we will be with the Lord forever. Therefore encourage one another with these words."

—1 Thessalonians 4:16-18

19 The Lord Is Coming

OUR HUMAN CONDITION

We lack a context of hope in which to place our daily lives. We see only dead ends. We long to be encouraged at home, at work, even at church. Can anything make a difference?

ASSIGNMENT

First Thessalonians is considered the first existing letter Paul wrote and the oldest book in the New Testament. Begin by reading the letter aloud. Remember that Thessalonica was an infant church in Macedonia that experienced Roman, secular, and Jewish persecution. Paul bragged to other churches about the Thessalonians' faith.

Day 1 1 Thessalonians 1–5
Day 2 Acts 17:1-15; 1 Thessalonians 1 (faith and example of the Thessalonians)
Day 3 1 Thessalonians 2 (Paul's ministry in spite of opposition)
Day 4 1 Thessalonians 3 (Timothy's encouraging report)
Day 5 1 Thessalonians 4–5 (call to purity, the coming of the Lord, encourage one another)
Day 6 Read and respond to "The Word of the Lord" and "Marks of Obedient Community."
Day 7 Rest

PRAYER

Pray daily before study:
"My trust is in you, O LORD;
you are my God.
I am always in your care" (Psalm 31:14-15, TEV).

Prayer concerns for this week:
Bob's mother-in-law, daughter

ENCOURAGE

Day 1 1 Thessalonians 1–5

4:11-12 lead a quiet life, mind your own business, work with your hands. not be dependent on anybody.

4:13 do not grieve like the rest of men. who have no hope.

5:21 Test every thing.

Day 4 1 Thessalonians 3 (Timothy's encouraging report)

Day 2 Acts 17:1-15; 1 Thessalonians 1 (faith and example of the Thessalonians)

Day 5 1 Thessalonians 4–5 (call to purity, the coming of the Lord, encourage one another)

5:10 He died for us so that, whether we are awake or asleep, we may live together with him.

Day 3 1 Thessalonians 2 (Paul's ministry in spite of opposition)

Day 6 "The Word of the Lord" and "Marks of Obedient Community"

THE WORD OF THE LORD

After Paul and Silvanus (Silas) got out of jail in Philippi, they said farewells at Lydia's house, and with Timothy made their way to Thessalonica. This port city was the most important trade center in northern Greece (Macedonia). Thessalonica's harbor was in the northern reaches of the Aegean Sea on the Thermaic Gulf. It was the midway point of the Via Egnatia, the last stop on the way to the Danube River. Although the city was the Roman capital of Macedonia, it remained a free Greek city with its own coinage and its own city magistrates.

As was Paul's custom, they went first to the synagogue, taught, preached, and interpreted the Scriptures each sabbath. He explained that Jesus was the promised Messiah, that it was necessary for the Messiah to suffer (Isaiah 53:3-5), and that Jesus had been raised from the dead (Acts 17:3). Some Jews were converted; so were a good number of "devout" Greeks and "not a few of the leading women" (17:4).

Jealous Jews and ruffians caused a furor. They charged that the missionaries were "turning the world upside down" (17:6) and that they proclaimed a "king" other than Caesar. Paul escaped to Beroea and then hurried southward to Athens, where Timothy joined him. Later, Paul went on to Corinth (17:10, 15; 18:1).

News From Thessalonica

While Paul was preaching in Athens, he sent Timothy back north to encourage the fledgling group in Thessalonica. Why? Already they were suffering persecutions. Paul wanted to go back but could not. He sent Timothy, "brother and co-worker for God . . . , to strengthen and encourage" the new Christians (1 Thessalonians 3:1-4).

Paul was fearful the little band would fade under stress. "I sent to find out about your faith; I was afraid that somehow the tempter had tempted you and that our labor had been in vain" (3:5).

Before Paul wrote this letter, Timothy returned. Paul was overjoyed to learn from his young helper that the converts were holding fast. Paul was encouraged by both their loyalty to Christ and their affection for him and found strength for his own persecution through their faith (3:7).

Words of Encouragement

Paul uses several strategies for undergirding the faith of the Thessalonians. Over and over he thanks God for them (1 Thessalonians 1:2; 2:13; 3:9). He remembers their labors of love (1:3). He recalls how they received the Holy Spirit and how they (the Gentiles) turned from Greek and Roman gods (idols) "to serve a living and true God" (1:9). He believes they were "chosen" by God (1:4) just as Abraham and his

NOTES, REFLECTIONS, AND QUESTIONS

This language from 1 Thessalonians 1:9-10 is probably part of an early creed that expresses the meaning of conversion for the Gentiles: "how you turned to God from idols, to serve a living and true God, and to wait for his Son from heaven, whom he raised from the dead—Jesus, who rescues us from the wrath that is coming."

descendants had been chosen. He assures them of the coming again of the Lord Jesus. He is proud of their "steadfastness in hope" (1:3).

Paul will have only one thing to boast of before the Lord Jesus. He will have only one thing to present on the day of judgment—the converts from his ministry.

In some churches, such as Corinth and Galatia, critics said Paul was a second-class preacher and less than a true apostle. We don't see signs of that in Thessalonians; yet for Paul, the integrity of the gospel was always linked to the integrity of the messenger. So he reminds the Thessalonians of his labors, perhaps as a way of affirming his love (2:9). He preached without trickery or guile, never seeking praise or money (2:5-6).

Paul wanted no one to be "shaken" by persecution. He reminded them persecution was to be expected (3:2-3). The Thessalonians stand as "imitators" of the churches in Judea. "You suffered the same things from your own compatriots [Greek and Roman townspeople] as they [the Jewish Christians in Judea] did from the Jews" (2:14). Paul boasts that their faith gives inspiration to others throughout Greece, in fact in churches everywhere (1:7-8). That faith is grounded in the hope of the coming of Jesus (1:10). Paul reassures them that hope is not in vain.

Paul uses the tenderest words of love and fellowship for additional affirmation. He feels like an orphan away from them (2:17). He and his associates have shared "not only the gospel of God but also our own selves, because you have become very dear to us" (2:8).

Purity of Life

When Paul moved in his letter to moral instructions (1 Thessalonians 4:1), he was specific. First, he pleaded for sexual purity (4:3-8). Within the Gentile world, sexual promiscuity was rampant. Certain mystery religions had sexual encounter as part of their initiations. Temple prostitutes, male and female, served some Greek temples. A few Greek philosophers advocated restraint from wild passions. Judaism taught family fidelity under Torah. In practice, however, the social temptations were severe.

"Abstain from fornication," Paul urged (4:3). Do not "exploit" a Christian brother or sister. His appeal is not so much to laws or rules as it is to the indwelling of the Holy Spirit, which makes for holiness of life. Inner cleansing and inner freedom were part of Paul's salvation experience and part of his gospel. Paul called that purifying power of the Holy Spirit "sanctification"—being made holy (4:3).

Three sources of inner strength help these Christians be pure—the indwelling of Christ's Spirit; the power of self-control, which is a fruit of the Holy Spirit (Galatians 5:23); and the fear of the Lord, who is "an avenger in all these things" (1 Thessalonians 4:6). Don't forget that the agreement

NOTES, REFLECTIONS, AND QUESTIONS

First Thessalonians 2:14-16 is regarded by some scholars as a later addition because the sharp words here about Jews differ from the way Paul usually speaks about Jews. One interpretation of it is that it refers to the fall of Jerusalem (A.D. 70) as God's punishment for killing Jesus.

at the Jerusalem Council did not demand circumcision but did insist on sexual purity for Gentile Christians (Acts 15:19-20).

Messages in the media and society go against sexual purity. How has the church's message been influenced by those messages?

In what sense have sexuality and sex become false gods in our society?

How can we encourage sexual purity in our Christian fellowship?

Christ's Return

Since Christ had not yet returned, the Thessalonians were worried about those who had already died. Would they live, or was it too late? In the first burst of Holy Spirit enthusiasm, they had expected the immediate second coming of Christ. Paul reassured them in two ways.

First, do not grieve as those "who have no hope"; for "through Jesus, God will bring with him those who have died" (1 Thessalonians 4:13-14). When the Lord gives the cry of command, "the dead in Christ will rise first" (4:16). "We who are alive . . . will be caught up in the clouds together with them to meet the Lord in the air" (4:17). "Encourage one another with these words" (4:18).

Paul's message was that the Messiah had suffered and died but God had raised him up and that he would come again in the total peace and victory promised by the prophets. But when? Paul, without directly quoting Jesus, knew the central teaching: No one knows the time. That was his second form of reassurance. Paul's point is that the dead will not miss out but the opposite: They will be raised first. Then the living will join them.

Paul used two allusions for the coming of Christ—"as labor pains come upon a pregnant woman" (5:3), an image often used by the ancient prophets, and "like a thief in the night" (5:2), an image used by Jesus. Paul's point: Do not fall asleep (spiritually), but "keep awake and be sober" (5:6). We are not children of the night, drunk or sleepy; we are children who "belong to the day," to the light that marks the Christian (5:5). Be ready. Paul urges us to put on "the breastplate of faith and love and for a helmet the hope of salvation" (5:8). Remember the prophet who said,

> "He [God] put on righteousness like a breastplate,
> and a helmet of salvation on his head" (Isaiah 59:17).

Ephesians 6:13-17 builds this metaphor into full Roman armor.

NOTES, REFLECTIONS, AND QUESTIONS

One of the Dead Sea Scrolls, "The War Between the Children of Light and the Children of Darkness," describes a war between the righteous and the wicked. This "War Scroll" identifies Jews from the tribes of Judah, Benjamin, and Levi as the children of light and their enemies as the children of darkness. The scroll may date from the early Roman occupation of Judea. The eventual victory of the children of light over the children of darkness will signal the beginning of the messianic age. Notice Paul's use of similar language in First Thessalonians.

What does "being ready" for Christ's return mean to you?

Being faithfull & full of hope

Paul ends his letter as he began, with the grace of our Lord Jesus Christ (5:25-28).

MARKS OF OBEDIENT COMMUNITY

The faith community lives in perpetual readiness for the Lord's coming. When discouraged, we do not falter. We build one another up, remembering the promises of God. We hold one another accountable, asking one another about our faithfulness. Sometimes we console, sometimes we chastise, but always we encourage.

The best encouragement is a reminder of God's power, but sometimes that sounds preachy or pious. How can we do this effectively?

At harvest time, good & bad will be sorted, bad will be burnt.

Paul often spoke of Christ's resurrection and of his coming again. How can we do this in a helpful way?

Living God; giver of talents; multiply talents

What have you noticed gives fresh encouragement to your DISCIPLE group? to your church?

sharing experiences & understanding

How can you be a congregation of encouragement both *in* and *through* the congregation? Who needs encouragement? What kind of encouragement? How can all be made to feel their contribution to life in commmunity is valued?

Encourage those in ministry & support them.
Learn the word of God & improve self control

IF YOU WANT TO KNOW MORE

Letter: Write a letter of encouragement to someone who is having a tough time (family, church member, government official). Express words of support.

Memorize a text of encouragement so you can repeat it to yourself, perhaps to others. Examples: Isaiah 40:31; Romans 8:28; 8:37-39; 1 Thessalonians 5:9-10.

NOTES, REFLECTIONS, AND QUESTIONS

The faith community lives in perpetual readiness for the Lord's coming.

WORK

"You yourselves know how you ought to imitate us; we were not idle when we were with you, and we did not eat anyone's bread without paying for it; but with toil and labor we worked night and day, so that we might not burden any of you."

—2 Thessalonians 3:7-8

20 Honest Labor

OUR HUMAN CONDITION

Because we allow society to tell us what work is valuable and what work is not, we miss the real issue—whether we are using the time God gives us productively.

ASSIGNMENT

Pretend you are hand-carrying this letter to new Christians. Read it aloud, to someone else if possible, giving brief interpretations as you read. Bear down hard on the value of hard work, holding steady, being faithful. On Day 5, read the two Thessalonian letters straight through to be reminded of the similarities and differences in tone and subject matter.

Day 1 2 Thessalonians 1–3 (living until Christ comes)
Day 2 2 Thessalonians 1 (God's judgment)
Day 3 2 Thessalonians 2 (day of the Lord delayed)
Day 4 2 Thessalonians 3 (warning against idleness)
Day 5 1 Thessalonians 1–5; 2 Thessalonians 1–3
Day 6 Read and respond to "The Word of the Lord" and "Marks of Obedient Community."
Day 7 Rest

PRAYER

Pray daily before study:

"Let us, your servants, see your mighty deeds;
let our descendants see your glorious might.
LORD our God, may your blessings be with us.
Give us success in all we do!" (Psalm 90:16-17, TEV).

Prayer concerns for this week:

Day 1 2 Thessalonians 1–3 (living until Christ comes)

2:9 purpose of true miracles to help, to heal, to point us to God.
3:13 Never tire of doing what is right

Day 2 2 Thessalonians 1 (God's judgment)

Day 3 2 Thessalonians 2 (day of the Lord delayed)

Day 4 2 Thessalonians 3 (warning against idleness)

Real faith, doctrine of election is for christian comfort.
Christ belief is God chose us vs other religion "free will" we choose God.
"No student is above the master". if Jesus suffered & then was taken to glory, we will follow that same route.
faith → turn, serve, wait.
idols → anything you rely on → hope, security & peace. Don't save, they enslave

Day 5 1 Thessalonians 1–5; 2 Thessalonians 1–3

2:6 not looking for praise from men
2:19 what is our hope, joy, & crown in which we will glory? Is it not you?
5:10 He died for us so that, whether we are awake or asleep, we may live together with him.
5:15 Make sure no one pays back wrong for wrong, but always try to be kind to each other & to everyone else.
Be joyfull always. Give thanks in all circumstances.

Day 6 "The Word of the Lord" and "Marks of Obedient Community"

5:21 Test everything

THE WORD OF THE LORD

Second Thessalonians is heavy with problems for scholars. On one hand, it is full of Paul's thoughts; on the other hand, it contains several concepts not found elsewhere in Paul's writings and deals with church issues that emerged later. Whether Paul wrote the letter or some disciple of Paul modified the letter or wrote it in Paul's name, we do not know. But the word of authority is present.

The opening is identical to First Thessalonians. Silvanus (Silas) and Timothy join in the greeting. Notice that the church is not *of* God but *in* God. The letter opens with grace and peace from God our Father and the Lord Jesus Christ and closes with a blessing of peace and grace. Grace and peace are the heart of Paul's gospel. Grace (*charis*) was hard for ancients and is hard for moderns to believe. We want to earn our respectability. Or we feel we have a rights entitlement. Because we do not understand the depth of our self-centeredness, the brokenness of our relationship with God, we cannot comprehend the impossibility of our saving ourselves by our own actions. Grace is God's work in Christ Jesus to give to us the undeserved favor of God. Grace puts things right; grace is love's unmerited initiative that frees us to love God in return.

We do not fathom *peace* until we shudder before *wrath.* When things are not in line with what God wants, nothing is right. By the act of God in Christ Jesus, wrath is replaced by a healthy, right relationship. Peace is rightness with God, in which inner tranquillity is matched by outer harmony. To live "in Christ" is to live in undeserved favor, in harmony and accord with God's plan of righteousness and compassion.

Thanksgiving

Prayers of gratitude for the Thessalonian Christians are constant. The writer always gives thanks to God for them because their faith is growing, and because they show love for one another (2 Thessalonians 1:3). Wherever they went, the apostles bragged on the church in Thessalonica, for the members held steady amid persecution. The prayer here is that the Thessalonians will be worthy of the Kingdom. Jesus associated suffering with the Kingdom, and so did Paul as we see in Acts 14:22: "It is through many persecutions that we must enter the kingdom of God."

The law of Moses and the prophets of Israel insisted that God's judgment is just. God is righteous. Somehow the people who are afflicting the believers will be afflicted (2 Thessalonians 1:6). Judgment will come "when the Lord Jesus is revealed from heaven with his mighty angels in flaming fire" (1:7). The day of the Lord in the prophets now becomes the day of Christ's coming.

NOTES, REFLECTIONS, AND QUESTIONS

Second Coming of Christ

The letter deals with bewilderment over Christ's return. Paul and others had preached sermons, written letters, and discussed the matter; but people were still confused. Some believers in Thessalonica thought, from Paul's sermons and letters (or from some bogus letters that may have been circulating), that the Lord's day had already come; and they were alarmed (2 Thessalonians 2:1-2). Others were worried about those who had died (1 Thessalonians 4:13-15). Still others were weakened in faith by the fear that Christ was not coming at all. This last concern has troubled Christians for two thousand years. As early as 1 Corinthians 16:22 with its prayer, "Our Lord, come!" and for all time since, the faithful have prayed "Come, Lord Jesus!" (Revelation 22:20). Second Peter's explanation is that "with the Lord one day is like a thousand years" and that God is patient, wanting all to come to repentance (2 Peter 3:8-9).

But in Second Thessalonians the delay involves forces of evil. A "lawless one" must be revealed and destroyed (2 Thessalonians 2:8). He is not Satan, although he is working with Satan. Perhaps the lawless one was ancient Jewish imagery revolving around the forces of evil in last times. The letter urges the Thessalonians to remember they are the "first fruits" of the coming salvation (2:13). Therefore, no matter what they are told by false teachers, and no matter how long the wait, "stand firm and hold fast to the traditions that you were taught by us, either by word of mouth or by our letter" (2:15).

Work

Enthusiasm about Christ's expected return caused misunderstandings. Paul had preached that the messianic reign foretold by the prophets was near at hand. Jesus, the Messiah, ushered in the first wave of victory with his crucifixion and resurrection. The Holy Spirit in the believer's heart gave a foretaste of the heavenly fellowship. Soon, very soon, God would redeem all creation through Jesus Christ.

What should believers do in the meantime? Some in Thessalonica and some across the centuries allowed this teaching to cut the cord of responsibility. Some sat all day in others' houses talking about religious things, eating off someone else's table. Others in great but misguided faith quit their jobs, stopped maintaining their homes, and waited prayerfully and patiently for the Parousia, Jesus' coming. Such behavior is a grievous error (2 Thessalonians 3:6-13). People either serve sin, or they serve the Savior. Faith in the Messiah who has come and who will come again requires the believer to work—and to work hard! To earn salvation? No, for the unmerited love of God saves. To bring in the Kingdom? No, for God, in perfect freedom and power, will redeem the creation according to divine plan. But Christians are on the Lord's side in the redemptive battle against evil. Bringing all

NOTES, REFLECTIONS, AND QUESTIONS

NOTES, REFLECTIONS, AND QUESTIONS

people to Christ has an urgency about it. Believers lean forward, eagerly participating in the holy struggle. Besides, it is just as presumptuous to say, "Christ is coming today," as it is to say, "Christ is coming tomorrow." God is full of surprises.

In the "not yet" of our redemption, we are to teach, pray, convert, serve, and most certainly work. We have the example of Paul, who took pride in the hard physical work of cutting and sewing leather panels for tents. Combined with his missionary activity, he worked night and day (3:8).

Partly out of self-respect, partly out of respect for the dignity of the gospel, Paul wanted to earn his own keep by working with his hands. He elevated work. Labor is honorable.

How does our society look on hand labor?

Labor is valued by demand & supply

The author of Second Thessalonians wanted the secular community to respect him and thereby honor the gospel. He thought sheer idleness to be an offense to God and went so far as to urge his friends in the church to "keep away from believers who are living in idleness" (3:6). "Do not regard them as enemies" (3:15). But teach them, exhort them, and "warn them as believers" that they have Christian responsibility. "Busybodies" are not strong disciples of Christ. "Anyone unwilling to work should not eat" (3:10-11). Of course this teaching did not mean the sick, the elderly, and persons with disabilities. In fact, that was another reason to work hard, so Christians could help others.

What guidance do these teachings offer for our day?

Missionary zeal could result in supporting those who are in the field

A special issue held the mind of the writer. As an apostle, a messenger called by God to proclaim the gospel, he had a right to sustenance. Paul had mentioned that right to his church in Corinth (1 Corinthians 9:1-18). He could have expected and received room and board. In fact, in Paul's day, it was assumed that a real leader charged fees, got paid.

Why make such a big issue of earning one's bread? To show love by not being a burden (2 Thessalonians 3:7-8) and to avoid any hindrance to the gospel. Sometimes religious leaders were in it for the money. The prophet Micah blasted Jerusalem's priests and prophets who served only when they got paid (Micah 3:11).

The apostle wanted only one thing—for the gospel to bear fruit. And it did. People in Thessalonica were converted. "What is our hope or joy or crown of boasting before our Lord Jesus at his coming? Is it not you? Yes, you are our glory and joy!" (1 Thessalonians 2:19-20).

MARKS OF OBEDIENT COMMUNITY

We are not afraid to work with our hands, for livelihood, to help others, or to serve the church. God works; we work. We are eager to include in our fellowship people who do all sorts of work. We struggle to build a society where good jobs with fair pay are available to all.

What is the job situation in your area?

There are a mix of situation. College is expensive 4 student loans are a burden.

What action or ministry regarding jobs is called for from you, your DISCIPLE group, or your congregation?

Vocational guidance, teach

We teach children that hard work is honorable, that work brings joy and satisfaction.

Discuss a plan for a work project such as Habitat for Humanity, a local repair project, or as mission volunteers where your DISCIPLE group could give hands-on assistance. Record your decision.

How can your congregation extend greater hospitality to people who work with their hands?

Be welcoming

Sometimes, gospel work can be performed by "tentmakers." Example: laity who start new churches. Any ideas?

Disciple group is preparing laity

IF YOU WANT TO KNOW MORE

Look up the terms *grace* and *peace* in a Bible dictionary.

Letter: Write a letter to someone you know who is working hard, perhaps without pay. Affirm her or his labor. Or write someone who ought to be working hard but is floundering, perhaps because of lack of focus, training, or opportunity. Offer whatever is needed—prayer, intervention, recreation, affirmation, training, moral support.

Or share with your group a letter you received regarding your work.

NOTES, REFLECTIONS, AND QUESTIONS

Obedient community honors the worker and understands work as graced with a sense of urgency.

REJOICE

"Rejoice in the Lord always; again I will say, Rejoice!"

—Philippians 4:4

21 Seeing the Good

OUR HUMAN CONDITION

We have difficulty seeing good in all situations. We feel no honor in suffering. And as for putting others ahead of ourselves, let them go first. When something good happens, then we'll say thanks. Until then, we prefer reality.

ASSIGNMENT

Read Philippians aloud to someone if possible. Notice the intimacy, the affection in this letter. Look at Paul's way of seeing good coming out of bad. See how he uses trouble as opportunity for witness and praise. Read Philippians like a poem, a hymn, even a creed.

Day 1 Philippians 1–4
Day 2 Acts 16; Philippians 1 (Paul and Silas in Philippi, Paul's chains advance the gospel)
Day 3 Philippians 2 (imitating Christ's humility and obedience)
Day 4 Philippians 3 (pressing on toward the goal)
Day 5 Philippians 4 (instructions for Christian maturity)
Day 6 Read and respond to "The Word of the Lord" and "Marks of Obedient Community."
Day 7 Rest

PRAYER

Pray daily before study:

"Fill us each morning with your contant love,
so that we may sing and be glad all our life"
(Psalm 90:14, TEV).

Prayer concerns for this week:

Day 1 Philippians 1–4

slaves carrying word of God.
Phillipi church;
Christ4 culture collide; a slave girl, a jailor, a merchant woman.
Paul's thankfullness is Godward.
James 1:17 every good & perfect gift is from above.
Thankfullness in all circumstances (chain)
Joy for all that God does continually.

Day 2 Acts 16; Philippians 1 (Paul and Silas in Philippi, Paul's chains advance the gospel)

Jailor & family saved; Lydia became a christian.
:29 Epaphroditus was a missionary. we
30 need to encourage & support them.
No coasting, press on to grow more & more in christian love. Paul praying for love guided by knowledge of JC through scripture & discernment. = mature christian.
Truth without love = law
Love without Truth = never calls for repentance. Pursuit of servant-hearted excellence pursuing JC.

Day 3 Philippians 2 (imitating Christ's humility and obedience)

Playing second fiddle. No harmony without second fiddle.
Christian mind = believe in JC, make his life your study.

Day 4 Philippians 3 (pressing on toward the goal)

3:2,3 what believers do is a result of faith, not a prerequisit to faith.
God values the attitude of our hearts above all else.
do everything as a loving response to His free gift of salvation.
3:6 Paul's expectations of what the messiah would be like, didn't match Jesus & hence he was prosecuting
3:16 Live up to what we already know. Don't be side tracked by an unending search for truth

Day 5 Philippians 4 (instructions for Christian maturity)

4:6-7 Do you want to worry less? Pray more.
4:8 what we put into our minds determines what comes out in our words & actions.
4:12-13 detach himself (Paul) from non-essentials.
S

Day 6 "The Word of the Lord" and "Marks of Obedient Community"

THE WORD OF THE LORD

Paul knew jails. He knew the inside of the prisons in Philippi, in Ephesus, in Caesarea, in Rome. Of course he never allowed imprisonment to stop his ministry. In fact, he intensified it with steadfast prayer and by witnessing to jailers and prisoners. He sent and received a steady flow of messengers and letters, constantly giving guidance, instruction, and encouragement. When Paul wrote Philippians, which may contain a fragment or two from his other letters, he was in prison awaiting trial (Philippians 1:7).

You can speculate on the place. Scholars do. If you prefer an earlier dating and stress the flow of visitors, you may choose Ephesus. In that case, you would say "the emperor's household" (4:22) was part of the vast administrative staff of government officials serving in all great Roman cities. A praetorian guard ("imperial guard," 1:13) would have been in Caesarea and Ephesus as well as in Rome. Tradition prefers Rome, because of the heavy sense of finality, of completion of his mission as well as the emphasis on the emperor, staff, and guard.

The church in Philippi was Paul's baby, his first church in Europe. Roman and Greek gods stood in a score of temples; Zeus was on the coins; retired Roman soldiers (pensioners) walked the streets. Rome established the colony to strengthen the east-west road to Asia and to help fortify the northern Macedonian border. Paul, Timothy, Silas, and Luke began their mission with a few women, Jews, and God-fearers (Gentiles who attended synagogue but were not full converts to Judaism) who prayed on sabbath by the river (Acts 16:11-15).

Disturbing the Peace

Gone were the tolerant days of the Roman Republic (500 B.C.–60 B.C.). Gone were the open, progressive days of Caesar Augustus (27 B.C.–A.D. 14). Now, each succeeding emperor seemed more dictatorial, more self-inflated, more insecure, more paranoid than his predecessor. Caligula declared himself a god (A.D. 38) and tried to put his statues in the Jerusalem Temple. Claudius expelled Jews and Jewish Christians from Rome (A.D. 49). Nero blamed the Christians for a fire that devastated Rome and martyred thousands in retribution (A.D. 64). An early tradition puts the martyrdom of both Paul and Peter at this time.

Rome had two concerns that Judaism, and especially the new Jewish-Christian groups, violated. First, Rome wanted to maintain the peace. Rebellion, even rioting or street confusion, brought Roman guards running. When Paul healed the psychic slave girl in Philippi, her owners, upset at losing their livelihood, brought charges, saying, "These men are disturbing our city" (Acts 16:20).

The second concern was more intense. Worship of the gods of Rome was essential for civic order. Persons could worship

NOTES, REFLECTIONS, AND QUESTIONS

Philippian Correspondence

- Paul in prison
- Philippians send Epaphroditus with money
- Paul's letter to Philippi (now lost) reports Epaphroditus's illness
- Philippians' letter to Paul
  —concern for Epaphroditus
  —regret that he was unable to help more
  —some problems in the congregation
- Letter from Paul sent with Epaphroditus
  —thanks for their help
  —promising to send Timothy later
  —promising to come himself when released from prison

The emperor Claudius, who ruled the Roman Empire A.D. 41–54, blamed the Jews for causing riots and ordered them, including many Jewish Christians, to leave Rome in A.D. 49 (Acts 18:2).

many gods, be initiated into secret mystery religions, discuss philosophy with the Stoics or the Epicureans, so long as they also acknowledged the gods of Rome. Foreign religions (those brought to Rome by their devotees from various parts of the empire) were regarded with suspicion, often harassed, then expelled, then tolerated. Roman religion was a civic, public matter, not a matter of personal devotion to the gods. Despite being granted special status, the Jews were always suspect because of their strange ways and their worship of only one God.

Christians too were troublesome. Their enthusiasm over Christ as Lord implied conflict with Caesar as lord. Christians violated civil religion by refusing to attend imperial celebrations. The charge against Paul and Silas in Philippi stated, "They are Jews and are advocating customs that are not lawful for us as Romans to adopt or observe" (Acts 16:20-21).

You can imagine how upset the authorities in Philippi were when an earthquake set Paul and Silas free from jail. But they were even more upset when a career Roman soldier was baptized, "he and his entire family" (16:33). The point is that ridicule, economic oppression, beatings, and persecution were not unusual for the Philippian Christians or for Paul. Paul considered it an honor to be persecuted for the sake of the gospel and said so to the Philippians: "He [God] has graciously granted you the privilege not only of believing in Christ, but of suffering for him as well—since you are having the same struggle that you saw I had and now hear that I still have" (Philippians 1:29). All are in the redemptive struggle together. All are suffering together in innocent faith and love.

When have you ever had the opportunity to stand up for Jesus Christ amid scorn? What did you do?

in college but was unable to defend
questions because of lack of depth in knowledge

Paul always asks whether actions and events are helping the gospel mission. Is prison helping? Yes, he affirms. "What has happened to me has actually helped to spread the gospel" (1:12). He wanted the Philippian church to know that the entire imperial guard knew he was in jail "for Christ," not for robbery or murder (1:13). Other "brothers and sisters" in Christ, in the jail and in the house churches of the city, were being enriched, being strengthened by his imprisonment. They "dare to speak the word with greater boldness and without fear" (1:14).

When has someone else's boldness in witnessing strengthened your faith?

Missionary in remote parts of India

NOTES, REFLECTIONS, AND QUESTIONS

A *praetorium* was the official residence of a Roman ruler—the emperor's palace in Rome and the residence of any provincial ruler. *Praetorian guards* were the soldiers who guarded those residences. These statues show styles of uniforms, including weapons, shields, and headdress.

The world thinks that when God is with someone, that person is going to prosper. When people are sick or have trouble or are poor, God—if there is a God—is not with them. Either they have done something wrong, or God is weak or absent. Christians understand that God is present in our trouble. God uses weakness and pain to help build up people and honor God's name.

Where do you see evidence that people today still think riches are reward for virtue and poverty equals sinfulness?

Definitely in India. Debit & Credit

Another good thing was happening in Philippi. Because Paul was absent from the churches, other preachers and teachers were picking up the slack (1:15-17). Not all preachers were perfect, of course. Some were competitive; others were totally sincere, supportive of Paul, and witnessing out of love. But some were using Paul's imprisonment to discredit him. Apparently he had no quarrel with what they preached. So, he could overlook their motives. "What does it matter?" Paul asked with grace. "Christ is proclaimed in every way, whether out of false motives or true; and in that I rejoice" (1:18).

Gifts From Philippi

Paul loved the people in the Philippian church, and they loved him in return. The phrase "you hold me in your heart" (Philippians 1:7) can also be translated "I have you in my heart" (1:7, NIV). The expression is true both ways. They were "my brothers and sisters, whom I love and long for, my joy and crown" (4:1).

In every city, Paul worked to pay his way. But the Philippian church sent him love gifts by Epaphroditus to sustain his ministry in Thessalonica and Corinth. Paul was grateful, especially because it showed how much love for God was in their hearts. Apparently this was the only church that did so (4:15-18).

Ever since the Jerusalem Council Paul had been gathering an offering for the poor Jewish Christians in Judea. In fact, his final imprisonment in Rome was the result of his stubborn insistence on returning to Jerusalem. He wanted to take the money from Philippi, Thessalonica, Corinth, Ephesus, and elsewhere to the heart of the church.

And who led the way in the offering for the poor? The Philippians, of course. In addition to their love gifts for Paul, they set aside money for "the saints" in Jerusalem. When Paul wanted to encourage the Corinthian Christians to give generously, he wrote, "We want you to know, brothers and sisters,

NOTES, REFLECTIONS, AND QUESTIONS

about the grace of God that has been granted to the churches of Macedonia. . . . For, as I can testify, they voluntarily gave according to their means, and even beyond their means, begging us earnestly for the privilege of sharing in this ministry to the saints" (2 Corinthians 8:1-4). What a witness! Paul continually held the Philippians up as an example.

How can the example of other Christians inspire us to greater generosity today?

Problems in the Congregation

Paul addressed the church problems with apostolic candor. Some people wanted to be *really* sure of their salvation. They wanted to be super-Christians. Perhaps if they were to keep both sabbath and Sunday or if they were circumcised, they would be doubly sure. Paul got downright angry on this issue when it arose in Philippi, as it did also in Galatia: "Beware of the dogs, beware of the evil workers, beware of those who mutilate the flesh!" (Philippians 3:2-3). He was blasting the people who wanted to circumcise adult Gentile converts. They were adding extras, some work of their own, to the undeserved favor of God, to the grace of Christ.

"If you want to do it, do it right," says Paul. He recalls his Hebrew home, his family tree going all the way back to Benjamin, son of Jacob, son of Isaac, son of Abraham. If you want to earn righteousness, be circumcised on the eighth day as Paul was. Then become a Pharisee, trying to keep hundreds of laws with a mountain of interpretation (3:4-5). Paul did it and was "blameless" (3:6). If you want to brag to God about how righteous you are, you have a long way to go to equal Paul. But in Christ, he said, it's all worthless. Paul had so many noble traditions, the Law and the Prophets. They were glorious gifts. Yet Paul counts them all "as loss because of Christ" (3:7). Salvation in Christ is unmerited, and when finally completed, will be total and absolute. Don't dilute the gospel of grace, says Paul. Paul had no "righteousness . . . that comes from the law" but a right relationship with God "that comes through faith in Christ" (3:9).

Paul did not turn to Christ because he found the Law and life shaped by obedience to Torah a failure. Once he was "in Christ," he saw that his problem was not his prior failure but his success.

When are we tempted to act like super-Christians to boost ourselves?

NOTES, REFLECTIONS, AND QUESTIONS

NOTES, REFLECTIONS, AND QUESTIONS

Christ Our Example

Paul asked the congregation to be in unity, with one clear purpose. "Be of the same mind, having the same love, being in full accord and of one mind" (Philippians 2:2). Don't be conceited or have ambitions over one another, "but in humility regard others as better than yourselves" (2:3). Look after the interests of others (2:4). To make his point, Paul did not berate or scold. Instead, he quoted a Christian hymn that was circulating among the churches (2:6-11). It honored Christ, his suffering, his self-emptying, his servanthood. Christ would be their motivating example in caring for one another.

Christ, the Messiah, preexisted as part of God, in the essence of God (2:6). But Jesus Christ did not hold onto, grasp, exploit the prerogatives of holiness and power; instead, he became a servant. He gave up "the form of God" and voluntarily took on "the form of a slave," totally obedient to God. That unflinching obedience was what the world needed to reverse human rebellion. That obedience, even "to the point of death"—did Paul add the phrase "even death on a cross"?—mysteriously and wonderfully, in faith, puts people in right relationship with God and with one another.

Because of Christ's servanthood, God raised him from the dead and exalted him. The prophecy of Isaiah would be fulfilled in him.

> "Turn to me and be saved,
> all the ends of the earth!
> For I am God, and there is no other. . . .
> from my mouth has gone forth in righteousness
> a word that shall not return:
> 'To me every knee shall bow,
> every tongue shall swear' " (Isaiah 45:22-23).

Not only is Christ Jesus our salvation; his servanthood is our model for Christian living. Paul followed the hymn with a power *therefore*. "Do all things without murmuring and arguing" (Philippians 2:14). You will "shine like stars in the world" as an inspiration to others (2:15).

Rejoice Always

Paul's letters ring with rejoicing. To the Thessalonians he appeals, "Rejoice always" (1 Thessalonians 5:16). The worse his circumstances, the stronger his joy. "We rejoice in our sufferings" (Romans 5:3, NIV). His letter from prison to the Philippians literally sings: "Rejoice in the Lord always; again I will say, Rejoice" (Philippians 4:4). Paul does not deny reality, but he sees the glorious work of God as part of that reality.

A thrilling part of Paul's witness is his ability to sing amid sadness. Paul's hold on Christ's saving grace was so strong he could see hope at midnight, the love of Christ in all circumstances. He felt joy because the Philippians were concerned, because he could suffer on Christ's account, and because he could "do all things" through Christ who strengthened him (4:13). So he repeated, "Rejoice. . . Rejoice. . . . The Lord is near" (4:4-5).

MARKS OF OBEDIENT COMMUNITY

When trouble comes, the faith community reframes its attitude. We look for ways God can transform the experience into something worthwhile. We search for a new picture to emerge from within the circumstances. Our fellowship of caring provides a climate in which we can perceive new possibilities.

You can't make someone rejoice. What enables you or others to rejoice?

Faith; jouney so far; being of service to others; humble

What is to keep our rejoicing from being empty piety?

outside should be a true reflection of inside. Attitude is as important as action

Describe a time when you saw God working for good amid trouble.

He strengthens you through troubled experiences.

When has your DISCIPLE group or your church been able to sing praises amid hardship?

In what ways does the suffering of Christ assist you in your own suffering?

Reminds me of His sacrificial love in all situations. Come to me all you who are heavily burdened.

IF YOU WANT TO KNOW MORE

Glance through the Psalms looking for joy, exuberant praise, rejoicing even in trouble.

Letter: Write a letter witnessing to the working of Christ in your own life. Without denying your troubles, show that you can rejoice amid your difficulties. Substitute thanksgiving for complaining, testimony for self-pity.

NOTES, REFLECTIONS, AND QUESTIONS

Obedient community sees all experiences and situations as occasions for God's transforming power to work.

UNITY

"Now you are the body of Christ and individually members of it."

—1 Corinthians 12:27

22 The Body of Christ

OUR HUMAN CONDITION

We all bring with us our own ideas, interests, loyalties, and backgrounds, and our human inclination to seek our own advantage, hold on to our rights, and see ourselves as self-made. Can we come together?

ASSIGNMENT

Paul, in Ephesus, has welcomed visitors and received correspondence from Corinth. In his Corinthian letters, he responds to questions, complaints, and criticisms one by one, as if from a list. As you read, keep in mind the mix of people in the Corinthian congregation and their different backgrounds—Gentiles mostly; slaves, some newly-freed; a few Jews; and a handful of civic leaders. Most were poor and uneducated. Unity was no easy goal. Paul counsels unity for the purpose of the message—Christ crucified.

Day 1 Acts 18; 1 Corinthians 1–2 (Paul in Corinth, the power and wisdom of God)
Day 2 1 Corinthians 3–4 (divisions in the church, the temple of God's Spirit, servants of Christ, Paul's suffering)
Day 3 1 Corinthians 5–7 (sexual immorality, marriage)
Day 4 1 Corinthians 8–11 (food offered to idols, rights as an apostle, warnings from Israel's history, the Lord's Supper)
Day 5 1 Corinthians 12–16 (spiritual gifts, one body, love, speaking in tongues, the resurrection, collection for Jerusalem)
Day 6 Read and respond to "The Word of the Lord" and "Marks of Obedient Community."
Day 7 Rest

PRAYER

Pray daily before study:
"Remember me, LORD, when you help
your people;
include me when you save them"
(Psalm 106:4, TEV).

Prayer concerns for this week:

UNITY

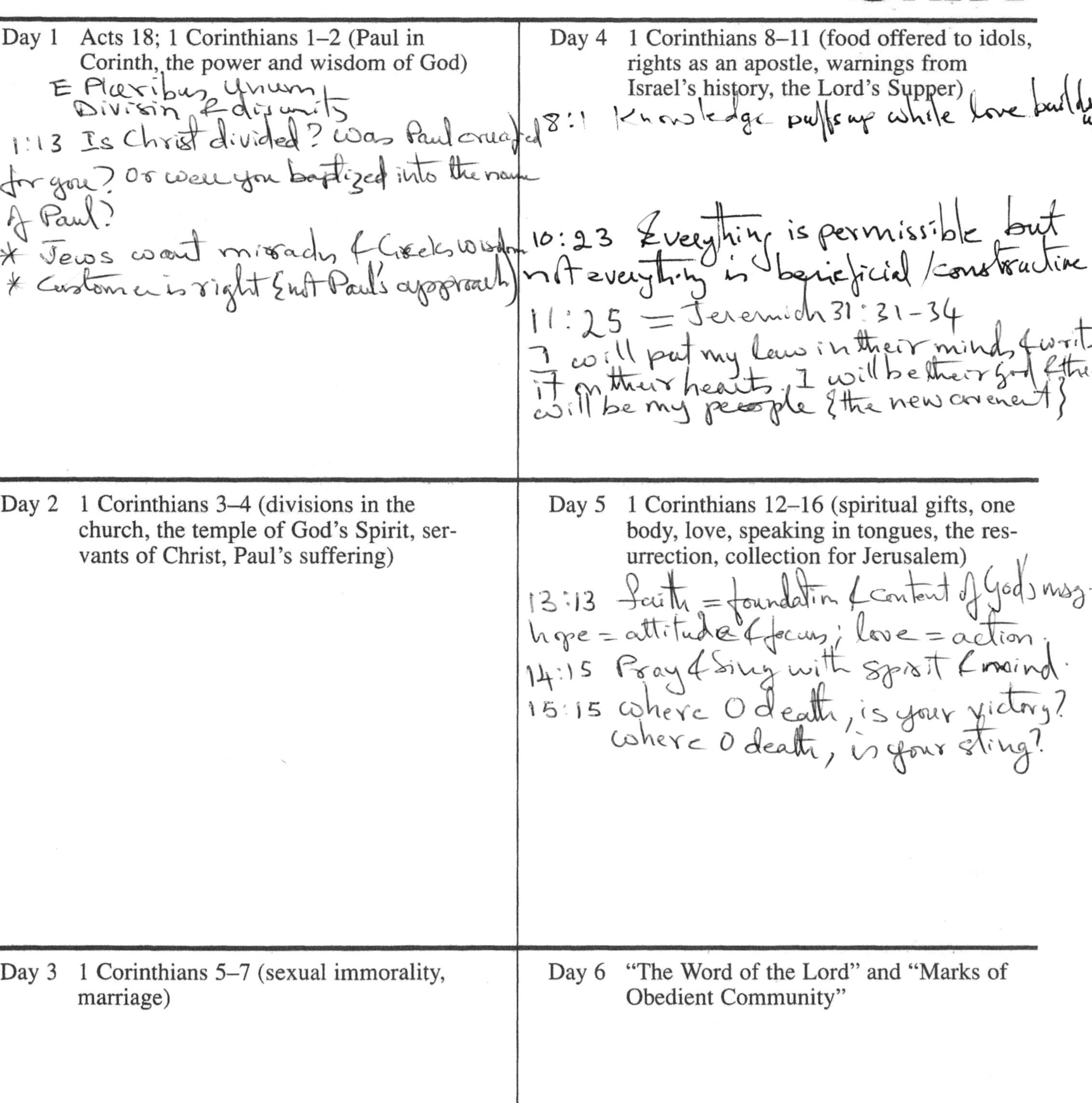

Day 1 Acts 18; 1 Corinthians 1–2 (Paul in Corinth, the power and wisdom of God)

Day 4 1 Corinthians 8–11 (food offered to idols, rights as an apostle, warnings from Israel's history, the Lord's Supper)

Day 2 1 Corinthians 3–4 (divisions in the church, the temple of God's Spirit, servants of Christ, Paul's suffering)

Day 5 1 Corinthians 12–16 (spiritual gifts, one body, love, speaking in tongues, the resurrection, collection for Jerusalem)

Day 3 1 Corinthians 5–7 (sexual immorality, marriage)

Day 6 "The Word of the Lord" and "Marks of Obedient Community"

THE WORD OF THE LORD

Corinth was a unique city; the Corinthian church was a unique church. Corinth linked two harbors and stood on the narrow isthmus between the Aegean Sea and the Adriatic Sea. So Corinth swarmed with traders from all over the world—Romans, Greeks, Asians, Jews, all kinds of people—two hundred thousand free and four hundred thousand slaves. It was known as a tough town full of drunkenness and prostitution, thievery and murder.

However, Paul experienced enormous success in Corinth. All sorts of people were converted. The gospel took hold and spread throughout Achaia (2 Corinthians 1:1). Luke records that Paul argued every sabbath in the synagogue, trying to convince Jews and Gentiles (Acts 18:4).

Soon the theological conflict in the synagogue reached a boiling point. Paul insisted Jesus was the Messiah; many Jews resisted. Paul left the synagogue and "shook the dust from his clothes." "From now on," said Paul, "I will go to the Gentiles" (18:6). When Paul became discouraged, God spoke to him in a vision, "Do not be afraid, but speak and do not be silent; for I am with you" (18:9).

After a year and a half in Corinth, Paul left and settled in Ephesus for three years, his longest work. So began a flurry of activity—emissaries and couriers, letters, even return visits to keep the church in Corinth faithful and flourishing.

Chloe's Delegation

Chloe, head of an important family, sent a delegation from the Corinthian fellowship to see Paul personally. "Chloe's people" (1 Corinthians 1:11) were either her family or her slaves. They reported a deteriorating situation in the church at Corinth. Factions claimed loyalty to Paul, to Peter (Cephas), to Apollos. Some smugly said they belonged only to Christ (1:12). With spiritual elitism, some boasted of religious "knowledge," others of privileged Holy Spirit "experiences."

Chloe's people reported disruptions in worship (11:17-34). Not everyone got off work at the same time. Slaves often came late. Early arrivals, probably the rich people, gorged themselves at the Lord's Supper fellowship meal, sometimes getting drunk on the wine, leaving little for others. The issue was not hunger but selfishness and actions that emphasized the division between rich and poor.

The fellowship meal was important because it showed equality in Christ. Slave ate with free; young ate with old; Jew ate with Greek; women ate with men. The power of Pentecost was present. The meal concluded with the bread and cup of the Lord's Supper. Paul used a rabbinical phrase, "For I received," which was usually followed by a quotation from another rabbi (11:23). But the words that followed Paul's use of the phrase were the words from Christ: "For I received from the Lord what I also handed on to you, that the Lord

NOTES, REFLECTIONS, AND QUESTIONS

Jesus on the night when he was betrayed took a loaf of bread, and when he had given thanks, he broke it and said, 'This is my body that is for you. Do this in remembrance of me' " (11:23-24). Observe that Paul uses these holy words to instruct. "So then, my brothers and sisters, when you come together to eat, wait for one another" (11:33). They celebrated the fellowship meal and the Lord's Supper when they met. But in view of the problems, Paul urged that the need for food be met at home (11:34), thereby beginning (so far as we know) the separation of the Lord's Supper from the church supper.

Paul Addresses Problems

Factions. Concerning factions, why do you boast? "Has Christ been divided? Was Paul crucified for you? Or were you baptized in the name of Paul?" (1 Corinthians 1:11-13). The point of God's grace is vulnerability, humility, even weakness. Paul deliberately did not use sophisticated Greek rhetoric or rabbinical reasoning but preached simply "so that the cross of Christ might not be emptied of its power" (1:17).

Paul used three arguments. The cross itself is foolishness (1:18, 21). Jews could not believe Messiah would be crucified; Greeks could not believe a man could be raised from the dead. Christ crucified is "a stumbling block to Jews and foolishness to Gentiles" (1:23). Don't boast of wisdom. Boast of being saved by the foolishness of God. Besides, God's wisdom makes all human wisdom into "folly" (1:25). Who can boast of wisdom in the face of God? Paul ridicules the Corinthians—their wealth, their power, their wisdom. Most of them were slaves. Few knew the Jewish Scriptures. "Not many of you were wise [even] by human standards, not many were powerful, not many were of noble birth" (1:26). Glory in your weakness! God chose you in your weakness to show that the power of salvation belongs to God.

Paul used himself as an illustration. In Corinth, he preached modestly. "My speech and my proclamation were not with plausible words of wisdom" (2:4)—yet people were converted, received the Holy Spirit—"so that your faith might rest not on human wisdom but on the power of God" (2:5).

Paul admits to a hidden wisdom that only the mature will understand, because it is not like the wisdom of this world. The mature know they receive strange and wonderful gifts from the Spirit. They cannot explain those gifts and powers to the "unspiritual," but those who have received the Spirit of Christ understand (2:6-16).

Unfortunately, writes Paul, you are acting like babies still on milk (3:1-2). How could you understand mature teachings when you bicker like children? Paul planted the church, Apollos nourished it, "but God gave the growth" (3:5-6). The leaders were servants; they will get paid as workers (3:8). But the glory belongs to God. Glory in Christ. Do it in unity. "I appeal to you, brothers and sisters, by the name of our Lord

NOTES, REFLECTIONS, AND QUESTIONS

Paul's Relationship With the Church at Corinth

- church in Corinth founded by Paul
- Paul in Corinth for eighteen months
- Paul in Ephesus for three years
- first letter to Corinth from Ephesus, now lost
- letter from Corinthians to Paul
- Chloe's people visit Paul in Ephesus
- second letter to Corinth, answering concerns in the letter and questions asked by visitors
- Paul's quick "painful visit" to Corinth
- "severe" letter to Corinth, perhaps delivered by Titus
- trip to Macedonia to meet Titus
- fourth letter to Corinth, the letter of reconciliation
- visit to Corinth to receive the Jerusalem offering

Jesus Christ, that all of you be in agreement and that there be no divisions among you" (1:10).

Sexual Immorality. Upon arriving in Ephesus, Paul wrote back to Corinth about problems in the church. This letter, now lost, apparently warned against two things, enthusiasm gone awry and sexual immorality. The letter was misunderstood, so in 5:9-13 Paul clarified. "I wrote to you in my letter not to associate with sexually immoral persons—not at all meaning the immoral of this world, or the greedy and robbers, or idolaters, since you would then need to go out of the world. But now I am writing to you not to associate with anyone who bears the name of brother or sister who is sexually immoral or greedy, or is an idolater, reviler, drunkard, or robber" (5:9-11). Paul did three things. He did not judge the world, for "God will judge those outside" (5:13). Second, he did not expect Christians, in daily commerce, in business and normal life, to avoid non-Christians (5:10). Third, Paul did not want sexual sins to be emphasized over other equally grievous faults, so he deliberately expanded the list.

Sex was a constant temptation in Corinth because immorality was so prevalent. Paul did not preach against the sins of society; he spoke to the church people. He insisted that the man who was living with his stepmother without shame be put out of the church. First Corinthians 5:2 suggests that this man was looked up to as a truly free person, an experimenter who pushed to the limit Christian freedom from ordinary rules. Paul was saying Christians were to live above promiscuity and sexual immorality and to exclude those who flouted these standards (5:12-13).

Marriage. Notice that Paul deals with issues point by point. "Now concerning" begins a new matter. He must have said, "It is good" or "It is better" for a man not to touch a woman. Paul now clarified. He did not mean a person should not marry. He did not mean married couples should not have sexual relations (7:1-6).

With great care and with full equality, Paul balanced each sentence to assure both wife and husband that they should give conjugal love to each other graciously and considerately. Couples could abstain, by mutual consent, for prayer or fasting, but not for too long, lest Satan tempt them. Never in Paul, as a Jew grounded in Jewish tradition, is sex considered sordid or evil. But never could he abide the abhorrent infidelities and promiscuous practices of the Gentiles.

If Christ were coming soon, very soon, why change your status? Single could remain single, married remain married (7:26-27). But Paul did not want people to sin. If they yearned to marry, do so. As for himself, he was free of all encumbrances to preach the gospel to a dying world (7:7, 32-34). Paul was fighting two opponents, libertines—those who fornicated, committed adultery, had sex with male and female temple prostitutes or prostitutes of the streets. Such sex joined Christ in one flesh with a prostitute. "Do you not

NOTES, REFLECTIONS, AND QUESTIONS

know that your body is a temple of the Holy Spirit within you?" (6:19).

The other opponents were Greek-speaking gnostics and Jewish ascetics who perceived that all sexual activity was wrong. Not so, he argued. For in marriage, husband and wife become one flesh together in Christ, even a believer with an unbeliever. They may be made holy, one through the other (7:8-16).

Meat Offered to Idols. "Now concerning food sacrificed to idols" starts his discussion not only about food but about upbuilding the church (8:1). Animals were taken to pagan temples, killed in sacrifice, with a small portion of blood or fat being burned. The priests would retain a portion. Most of the meat would be sold in temple-run meat markets. When you ate in a friend's home or at a gathering, you might not know where the meat came from.

None of the Christians went to the temples anymore for sacrifice. They would not deliberately eat sacrificed meat. But some church members meticulously bought meat in nonritual shops, ate only unsacrificed animals, and were careful in which homes they dined. They avoided any connection to worship of idols. Only months before, they had eaten sacrificed meat; now they wanted to abstain totally. They were critical of Christian friends who ate that food.

Other church members laughed at them. Idols were stone and wood. The sacrifices were foolishness. Meat is meat. Those who worried about meat offered to idols were moralists, trapped by their squeamish concerns. Christ had set them free. "Let us enjoy our freedoms," they said.

For Paul, the issue was respect and love. Paul abstained because he did not want his freedom to be a stumbling block to others (8:9). Some, who used to sin in idol worship (or gambling or drunkenness or lewd activities) had to be totally separated from any part of it in order to resist. Can others respect how hard their brothers and sisters are trying? Paul wrote, " 'All things are lawful,' but not all things are beneficial" (10:23). Those who are free should be thoughtful of those with a sensitive conscience. Though Paul agrees with those who eat the meat (8:8), he will not insist on doing so. He would abstain from meat if it offended others in the group. Paul is concerned for persons' faith (8:9-13). To promote the gospel, Paul was intentional in everything he did: "I have become all things to all people, that I might by all means save some" (9:22).

How do you experience your freedom through not offending "a weak conscience"?

So Paul disciplined and focused himself to be faithful and to encourage others. He could lay aside his rights if doing so would help a fellow Christian, but he did not think of it as giving up his freedom.

NOTES, REFLECTIONS, AND QUESTIONS

NOTES, REFLECTIONS, AND QUESTIONS

The Worshiping Community. Some Corinthians quoted Paul, "In Christ there is neither male nor female," then proceeded to throw out all social practices. They abandoned normal hairstyles, ignored customs of clothing and courtesy. A revolution had occurred in Corinth; slaves and free citizens were eating at the same table; women and men were praying, testifying, and teaching together. But some claimed gender didn't matter in Christ. Men quit cutting their hair; women let their hair fall down like prostitutes. The result was confusion. Paul urged that social customs and normal distinctions between men and women be observed. Why? To avoid contentiousness (11:16).

The passage "women should be silent in the churches" (14:33-36) was probably added by disciples from a later period. (Scholars differ on this point.) The passage disrupts the flow of Paul's discussion about speaking in tongues, and it conflicts with Paul's emphasis on equality. Attention to hair and head coverings for men and women allowed both women and men to pray aloud and prophesy (11:5, 13). If these words are Paul's, they attempt to keep social decorum in a lively and sometimes conflicted congregation.

Spiritual Gifts. "Now concerning spiritual gifts, brothers and sisters. I do not want you to be uninformed" (12:1). Often when the Holy Spirit falls on a congregation, some people speak in tongues. Prayer language, ecstatic verbalizing, speaking only to God in unknown language, was happening in Corinth. Such experiences should not be confused with Pentecost, where the apostles spoke in understandable languages to show the gospel was to go to all nations (Acts 2:6-8).

Paul sometimes spoke in tongues (1 Corinthians 14:18). But that gift of the Holy Spirit was the least (12:28) and should be carefully disciplined. But do not criticize those who have prayer language so long as they do not disrupt worship or become judgmental. Speak with the mind mostly. Prophesy the truth so unbelievers can believe. The really important work of the Spirit was to help a believer say "Jesus is Lord" (12:3). Then other wonderful gifts would be given, a rich variety (12:28). Not everyone received all these gifts (12:11, 29-30). But all could receive the Holy Spirit, which is Christ Jesus' Spirit, by surrendering their hearts in total trust and obedience to him. The greatest gift is the ability to love (13:1). Above all, consider the church as the body of Christ, made up of a variety of parts, working together in love and harmony to help others find the Lord (12:12-27).

Resurrection

Bewilderment about resurrection caused some new converts doubt (1 Corinthians 15:1-5). Paul reminds them of his sermon, a message he had "received." He preached that Christ had died, was buried, was raised from the dead. Christ appeared to many apostles, but "Last of all, as to one untimely born, he appeared also to me" (15:8). But the Corinthians had questions: "How are the dead raised? With what kind of body do they come?" (15:35).

Paul responded. Christ was raised first; the full resurrection of Christ's people will take place when Christ returns. Sin has been conquered in Christ. God will give us new bodies, bodies appropriate for the new Kingdom. When God puts all enemies underfoot, the last enemy to be destroyed will be physical death. Then and only then, through the power of Jesus Christ, will we be able to shout, "Death has been swallowed up in victory" (15:54).

MARKS OF OBEDIENT COMMUNITY

The world thinks harmony requires similarity, uniformity. (We get along well because we're all alike.) That's why clubs are formed. The faith community experiences unity amid diversity. More important, the variety of experiences and gifts enhances the capabilities of the body to serve. Our unity is always at the service of the gospel. Difference not only provides interesting richness but also supplies a vast array of talents. But the glue that holds us together is the love born of Jesus Christ.

Consider your DISCIPLE group. What signs do you see of unity amid diversity?

___

How far has your congregation stretched to include different kinds of people? What people are still excluded?

___

___

How willing are you to set aside your rights for the good of another?

___

___

How is emphasis on unity amid diversity in your congregation clearly connected to bearing the message of Christ crucified?

___

___

IF YOU WANT TO KNOW MORE

Letter. Unity requires reconciliation. Write a letter offering apology or expressing sorrow over an incident of conflict. Suggest a compromise. Offer a plan to make things right.

NOTES, REFLECTIONS, AND QUESTIONS

First Corinthians 15:3-7 is the oldest identifiable piece of Christian tradition we have because Paul "received" it when he became a Christian. That was around A.D. 35. Already then, this piece of tradition was fixed. It is bedrock.

The faith community seeks unity amid diversity for the sake of the gospel.

PAIN

"I fear that when I come, I may find you not as I wish, and that you may find me not as you wish; I fear that there may perhaps be quarreling, jealousy, anger, selfishness, slander, gossip, conceit, and disorder."

—2 Corinthians 12:20

23 Crisis in Confidence

OUR HUMAN CONDITION

We misunderstand or are misunderstood. It hurts. So we become defensive and withdraw trust. That's painful too.

ASSIGNMENT

More correspondence from Paul, more problems in Corinth. Chapters 10–13, a severe letter; Paul chastises. Chapters 1–9, a reconciling letter; Paul builds bridges. Look for humility. Study stewardship.

Day 1 2 Corinthians 10–13 (Paul defends his ministry, his sufferings as an apostle, strength in weakness, examine yourselves)
Day 2 2 Corinthians 1–2 (thanksgiving, concern for the church)
Day 3 2 Corinthians 3–4 (ministers of a new covenant, treasure in clay jars)
Day 4 2 Corinthians 5–6 (a house in heaven, ministry of reconciliation, now is the acceptable time)
Day 5 2 Corinthians 7–9 (Paul's joy at the church's repentance, generous giving)
Day 6 Read and respond to "The Word of the Lord" and "Marks of Obedient Community."
Day 7 Rest

PRAYER

Pray daily before study:
"Turn to me, LORD, and be merciful to me,
because I am lonely and weak.
Relieve me of my worries
and save me from all my troubles.
Consider my distress and suffering
and forgive all my sins" (Psalm 25:16-18, TEV).

Prayer concerns for this week:

PAIN

Day 1 2 Corinthians 10–13 (Paul defends his ministry, his sufferings as an apostle, strength in weakness, examine yourselves)

Reading Scripture
1 Freedom
2 Old & new testament continuity
3 Election & promise
4 Word as directed to church
5 New eyes

Day 2 2 Corinthians 1–2 (thanksgiving, concern for the church)

2: 12-17 For we are the aroma of Christ to God among those who are being saved and among those who are perishing.
Aroma produced in suffering.
Who is sufficient for these things? God is.

Day 3 2 Corinthians 3–4 (ministers of a new covenant, treasure in clay jars)

Truth without love; Love without truth.
For the letter kills, but the spirit gives life.
4:6 Let light shine out of darkness
Do everything to the glory of God
Live your life in the light of eternity
7 Jars of Clay (frail, fragile, easily broken)

Day 4 2 Corinthians 5–6 (a house in heaven, ministry of reconciliation, now is the acceptable time)

Fear of the Lord. Joseph's brothers on finding out Joe's identity.
5:14 Love of Christ controls/constrains us
The Gospel is that God counts our sins against Jesus not us.

Day 5 2 Corinthians 7–9 (Paul's joy at the church's repentance, generous giving)

Charles Spurgeon in response to an atheist's taunting: like Elijah; "Let God, the God of orphanages, answer by orphanages. Let Him be God".
James 1:27 Pure religion & undefiled is to help widows, orphans, & those in need.
Jesus' self giving informs our standard of giving.
Give proportional out of what God gave you already.
Matth 10:42 God will not forget even a cup of water given in His name.

Day 6 "The Word of the Lord" and "Marks of Obedient Community"

9:6 He who sows sparingly will also reap sparingly & he who sows bountifully will also reap bountifully.
Matt 11 Jesus say about Woman's perfume anointing: He who is forgiven much loves much but he who is forgiven little loves little.
Manna was equally apportioned regardless on how much each person picked up.
9:7 God loves a cheerful giver.
Psalms 112:6-9 his righteousness endures forever
If you are giving to God (not charity or Church) you are a cheerful giver. Ex 16:17-18

THE WORD OF THE LORD

NOTES, REFLECTIONS, AND QUESTIONS

First Corinthians reports that in addition to "Chloe's people" other Corinthian Christians—Stephanas, Fortunatus, and Achaicus—had visited Paul (1 Corinthians 16:17). This group added to the concerns later addressed in that letter but "refreshed" Paul's spirit. They made up for the loneliness Paul felt in being absent from his Corinthian friends. Some of them surely hand-carried Paul's letter (First Corinthians) from Ephesus back to Corinth.

Communication continued, but the relationship deteriorated. In response to reports from Chloe's people, Paul sent Timothy to Corinth to assess and try to ease the situation in the church there. By the time Timothy arrived, the congregation had already received and read Paul's letter, First Corinthians. The letter had done little to reduce the quarreling in the congregation or their suspicion of Paul. Paul's proposed visit, announced in his letter (16:5-7), had not materialized. Sending Timothy in his place had not sufficed. The church was doubly critical. Paul had not come, and he seemed to have vacillated in his plans.

Timothy returned to Ephesus to tell Paul the bad news. Neither his visit nor Paul's letter had brought reconciliation. Paul decided to make a hurried visit to try personally to heal the wounds. Unfortunately his visit was both short and "painful" (2 Corinthians 2:1). It even worked to his critics' advantage. Paul had not meant to cause them pain. "I wrote you out of much distress and anguish of heart . . . to let you know the abundant love that I have for you" (2:4). The visit hurt Paul. He was wronged by a man in the congregation (2:5-8; 7:12). Yet he hoped the church would accept this man back, forgiving him as Paul has forgiven him. We must not be "outwitted by Satan" (2:11).

Severe Letter

Some scholars think Second Corinthians contains two of Paul's letters—his third, the "severe" letter (2 Corinthians 10–13), and his fourth, a reconciling letter (1–9). The third letter was written out of much pain. Paul sent the letter by Titus. So anxious was Paul about how the letter was received that he hurried to Troas to await Titus's ship. When Titus failed to return, Paul "could not rest"; so he set sail to Macedonia to find his fellow worker (2:12-13). He arrived at Neapolis, Philippi's port, and the two reunited. The news was good! Attitudes toward Paul had changed; the Corinthians were longing to see him. They had dealt with the offender, and their welcome of Titus proved them worthy of Paul's boasting about them. Paul was elated; for the pain, the grief, the hard letter, the repentance had all worked for good (7:5-13). "For godly grief produces a repentance that leads to salvation and brings no regret, but worldly grief produces death" (7:10).

Look at the painful or "severe" letter (10–13). Paul's

language is biting, both ridiculing and mocking. He is in a fighting mood. Some opponents were destroying the converts he had intended to present to Christ. They were meddling with people's salvation. The address, salutation, and thanksgiving of this letter are missing, perhaps so the third and fourth letters could be combined. Paul was charged with cowardice, with weakness and ineffectiveness. Opponents claimed, "His letters are weighty and strong, but his bodily presence is weak, and his speech contemptible" (10:10). He was accused of being a second-rate apostle asking for money.

On the Defensive

Paul, for the sake of the church, had to defend both his apostleship and the gospel he proclaimed. He declared war against false apostles and false ideas (2 Corinthians 10:3-5). He wrote that he was not "trying to frighten" them with his letters (10:9). He was working where God assigned him. He was not in someone else's territory, for he was the first one to bring "the good news of Christ" to Corinth (10:14). That was bold! He won't take credit for the work of others, but he will boast about his own work (10:12-16). His goal, like the father of a bride, was to present his fledgling church like a virgin to the Bridegroom, who is Christ (11:2). But he feared that goal was threatened by "super-apostles" who were preaching a gospel and a Jesus different from his (11:4-5).

Apparently Paul's critics considered his tentmaking to support himself degrading. Paul responds with irony, "Did I commit a sin by humbling myself so that you might be exalted, because I proclaimed God's good news to you free of charge?" (11:7). But he had no intention of bowing to his critics: "What I do I will also continue to do, in order to deny an opportunity to those who want an opportunity to be recognized as our equals in what they boast about" (11:12).

Foolishness of Boasting

Paul wrote that it was foolish to boast; but since his opponents were acting foolishly, Paul played the fool for a moment (2 Corinthians 11:1, 17, 21). You seem to like fools; for in your wisdom, you allow deceitful workers who claim credentials to make slaves of you, that is, lay Jewish practices on you; prey upon you, that is, reach for your money; or put on airs, that is, pretend to be super-apostles. With some sarcasm, Paul said in effect, "I guess we were not bold enough to do all that!" Then he recounts his own credentials (he is playing the fool). Are they Hebrews, sons of Abraham? "So am I" (11:22). "Are they ministers of Christ?" (11:23). I have worked harder, had more imprisonments, more floggings than any of them. Who is weak? Paul lists his sufferings (11:23-28). Then he turns the argument. If he must boast, he will boast not of strength but of weakness. He had been so weak (and yet so bold) that he had to escape Damascus in a basket (11:30-33).

NOTES, REFLECTIONS, AND QUESTIONS

NOTES, REFLECTIONS, AND QUESTIONS

Were the troublemakers bragging about visions and spiritual experiences? Paul gave testimony to being taken up to "the third heaven" and "caught up into Paradise" (12:2-4). Yet, to emphasize how God works in weakness, just as God worked through the weakness of the cross, Paul was given "a thorn . . . in the flesh" (12:7). We stand amazed that, accused of weakness, Paul would reveal even greater weakness. Though Paul appealed to God, the thorn was not removed. Paul explained: God's power "is made perfect in weakness" (12:9). What was Paul driving at? Salvation is built on weakness—the weakness of the cross, the weakness of the apostles, and Paul's own weakness shown in humility. "I am nothing," but "I am not at all inferior to these super-apostles" who also are nothing (12:11).

Now Paul denied being crafty with a clear question: "Did I take advantage of you through any of those [Timothy, Titus] whom I sent to you?" (12:17). No. "Everything we do, beloved, is for the sake of building you up" (12:19). Now he shifts the spotlight onto them. "I fear that there may perhaps be quarreling, jealousy, anger, selfishness, slander, gossip, conceit, and disorder" among you (12:20). Paul warns that when he comes, he will be bold to see how strong they are in faith and love and unity.

Letter of Reconciliation

When Paul met Titus in Macedonia following the "severe" letter, he was so relieved over Titus's good report that he immediately wrote a fourth letter (2 Corinthians 1–9), which he sent by Titus and two other companions (8:16-24). This was a letter of reconciliation. The crisis had passed. Paul had not wanted to make another painful visit. Now he would come, rejoice, and receive the offering for the destitute Christians in Jerusalem. Notice the wonderful words of consolation. The "God of all consolation" has comforted Paul so he in turn can console others (1:3-4). The sufferings of Christ comfort us all so we, through Christ, can comfort one another. If we share one another's suffering, we can share one another's comfort (1:7).

Paul's itinerary changed from time to time, but his full commitment to do God's will as a messenger never changed. He does not waver regarding Christ. Nor does God waver. God is faithful; we know that from the prophets. Jesus Christ is not " 'Yes and No'; but in him it is always 'Yes' " (1:17-19). Just think, God forever and always says yes to us in Jesus Christ. We are established in that *yes* by faith, anointed in baptism, and through the Holy Spirit have received the down payment of our total redemption. That *yes* will never be taken away.

How do you experience the *yes* of Christ?

Paul reviews some of his preaching in 2 Corinthians 3–4. He plays with the idea of a message written on paper or on stone. Some professionals carried letters of recommendation, written on paper, like Romans 16:1-3 for Phoebe. But the Christians in Corinth were Paul's letter, for the Spirit of Christ was written on their hearts (2 Corinthians 3:2-3). Paul, in rabbinical fashion, shifts from written material and old covenant to living material and new covenant (3:6). Had not the Lord through Jeremiah the prophet promised, "I will make a new covenant with the house of Israel and the house of Judah. . . . I will put my law within them, and I will write it on their hearts; and I will be their God, and they shall be my people" (Jeremiah 31:31-33)?

No one knew better than Paul that rules are cold and relationships are warm. To know the Law is impersonal; to know Christ is vitally personal. The stone tablets of Moses came in glory; how much more glorious is the ministry of the Holy Spirit (2 Corinthians 3:8). In Exodus 34:29-35, when Moses came down from Mount Sinai, he put a veil over his face because the glory of the Lord shone so brightly on his face that the people were afraid to come near. Here Paul reinterprets Scripture to his purposes. Moses put a veil over his face to hide the temporariness of the Law, so Jews still have a veil over their understanding. But Christ has removed the veil so that we see the glory of the Lord (2 Corinthians 3:12-14).

Paul now is inspired. "We do not lose heart" (4:1). If some cannot see, cannot hear, cannot penetrate the veil of the gospel, it is their own fault as unbelievers (4:4). Everything that contains the gospel is human and therefore fragile and weak—apostles, teachers, the church. But that does not weaken the gospel, for it rests upon the righteousness of God. "We have this treasure in clay jars, so that it may be made clear that this extraordinary power belongs to God and does not come from us" (4:7). No matter how frail the preacher, no matter how fragile the church, we rest upon the power of God. So Paul argues we are indestructible. "We are afflicted in every way, but not crushed; perplexed, but not driven to despair; persecuted, but not forsaken; struck down, but not destroyed" (4:8-9). Even death, which was a constant companion for Paul, cannot defeat us. If our earthly "tent" is taken down, we have a new "house" in heaven (5:1). We are even eager. Death holds no terrors.

The Offering

Paul was concerned with the offering for the saints in Jerusalem. He mentioned it in several of his letters. His trip to Jerusalem to deliver the money cost him his freedom. He was warned by his own intuition and by Agabus, the prophet who took Paul's belt and tied it around his own feet and hands: "This is the way the Jews in Jerusalem will bind the man who owns this belt" (Acts 21:11). Paul even had doubts whether

NOTES, REFLECTIONS, AND QUESTIONS

he would be welcomed when he arrived with the offering (Romans 15:30-31).

Why did the offering take on such significance? Three reasons. First, Paul was responding to the request to remember the poor made at the Jerusalem Council (Galatians 2:10). He was eager to follow through. No matter the cost, he would deliver the gift personally.

Second, some critics suggested Paul might be keeping some of the money for himself. Paul bent over backward to maintain absolute integrity, not only for his own sake but for the sake of the gospel. He carefully chose three people to go with him—Titus, a man without reproach, plus two other men, one chosen by the churches. He would deliver every coin. Word would go throughout the Christian world of his faithful stewardship. "We intend to do what is right not only in the Lord's sight but also in the sight of others" (2 Corinthians 8:21).

The third reason was most important. The unity of the church hung in the balance. Could Jewish Christians and Gentile Christians hold together? Would Christianity be only a Jewish sect? Would it divorce itself from its Jewish roots and become another Greek-Roman religion? The Jerusalem Christians had mothered the church in suffering. Now the Gentile wing could pour back sacrificial love in return. The handclasp between Paul and James at the council would be reenacted when Paul laid the money at his feet. The covenant, the bond between Jew and Gentile, would be ratified. The Gentile mission had been authorized by the apostles. The offering, from the heart in Christian love, secured Paul's ministry and the Gentile mission.

A New Appeal

After an early burst of enthusiasm, the Corinthians had lost interest. Paul's absence, their skepticism over the project, and internal strife put the collection on hold. So Paul, with the integrity of the church at stake, had to appeal afresh. Underlying all of his appeals was the assurance that Jesus Christ became poor for their sakes, taking on flesh and the cross so that they might become rich through his offer of salvation (2 Corinthians 8:9). This thought became a doxology: "Thanks be to God for his indescribable gift!" (9:15).

To help them with their giving patterns, Paul sent suggestions rooted deep in Jewish piety. Emotion wanes; discipline prevails. An earlier letter advocated systematic weekly giving (1 Corinthians 16:2), an idea based on "first fruits" giving (Exodus 23:19). Giving as God has prospered you sprang out of the tithe (Malachi 3:10). Trusting God to provide for needs recalled the manna in the wilderness (Exodus 16:18).

We assume the effort was successful, for when Paul wrote to Rome, he specifically said, "I am going to Jerusalem in a ministry to the saints; for Macedonia [Philippi, Thessalonica]

NOTES, REFLECTIONS, AND QUESTIONS

and Achaia [Corinth] have been pleased to share their resources with the poor among the saints at Jerusalem" (Romans 15:25-26).

MARKS OF OBEDIENT COMMUNITY

The faith community learns to disagree without discord, communicate differences without conflict. When the group takes on the self-emptying nature of Christ, people try to avoid self-adulation, try to honor others. When Christians are driven by the mission, they tend to work together; for success requires unity of spirit. In a healthy fellowship, differences can be resolved without bitter conflict.

What causes crises in confidence in congregations? between leaders and members? among the members?

What can be done when troublemakers divide the fellowship?

Tough decisions must be made. People have different opinions. Strong personalities clash. Turf issues, leadership tugs—all tear at harmony. How can a group make difficult choices without rupturing the fellowship?

What insights from Paul can assist reconciliation within a congregation in conflict?

IF YOU WANT TO KNOW MORE

Look up examples in the Gospels when Jesus inspired cheerful giving. List some of them.

Write a stewardship or tithing testimony.

Letter: Appeal for funds for a mission-related cause. Write a letter to someone in your church or community listing reasons for giving to a particular mission project. Support your request with your testimony or testimony from others.

NOTES, REFLECTIONS, AND QUESTIONS

The faith community knows that it bears the gospel in weakness and counts on the power of God to overcome that weakness.

FAITH

"I am not ashamed of the gospel; it is the power of God for salvation to everyone who has faith. . . . For in it the righteousness of God is revealed through faith for faith; as it is written, 'The one who is righteous will live by faith.' "

—Romans 1:16-17

24 God's Saving Righteousness

OUR HUMAN CONDITION

We let go of our guilt with great difficulty. Somehow guilt allows us to think we're in control and that eventually we'll be good enough to be free of it. The risk of letting go is scary.

ASSIGNMENT

Romans is the deepest, most profound of all the letters. Read slowly, word for word, and reread. Look for power-laden words: *grace, peace, sin, righteousness, wrath, gospel, freedom, justification, salvation.* Watch for echoes and quotes from the prophets, Torah, and the psalms.

Day 1 Romans 1:1-17 (the power of the gospel)
Day 2 Romans 1:18–2:16 (righteous judgment)
Day 3 Romans 2:17–3:31 (advantage of the Jews, righteousness through faith)
Day 4 Romans 4 (faith of Abraham)
Day 5 Romans 5 (results of justification, peace with God, Adam and Christ)
Day 6 Read and respond to "The Word of the Lord" and "Marks of Obedient Community."
Day 7 Rest

PRAYER

Pray daily before study:
"LORD, hear my prayer!
In your righteousness listen to my plea;
answer me in your faithfulness!" (Psalm 143:1, TEV).

Prayer concerns for this week:

Day 1 Romans 1:1-17 (the power of the gospel)

1:16 & 17: "For I am not ashamed of the gospel." (A True believer) Paul's complete conviction & certainity of the gospel. Both to Jews & gentiles (one gospel).
Gospel 1) Jesus Christ fulfillment of Old Test. prophesies
2) Life & death of Jesus Christ. 3) Resurrection,
4) His exultation & judgement
5) Absolute Truth
Gospel saves all who believe.

Day 4 Romans 4 (faith of Abraham)

4:13-15 Justified Abraham through faith. 430 yrs befor 10 cmds. 70 yrs of exile.
1 John 4:10 not that we loved God; but that he loved us & sent his Son
Romans 5:8 while we were still sinners, Christ died for us.
Faith = belief; it is a response to a revelation, it is embrace of truth, it is trust in a person.
Abraham & Walk to Emmaus

Day 2 Romans 1:18–2:16 (righteous judgment)

1:21-23
Atheism comes from a moral suppression of the truth. failing to glorify & be thankful to Him.
Smart people believe in superstition, scientology, Dianetics, Feng Shui, Rajneesh
It leads everything else go haywire in our thinking & in our living.
idolatry = there is a God we want & there is a God who is; we will invent the God we want.
Leads to wrong thinking & wrong behavior
2:1-3 judge not. deflecting; corresponding
2:14-15 Law written on gentiles heart.

Day 5 Romans 5 (results of justification, peace with God, Adam and Christ)

Day 3 Romans 2:17–3:31 (advantage of the Jews, righteousness through faith)

2:17-28: The Jews & the law
3:27-31: Everything you do is the result of God's grace in you, not the cause of it.
Boasting is excluded = humility.
26 - God justifies; 24 Being justified as a gift by His grace; Justification is based on the atoning sacrifice of Jesus Christ.
28: Justified by faith!
God requires faith of those who would be justified, and He gives that faith by His grace.
Ephesians 2:8-10: Saved by grace; For we are His workmanship, created in Christ Jesus for good works.
Any time we are looking to our works turns our face away from our Savior

Day 6 "The Word of the Lord" and "Marks of Obedient Community"

THE WORD OF THE LORD

Paul's letter to the Romans is different from his other letters. He wrote it to Jewish and Gentile converts in the house churches in the empire's capital, but he did not know them. He had eaten and slept in homes in Thessalonica, been locked up in jail in Philippi, preached in the synagogue in Corinth. But Rome's church he did not start, did not know personally, had never visited. His salutation therefore is long and introductory. Paul feared the Roman Christians would question the soundness of his gospel and doubt the legitimacy of his apostleship.

Paul's apostolic mission comes not from human but from divine authority. Even before offering grace and peace, he presents himself as a called messenger (Romans 1:1). He is bold in initiating this correspondence. He inserts his message, uninvited, into the Roman community of faith.

Paul wants the Roman Christians to know he is under divine mandate; he is "set apart for the gospel of God" (1:1). Then he highlights his gospel to show he is not a maverick. Paul is establishing his right to be heard.

His thanksgiving affirmed the Roman believers. "Your faith is proclaimed throughout the world" (1:8). Already he was praying for them, asking that God would permit him to visit them. Paul wrote from Corinth where he was collecting the offering. He hoped to travel westward after delivering the money to Jerusalem. His prayer would be granted, but he would travel in chains.

Obligated to Preach

Paul is a debtor. He owes Christ Jesus for his salvation, and therefore he is obligated to preach the gospel to all Gentiles—Greeks, Romans, barbarians, the wise, and the foolish. Only then will he have fulfilled God's commission (Romans 1:14-15).

Paul and his gospel had been ridiculed and mocked (Acts 17:18, 32). But Paul declared, "I am not ashamed of the gospel" (Romans 1:16). By worldly standards the gospel has little to recommend it; in fact it offends the world. Still, though showered with slander, Paul would never be ashamed. The good news has power for salvation. It came first to the Jews (Peter, James, John, Paul, and all the saints in Judea) and then to the Gentiles. God revealed God's righteous love to those open to trust Jesus Christ.

The prophet Habakkuk asked God why the promised kingdom was delayed. What was taking so long (Habakkuk 1:2)? God answered,

> "If it seems to tarry, wait for it;
> it will surely come" (2:3).

Meanwhile, "the righteous live by their faith" (2:4). In the Septuagint, Paul's Bible, the word translated *faith* can also mean *faithfulness*. Versions of the Septuagint translate the

NOTES, REFLECTIONS, AND QUESTIONS

Roman milestones such as these in Transjordan were set up to mark distances throughout the Roman Empire. A Roman mile was slightly shorter than a standard mile today.

verse "the just shall live by my faith" or "the just [righteous] shall live by my [God's] faithfulness." Paul, sensing that in Christ Jesus God's faithfulness is extended to human trustfulness, grabs both ideas by writing, "The one who is righteous [made right by Christ] will live by faith [God's faithfulness held tightly by human trust]" (Romans 1:17). The theme of the letter is announced: All who place their obedient trust in Christ, Jew and Gentile, can rely on God's faithful love.

Wrath

The prophets understood wrath. God's wrath is not capricious anger, like some divine rage that erupts occasionally. Wrath is the holiness of God yearning for the wholeness of creation. Wrath is goodness offended by evil, compassionate love recoiling at hatred. Wrath stands over against sin, condemning it and ultimately destroying it. Humankind experiences wrath when life lacks accord, when human beings hate one another, when a person's soul is at war with itself.

Who stands under divine wrath? The ungodly (Romans 1:18). Who is ungodly? Everyone. Why? Because they know better. Everyone on earth can see the creation of the universe. Everyone knows what truth is, what fair play is, what concern for a neighbor is all about. People see the immensity of the heavens and infer God. Some Gentiles even amazed the Jews by caring for the sick and elderly, honoring parents, condemning adultery, obeying an inner law they had not learned from Moses. They know right from wrong. They have no excuse (1:20). Paul relies here on an old line of thought: From the created we can infer the Creator. And he relies on the fact of Gentile conscience. Where is Paul headed with his argument? To the claim in 3:20 that keeping the Law will not result in being made right with God. So, Gentiles with their conscience and Jews with the Law are in the same situation before God: All are sinners. Yet all can be made right with God through faith in Jesus Christ.

What does wrath do? The greedy can never rest. Those who shame their neighbors will be shamed in return (Habakkuk 2:15-16); violence will beget violence (2:17). Lust leads to "degrading passions" (Romans 1:26-27). God gives the disobedient up to their own passions. That is their punishment; that finally is their destruction. Paul does not *threaten* God's wrath. The situation *is* God's wrath.

What new thoughts are provoked in you by this explanation of wrath?

The point: Sins spring from self-corruption, which comes from refusing to honor God as God.

The plight is deeper yet, as Paul will make clear as the

NOTES, REFLECTIONS, AND QUESTIONS

letter moves along. Not only are we humans wrongly related to God, marked by self-seeking, but we are tyrannized by an enslaving power. Like a ship boarded by pirates, our minds have been taken over by that power. Sin has become for us a troublesome resident within us. Therefore sin is not mere transgression. If it were, the "answer" would be to stop transgressing—"Behave yourselves." But that is not possible (Romans 7).

Deeper and more tragic still, that power, sin, has a corporate quality that unifies us all in a web of wickedness. We participate in the sins of society. Sin draws forth the wrath of God and leads to that death of soul promised to Adam (5:14). The domain of sin holds us in bondage, making us do the opposite of our good intentions, even the opposite of God's holy law.

No Excuse

The wrath belongs to God. "Vengeance is mine, I will repay, says the Lord" (Romans 12:19). If we condemn others, we assume we are innocent; but we are not. In fact, our judging condemns us. Do we think we are blameless and can point a finger at others? That attitude stores up the severe wrath aimed at the haughty. Paul quotes a proverb that sounds like righteousness comes from works (2:6). But in context it reads,

> "If you say, 'Look, we did not know this'—
> does not he who weighs the heart perceive it?
> Does not he who keeps watch over your soul know it?
> And will he not repay all according to their deeds?"
> (Proverbs 24:12).

"God shows no partiality" (Romans 2:11). Evil will be repaid with wrath and fury; good, with eternal life. In love and kindness God knows our very being. When we stand naked and alone before God, we cannot judge another. We can only realize that God's kindness is meant to lead us to repentance.

The Gentiles know right from wrong. They will be judged accordingly. The Jews have the law of Moses. They will be judged by that Law. The Gentiles are as guilty without Moses as the Jews are guilty with Moses.

Paul is upset with those who boast special privilege. Jews who know the Law do not always obey it (2:17-23). "You . . . boast in the law" but "the name of God is blasphemed among the Gentiles because of you" (2:23-24). If you break the laws of Moses, of what use is circumcision? As the prophets said so often, the external, the physical do not count with God. God looks on the heart. Now Paul shocks! "A person is a Jew who is one inwardly, and real circumcision is a matter of the heart—it is spiritual and not literal" (2:29). When a Gentile somehow does what the Law is all about—that is, does the will of God—that Gentile is a real Jew; while the physical/ethnic Jew who does not do the Law is as good as a Gentile. Imagine the effect of that word!

NOTES, REFLECTIONS, AND QUESTIONS

God Is Faithful

NOTES, REFLECTIONS, AND QUESTIONS

When Paul asks, "What advantage has the Jew?" (Romans 3:1), we expect him to say "none." But to the contrary, he responds, "Much, in every way" (3:2). What advantage? They were entrusted with the Scriptures—the patriarchs, Moses, and the prophets—and with the promises of Scripture. Was that advantage wasted? No. God is faithful, even though people are not. God's Word would still be true even though everybody lied. Some people are unjust, but God's Word that God is just is true. Scripture tells the story of God's election of Israel. Did God deal falsely with Israel? At issue is the moral integrity of God. Paul quotes from Psalm 51, the penitential psalm attributed to David (Romans 3:4):

> "Against you, you alone, have I sinned,
> and done what is evil in your sight,
> so that you are justified in your sentence
> and blameless when you pass judgment" (Psalm 51:4).

In spite of human faithlessness, God is faithful. God's righteousness is steadfast. God will judge the world (Romans 3:6). Some people twist this argument, says Paul. Since sin shows God's justice and therefore brings glory to God, we ought to sin more. Let such people be condemned (3:8).

Paul wants to prove that everyone has sinned and stands under the wrath of God. He quotes or alludes to Ecclesiastes, Proverbs, Isaiah, and six psalms (Romans 3:10-18).

> "There is no one who does good,
> no, not one" (Psalm 14:3).

But just as God holds everyone equally accountable, so God offers the grace of right relationship to all. One solution for one problem. Everyone can be made right through faith in Jesus Christ. There is no distinction (Romans 3:22). Jesus' sacrificial death has power to save. God in Christ has "passed over the sins previously committed" (3:25). Boasting is excluded, not by any law but because boasting of oneself is not the style of faith (3:27-28). Justification comes through faith—for the circumcised and the uncircumcised. Is the Law made void? No, because people living in Christ uphold the Law as a matter of devotion (3:31).

Abraham

Abraham serves as Paul's example. Abraham was justified by the grace of God before he was circumcised. He simply trusted in obedient faith, and "it was reckoned to him as righteousness" (Romans 4:3). Circumcision was simply a seal or sign of his justification. Judaism itself, rightly understood, claims descent from Abraham not only by virtue of physical ancestry but also by virtue of sharing Abraham's trust in God. Abraham, therefore, is father to everyone, Jew or Gentile, who lives in obedient trust. The salvation history of the Jews came not through circumcision or from the Torah but from God's rectifying act to Abraham, who was obedient. "For this reason, it depends on faith" (4:16). Abraham hoped to be the father of many nations, and that hope is now being fulfilled as the gospel goes everywhere. Just as faith was reckoned as right relationship for Abraham, so it is offered to us in Jesus Christ, "who was handed over to death for our trespasses and was raised for our justification" (4:25)—putting us right with God. God, whose righteousness is revealed in Jesus Christ, is Israel's God, the God of Abraham.

Free Gift

"Justify" or "put right" alludes to a courtroom where a person is acquitted, pronounced free to go, no charges. It suggests alignment, being in right relationship. That is, the relation to God is made right. Justification is rectification. God in Christ gives us access to undeserved favor and therefore to peace with God. Christ's work, through faith, moves us from wrath to peace and to our hope of one day sharing the glory of God (Romans 5:2).

What Paul is saying next is astounding. Christ's death is literally God's love. Not God loving us because of who we are; rather, God loving us in spite of who we are—sinners, powerless to do what is right, enemies of God. Nothing about us merits God's love. Yet, "God proves his love for us in that while we still were sinners Christ died for us" (5:8). Now we can boast. We can boast of Jesus (5:11).

What thoughts does this paragraph provoke in you?

Paul compares Adam and Christ. Adam didn't sin any worse than the rest of us; but he was first, and humankind has been in rebellion ever since. Adam symbolizes pervasive human sin that leads to death (5:12). When the Law came, sin was recognized more clearly. Under the Law people rebelled more vigorously, so sin continued. Adam typified and inaugurated disobedience and death, which hold us also in their power, because we are all sinners. But also because we cannot escape the effect of Adam's sin.

In contrast, Christ lived obedience. Christ's obedience is God's free gift. Just as Adam's sin had pervasive power, exercising a kind of rebellious dominion over all humans, so Christ, through his obedience unto death, grants a new pervasive power, available to all, to live in peace with God. This free gift is even greater than Adam's sin, for it leads "to eternal life through Jesus Christ our Lord" (5:21).

Why did Paul select Adam? Because he represents universal humanity, neither Jew nor Gentile. *Adam,* which means "human being," symbolizes everyone. Christ Jesus is also universal. He is God's saving act, extended to everyone.

There is not one gospel for the Jews, another gospel for the

NOTES, REFLECTIONS, AND QUESTIONS

Gentiles. Paul puts Gentiles and Jews in one boat, a boat that is sinking. Then he offers one Savior, one gospel, to all.

MARKS OF OBEDIENT COMMUNITY

The faith community knows and claims the experience of justification. We learn how to talk about it within the fellowship and to others. We explore ways to explain how human beings have been put right with God through Jesus Christ.

What is your understanding of God's saving righteousness?

If you were to put into words what "being put right with God" means, how would you say it?

Why do we sometimes find it difficult to talk to others about the saving power of the gospel?

How can we prepare for the time when we have the opportunity to witness to others?

Put Romans 1:17 in your own words.

IF YOU WANT TO KNOW MORE

Letter: Write a letter of testimony to someone. Explain your understanding of grace. Your heart is light. You don't have to prove yourself anymore. You are loved. You can relax and do your work unhindered by guilt. You don't have to earn peace. God, in Jesus, has given it to you. Praise God's grace in Jesus Christ.

Study Paul's references to Adam and Abraham wherever they appear in his letters. How are they portrayed?

NOTES, REFLECTIONS, AND QUESTIONS

The faithful community, by faith, claims the experience of being made right with God and invites others to claim it.

GRACE

"There is no distinction between Jew and Greek; the same Lord is Lord of all and is generous to all who call on him. For, 'Everyone who calls on the name of the Lord shall be saved.' "

—Romans 10:12-13

25 Salvation for All

OUR HUMAN CONDITION

We're pulled in two directions. We desire to do right, but our actions undercut us. We intend only good but end up doing harm. We make up our mind, but we can't follow through. We long to feel whole.

ASSIGNMENT

Paul's logic is tightly reasoned. Read slowly and carefully. Try to follow Paul's argument about the salvation of Jews and Gentiles. Notice that both Jews and Gentiles will be brought together in Christ as the proper children of Abraham.

Day 1 Romans 6 (dead to sin but alive in Christ)
Day 2 Romans 7 (the Law and sin, conflict over willing and doing)
Day 3 Romans 8 (life in the flesh and in the Spirit, children of God, ground and assurance of hope)
Day 4 Romans 9–10 (God's promise to Israel stands, salvation for Israel and Gentiles, righteousness by faith)
Day 5 Romans 11 (the wild olive grafted in, gifts and calling of God irrevocable)
Day 6 Read and respond to "The Word of the Lord" and "Marks of Obedient Community."
Day 7 Rest

PRAYER

Pray daily before study:
"May all who come to you
be glad and joyful.
May all who are thankful for your salvation
always say, 'How great is the LORD!' "
(Psalm 40:16, TEV).

Prayer concerns for this week:

5:8 while we were still sinners, Christ died for us.

Every man wants to be happy, even the man who hangs himself.
Blaise Pascal

hokey — flimsy, fake, contrived

Reality of Resurrection.

Gal: 5:22-23

www. fpcjackson.org

GRACE

Day 1 Romans 6 (dead to sin but alive in Christ)

6:14 For sin shall not be your master, because you are not under law, but under grace.
6:23 For the wages of sin is death, but the gift of God is eternal life in Christ Jesus our Lord.
Power of resurrection in union with Christ. That's the basis for freedom from sin's power.
Lasting change → lasting hope

Day 2 Romans 7 (the Law and sin, conflict over willing and doing)

7:6 footnote: Let the Holy Spirit turn your eyes from your nonperformance & toward Jesus. Serving Him out of love & gratitude is the new way of the spirit.
What would Jesus want me to do?
I John 5:1-3 when we love God & observe His commandments.
Is law sin? renounce your self righteousness attempts at gaining God's acceptance.
Don't see the law as a tool by which we get acceptance with God
Law is good, equitable, & right.
Matt 5:17-19

Day 3 Romans 8 (life in the flesh and in the Spirit, children of God, ground and assurance of hope) Best chapter in the Bible

→ 6 Law demands perfection. No good in them we do.
8:39 nothing will separate us from the love of God.
In Christ 1) no condemnation, 2) set free, liberated, 3) we walk not according to flesh but according to spirit.
Law of spirit of life has set me free.
Free from performance mentality
8:7 when your thinking comes into conflict with God's word, who win? You or God's word.
Holy spirit dwell in you.
(of Jesus Christ)

Day 4 Romans 9–10 (God's promise to Israel stands, salvation for Israel and Gentiles, righteousness by faith)

9:32 righteousness by faith not by works (law).

10:14-15 missionary.

Day 5 Romans 11 (the wild olive grafted in, gifts and calling of God irrevocable)

Day 6 "The Word of the Lord" and "Marks of Obedient Community"

THE WORD OF THE LORD

NOTES, REFLECTIONS, AND QUESTIONS

Baptism, for Paul, was not an initiation into the church. It was not a rite, like circumcision on the eighth day. Baptism was not a sacrament of grace conferred on a person by the authority of the church. Baptism was not a dedication of a child to God by grateful parents. Baptism was not even a symbol of faith in Christ.

In Paul, baptism meant stepping down into the tomb, yielding, dying to the self-centeredness that is the heart of sin. Paul scarcely mentions forgiveness. That can seem too shallow, too superficial, like a parent washing dirt off a child's face. No, the stranglehold of human sin, the disease of human rebellion, is so deep and so pervasive that a person, surrounded by undeserved favor, standing in the presence of Almighty Holiness, must yield the center of his or her allegiance to the God and Father of the Lord Jesus Christ.

The death is not symbolic; it is real. The spiritual death of self is as real as Jesus' praying in Gethsemane, "Not what I want but what you want" (Matthew 26:39). Paul writes that our death to self and sin is, for us, experiencing the crucifixion of Christ within ourselves. We actually experience that same death of obedient trust and are joined into that crucifixion.

We are raised from the tomb, not merely cleansed or washed or forgiven but lifted in hope. We live in Christ's resurrection, in his freedom, in his victory over sin and death. In Christ, we stand in right relationship with God, free to trust and love, eager to obey and serve.

Salvation does not seem to occur on a timetable. Even Paul's water baptism seemed more like a seal to his conversion and call than the occasion for them (Acts 9:18). Both Scripture and Christian experience show that a person's water baptism, a person's confirmation, a person's conversion, a person's reception of the Holy Spirit may come at various times in one's experience. Paul's point: The saving work of Christ is made real in a believer's heart when that person dies to self in Christ's sacrificial love and is raised in trust in Christ's glorious resurrection.

How do you understand the experience of dying to self?

Slaves to Christ

What then? We are free to become Christ's slaves. It is clear to Paul that we will necessarily be slaves to something or to someone—to sin, which is serving the creature, or to the Savior, which is serving God. Everybody "obeys"—heeds, follows, looks to—something or someone. There is no autonomous self; we are always under some constraint. This doctrine rankles our human concepts of freedom, just as it did those of the ancient

Jews and Gentiles. Some Jewish believers protested to Jesus that as the children of Abraham, they were free. Jesus responded that, no, they were slaves, slaves to sin. Only if the Son set them free would they be truly free (John 8:31-36).

To slip into sin is to forget to whom we belong. "I am speaking in human terms," writes Paul (Romans 6:19). Just as you presented yourselves, "your members" (body, mind, spirit), as slaves to impurity (when you were slaves to self-centeredness), "so now present your members as slaves to righteousness for sanctification" (6:19). Notice his concluding word—*sanctification.* For Paul salvation is a process of being pulled toward God. We will see all through his letters that we "have been saved," we "are being saved," and we one day "will be saved." The Holy Spirit has begun a good work in us when we die to the power of sin and are raised in Christ; but we, like all creation, still "groan" for full redemption (8:22-23). We are being sanctified.

The Law

What has happened to Torah, all the instructions of the ancestors, of Moses and the prophets, all the oral traditions of the rabbis? Paul uses an analogy. Under Roman law and under our laws, a marriage places you in a legal contract. But when your spouse dies, that legal contract ends. That law is no longer in place for you. So "in the same way" you are no longer mated to sin, death, and the Law. You have died to that; you are married to a new spouse. You belong to another "in the new life of the Spirit" (Romans 7:6).

Now, as a Jew, Paul is worried still about the Law, the whole body of Jewish tradition. The integrity of God is at stake. Was the Law bad? "By no means!" (7:7). The Law is not our real problem; sin is our real problem. What does sin do when faced with rules? Sin rebels more. Were the instructions wrong? No. Paul says sin seized an opportunity (7:8). The Law kindles our passion to live outside the Law. The Law stimulates us, tempts us to look for loopholes, to try to get away with something, to break out of its restraint.

So the Law, although holy and good, wise as a parent's counsel, fair as a speed limit, does not have the power to overcome sin. Paul personalizes the conflict by confessing, "I can will what is right, but I cannot do it. For I do not do the good I want, but the evil I do not want is what I do" (7:18-19). The truthful teachings of God were good, but more was needed. Only a greater power can break the stranglehold of sin. The failure of the Law is not that it is incorrect, but that it lacks power to root out sin. The old idol of self-seeking must be replaced. A new resident power, the Spirit, must move into the human heart (8:15-17). Paul suggests that a believer leaves one form of slavery that leads to death and enters a new form of slavery that leads to life. With the good and gracious Spirit resident within, a person is freed to love God.

NOTES, REFLECTIONS, AND QUESTIONS

NOTES, REFLECTIONS, AND QUESTIONS

In the Spirit

When Paul writes of "the Spirit," "the Spirit of God," the "Holy Spirit," he always means the very being, the very Spirit of Jesus Christ. Surrendered human beings, dead to self and risen in Christ, live in Christ; and Christ lives in them. That Spirit is communal. One does not "experience the Spirit" in isolation. To be "in Christ" is to live expecting the coming harmonies of God with brothers and sisters of faith, to set one's mind on the Spirit in life and peace (Romans 8:6). For Paul, no other choices exist. We either live in ourselves, apart from God, broken in our relationships, at war within ourselves; or we live in Christ, in quiet obedient trust. "All who are led by the Spirit of God are children of God" (8:14).

In the Spirit, we no longer fight God, fight the universe, fight life and death; we cry "Abba! Father!" (8:15). Even that attitude is a gift, for the prayer comes from the Spirit of Jesus within us, linking with our spirit (8:16). We become children, heirs, joint heirs with Jesus, and we will ultimately receive the children's full inheritance.

All Creation Groans

We tend to think of sin and wrath as limited to humankind, although in our day especially we should know that sin ravages the land, contaminates the streams, and pollutes the air, even into the upper atmosphere. Paul alludes to the curse on the ground in Genesis 3:17. The universe is infected. "The whole creation has been groaning in labor pains until now" (Romans 8:22). The salvation that is to come will have an impact on the mountains and rivers, the plants and animals—God's new heaven and new earth.

We wait expectantly. We pray, "Our Lord, come!" (1 Corinthians 16:2). We are not yet fully saved, "for in hope we were saved" (Romans 8:24). We are so weak, sometimes not even knowing how to talk to God. But the Spirit helps us, sighing with prayers "too deep for words" (8:26).

Salvation for All

Paul, Jew of the Jews and apostle to the Gentiles, agonizes over the fact that Jews are not accepting the gospel while Gentiles are: "I have great sorrow and unceasing anguish in my heart" (Romans 9:2). What is most precious to Paul in all the world? His salvation and call in Christ Jesus! He has given up everything for Christ. Yet he would give up his own salvation if the Jewish people could be saved (9:3)! The Israelites have so much—adoption, the ancestors, the Exodus and Mount Sinai, the Psalms and the sacrifices, the prophetic witness, all pointing to Messiah (9:4-5). Did God fail?

No, "For not all Israelites truly belong to Israel" (9:6). What is Paul saying? Aren't all descendants of Abraham the chosen people? No. He uses stories of the ancestors to argue that being chosen has never been simply a matter of birth.

Abraham had other children "of the flesh"; but Isaac, not Ishmael, was the child "of the promise" (9:8). Rebecca had twins, but God chose Jacob over Esau before they were born, before Jacob could earn his status. Jacob was in the covenant; Esau was not.

What is happening? Is God unjust? No, writes Paul. God is free to be God and to work out his purposes as God determines. Paul quotes the law of Moses itself: "I will have mercy on whom I have mercy" (9:15; Exodus 33:19). God hardened Pharaoh's heart so freedom could be granted to the Hebrews (Romans 9:17; Exodus 9:16). It doesn't seem fair. But Paul reaffirms the greatness of God, the mystery of God's freedom, by using Jeremiah's analogy of the potter and the clay (Romans 9:21; Jeremiah 18:4). The potter decides what the clay will become. The decision is not the clay's; it is the potter's. The molding, the remolding, comes from the gracious caring hands of the potter who is determined to make something beautiful (Romans 9:19-23).

God Is Merciful

Paul insists God's mercy has reached out to Jews and Gentiles. He remembers Hosea said God will transform "not my people" into "my people." Paul, with Christ in his eyes, takes Hosea's words and changes Hosea's meaning to include the Gentiles, who once were "not my people" and now are becoming "my people" (Romans 9:25-26; Hosea 1:10; 2:23). What is Paul doing? He is driving a wedge between the spiritual and the physical in Israel. He is celebrating God's freedom to be merciful. He is opening the door for the Gentiles to become part of God's people. Moses cannot save anyone from Adam's sin. God freely shows faithfulness to save by acting once again—in the work of Jesus Christ.

The hints can be found in Torah. Did not Isaiah prophesy that God's word would go out to the Gentiles, to all nations (Isaiah 49:6)?

What happened to Israel? They leaned on legacy. They misunderstood their election. They *strived for* a right relationship, for righteousness, as if it were not by faith. Paul sees the irony in the way things are working out: Christian Gentiles attained righteousness because they believed the gospel. Jews strived for righteousness but missed it. They have stumbled over the stone. Is this stone obedient trust (Habakkuk 2:4) or the cross of Christ (1 Corinthians 1:23)? Or both?

Paul wants Israel to be saved. They have such a "zeal for God," but that zeal is "unenlightened" (Romans 10:2). Christ Jesus is the end of the Law—a troublesome expression because "end" can mean goal or termination. Many take Paul to mean Christ ends or terminates the Law for believers; but he probably means Christ is the completion, the fulfillment of the ancestors, the Exodus, the commandments, the monarchy,

NOTES, REFLECTIONS, AND QUESTIONS

NOTES, REFLECTIONS, AND QUESTIONS

the Temple, the land of promise, the prophets. Christ is the righteousness of God toward whom all covenant history has pointed. Trying themselves to establish right relationship with God, or believing they have it by birth, Israel is not able to yield in faith to God's new act in Christ.

Paul used a quotation from Moses to make a point (10:6; Deuteronomy 30:11-14). Moses' reference was to the Law, which was close by. We don't have to search for it; it is near at hand. So is Christ. We don't have to search. The Lord has come near to us. Notice that Paul leans on Moses literally: Just as Torah is on the *lips* and in the *heart* (30:14), so "if you confess with your lips that Jesus is Lord and believe in your heart that God raised him from the dead, you will be saved" (Romans 10:9). Just as God is no respecter of persons with wrath, so God is no respecter of persons with redemption. Just as there is no distinction in sin (3:22-23), so there is no distinction in salvation (10:12-13). Paul takes Joel 2:32 at face value and understands calling on the name of the Lord as the act of trusting God and God's deed in Christ. Those who live, Jew or Gentile, will live by the Spirit, not by inheritance.

The Wild Olive Shoot

Has God then rejected Israel? Paul drives his point home: "By no means!" (Romans 11:1). Paul is an Israelite, yet Paul is an apostle. When Elijah thought he was all alone, God reminded him that seven thousand others were faithful (11:2-4; 1 Kings 19:10, 18). When destruction came upon Israel and Judah, a remnant returned to Jerusalem, for God made "straight in the desert a highway" (Isaiah 40:3). All this work was done by grace, by a gracious God (Romans 11:6). Some of Israel have found grace; others have resisted (11:7-8).

But God works for good in all things. Resistance by Israel has opened the gates of grace to others. "Through their stumbling salvation has come to the Gentiles" (11:11). The covenant people of God are like an old olive tree. Some branches have broken off; and a new shoot from a wild olive (Gentile Christians) has been grafted in, sharing the rich root (traditions) of the olive tree, even though the shoot has no right to be there. Don't boast, Gentiles; just be thankful that through Christ you were grafted into the tree (11:18-19). "So do not become proud, but stand in awe" (11:20). In fact, if you become presumptuous, God will prune you off too (11:21-22)!

We have been disobedient, yet God has grafted us into the covenant people. So Israel, a part of whom are disobedient, will be grafted back in, one day. Their resistance has given Gentiles a place—"they are enemies of God for your sake" (11:28). Non-Jews should praise God for the mystery that gives us salvation. But the Jews are still the elected; "they are beloved" (11:28). Their calling of God is "irrevocable" (11:29). This mystery of salvation is beyond our comprehension. How "unsearchable" are God's judgments (11:33), how "inscrutable" God's ways.

MARKS OF OBEDIENT COMMUNITY

Right relationship with God comes not from our own striving for righteousness but by faith in God's saving act in Jesus Christ. Jew and Gentile are included in this mystery of God's salvation.

Describe your experience of coming to the realization that you could not, through your own efforts, be righteous.

In what sense did that experience free you to love God?

Paul assures us that God is keeping and will keep God's promises to Israel. How does that fact increase your trust in God's faithfulness?

We Christians are grafted into the root of Judaism. What richness do we draw from that root?

How can understanding of our connectedness break down walls of misunderstanding and hostility between Christians and Jews?

IF YOU WANT TO KNOW MORE

Write a few paragraphs that draw meaning out of Paul's olive tree analogy.

Letter: Write a letter as a group. Invite a Jewish rabbi or Jewish friend to talk with your group about current Jewish issues, to explain Torah and Jewish holy days, or to interpret the branches of contemporary Judaism.

NOTES, REFLECTIONS, AND QUESTIONS

Obedient community acknowledges that God is free to be God and to work out God's purposes as God determines.

THEREFORE

"I appeal to you therefore, brothers and sisters, by the mercies of God, to present your bodies as a living sacrifice, holy and acceptable to God, which is your spiritual worship."

—Romans 12:1

26 New Life in Christ

OUR HUMAN CONDITION

Freedom is in the air. So limits are passé. Rules are old-fashioned. Restrictions are uncomfortable. It's a competitive world, and we're on our own.

ASSIGNMENT

Therefore is pivotal; it signals the transition from theology to morality. Romans 1–11 explains God's work toward us, in us. Romans 12–16 tells how our faith should be manifest in our behavior.

Day 1 Romans 12 (marks of the Christian)
Day 2 Romans 13 (subject to authorities, love one another, put on Christ)
Day 3 Romans 14:1–15:6 (judge not, live to the Lord, don't cause another to stumble)
Day 4 Romans 15:7-33 (welcome one another, gospel for Jews and Gentiles, travel plans)
Day 5 Romans 16 (personal greetings)
Day 6 Read and respond to "The Word of the Lord" and "Marks of Obedient Community."
Day 7 Rest

PRAYER

Pray daily before study:

"I call to you, LORD; help me now!
Listen to me when I call to you.
Receive my prayer as incense,
my uplifted hands as an evening sacrifice"
(Psalm 141:1-2, TEV).

Prayer concerns for this week:

In Christ obedience is not an obligation to a never ending set of rules, but a joyful service in love to a person.

THEREFORE

Day 1 Romans 12 (marks of the Christian)

12:1-2 renewing of the mind gives discernment.

12:18 as far as it depends on you, live at peace with everyone.

12:21 Don't be overcome by evil, but overcome evil with good.

Day 2 Romans 13 (subject to authorities, love one another, put on Christ)

13:9 The golden rule.

Day 3 Romans 14:1–15:6 (judge not, live to the Lord, don't cause another to stumble)

14:19 Let us make every effort to do what leads to peace.

Day 4 Romans 15:7-33 (welcome one another, gospel for Jews and Gentiles, travel plans)

15:12 ...the gentiles will hope in Him.

Day 5 Romans 16 (personal greetings)

16:25-27 Blessings

Day 6 "The Word of the Lord" and "Marks of Obedient Community"

THE WORD OF THE LORD

NOTES, REFLECTIONS, AND QUESTIONS

Ethical behavior, for Paul, flows from faith like fresh water flows from a mountain spring. His powerful word *therefore* links what God has done for us in Christ to what we in Christ must do for God.

Paul had two kinds of theological opponents. One group, usually Gentile in background, wanted to believe their experience in Christ freed them from moral responsibility. Their view was, since they were saved, "all things are lawful" (1 Corinthians 6:12; 10:23). The other group, generally Jewish in background, anxiously held on to laws and traditions to make doubly sure they were right with God. Paul fought on both fronts, arguing that, in the unmerited grace of God in Christ, we are set right with God and therefore called into new life in a new community in a new age.

His *therefore* in Romans 12:1 and Galatians 5:1 is his hinge. The phrase "in view of God's mercy" (Romans 12:1, NIV) refers to everything Paul has written about righteousness and grace, reconciliation and faith in Romans 1–11. Now his ethical instructions begin. "Therefore . . . offer your bodies [selves] as living sacrifices, holy and pleasing to God—this is your spiritual act of worship" (12:1, NIV).

Paul remembers the animal sacrifices required under Torah. Sacrifices were brought as gifts to God. Sacrifice differed from slaughter because the blood, that is the "life" of the animal, was dashed against the altar. The "life" of the animal was offered to God on behalf of the lives of the people (Leviticus 17:2-7). Even as Paul wrote his letter, animal sacrifices were being offered for Israel in the Temple at Jerusalem. Paul, however, knew that animal sacrifice was no substitute for just and compassionate living.

Sacrificial Living

The Christian, with the enslavement to self-gratification finally broken by Jesus' sacrifice, is called to give an outpouring of self in daily, sacrificial living.

As a Pharisee, Paul was taught that daily obedience was the essence of keeping Torah. Pharisees, trying diligently to keep every last letter of the Law (Matthew 5:18), emphasized that the Law was to be kept in even the smallest aspect of life. God is everywhere; obedience should be everywhere. Now in Christ, obedience is not an obligation to a never-ending set of rules but a joyful service in love to a Person. Now, that joy, that sacrificial service, should pervade every room in the house of life. Once, all the "members" of our physical, mental, and spiritual bodies had been "instruments of wickedness." Now we present those same "members" as "instruments of righteousness" (Romans 6:12-13).

Just as our hearts have been changed (the Law now written upon them), so our behavior will be "transformed" (12:2). Unbelievers cannot see health and joy in godly behavior; their minds are blinded (2 Corinthians 4:4). But Christians think differently if their minds are renewed. Faith not only leads to life; it is life. Love is better than hate; integrity is better than lies; self-giving is better than greed. The power to live the godly life comes from Christ's cross and resurrection and our participation in it. It comes from the reign of God, hurling itself toward us. It comes from the Spirit of Jesus Christ in our hearts. People who are being transformed can see, can hear, can "discern what is the will of God" (Romans 12:2).

One Body, Many Members

The human body is an analogy for the church (Romans 12:4-5). To the Corinthians, Paul wrote, "The eye cannot say to the hand, 'I have no need of you' " (1 Corinthians 12:21). So the Roman Christians ought not to think of themselves more highly than they ought to think (Romans 12:3). Paul is less concerned about being important than he is about building up the body. Which gifts are more significant—healing? teaching? leading? giving? None. They are like eyes and ears, hands and feet; all are needed, all gifts for which the whole body is grateful. Therefore we ought to "love one another with mutual affection; outdo one another in showing honor" (12:10). Every Christian is a vital part of the body of believers. No one lives faithfully alone.

Why does Paul stress harmony in the fellowship (12:16)? Because the community is the foretaste of the messianic banquet. If God is at work creating a new heaven and a new earth where the entire cosmos will live in peace, we are to live like that now, insofar as we are able.

Paul knows God's wrath will stand against evil, judge it, condemn it, destroy it. Therefore, we are not to "repay anyone evil for evil" (12:17). We are to "leave room for the wrath of God" (12:19). Not only that; we are to do good to our enemies, feed them when they are hungry (12:20). Where did Paul learn this? From his tradition. A proverb of Israel reads,

> "If your enemies are hungry, give them bread to eat;
>   and if they are thirsty, give them water to drink;
> for you will heap coals of fire on their heads,
>   and the LORD will reward you" (Proverbs 25:21-22).

With kindness you may win your enemy over.

Governing Authorities

We might think Paul, in frequent trouble with the authorities, would be an advocate of civil disobedience. Not so, because Paul understood sin. No society can tolerate anarchy. Human greed left to its own devices will destroy everything. Look at the looting and violence when an earthquake or hurricane ravages a city and overwhelms authorities. People go crazy with corruption. No, Paul, Roman citizen—soon to be in a Roman jail—knew that civil governments are *servants* of God (not God) to keep order (Romans 13:4, 6). So be respect-

NOTES, REFLECTIONS, AND QUESTIONS

ful; give proper honor; pay your taxes. Let Christians, even if misunderstood, even if persecuted, respect authority.

Is any room allowed for disobedience? Yes, if fulfillment of God's will, the mission of the gospel, is at stake. Paul was whipped, stoned, and imprisoned for his preaching, teaching, and healing; but he continued his work undeterred.

Paul felt he was violating no law, Jewish or Roman. He always spoke respectfully before the magistrates, accepting any punishment they meted out. If it had not been for Roman soldiers and Roman fairness, Jewish leaders or angry mobs more than once would have destroyed Paul. Nearly five hundred soldiers escorted him from Jerusalem to Caesarea by night to avoid the forty zealots who swore to kill him (Acts 23:12-13, 23). Roman restraint held back the mob.

Paul interpreted the suffering he experienced as a messenger of God, working under Roman authority, in three ways: Suffering for the gospel caused some people to be converted; it gave glory to God. Suffering mixed his life's blood with the shed blood of Christ and with the blood of fellow Christians. Suffering paled before the glory that was yet to come (Romans 8:18). So Paul's message was to obey civil and criminal law, honor and respect people in authority, pay fees and taxes (13:5-7). Meanwhile, stubbornly continue healing, praying, preaching, and teaching. Later Christians, when bloody Roman persecutions became intolerable, prayed for the destruction of the evil empire ("Babylon" in Revelation); but they fought it with martyrs' blood, not with the sword.

Has God's Law been repealed? No, the Ten Commandments are eternally valid. As Torah itself said, and as Jesus and Paul reminded, the commandments are summed up thus: "You shall love the Lord your God with all your heart, and with all your soul, and with all your mind, and with all your strength" (Mark 12:29-30; Deuteronomy 6:5) and "Love your neighbor as yourself" (Mark 12:31; Leviticus 19:18). Love fulfills the Law (Romans 13:10).

Remember, wrote Paul, "Let us live honorably as in the day" (13:13), that is, in God's future that will bring salvation. Circling in Jewish-Christian thought was the notion of conflict between darkness and light (13:11-13). The believers are not fools living in debauchery, doing the works of darkness. To live in Christ means to live on a higher plane, in the light. Christ, the Lamb of God, who is coming soon, will usher in a world so filled with his light there will be no need for sun or moon. "There will be no night there" (Revelation 21:23-25). Therefore, "put on the armor of light" (Romans 13:12).

Religious Observances

Differences of opinion emerged among Jewish Christians over religious observances related to food and holy days. Paul emphasized the joy of fellowship and love. Don't judge; don't criticize; don't downgrade one another. Some still lit a candle

NOTES, REFLECTIONS, AND QUESTIONS

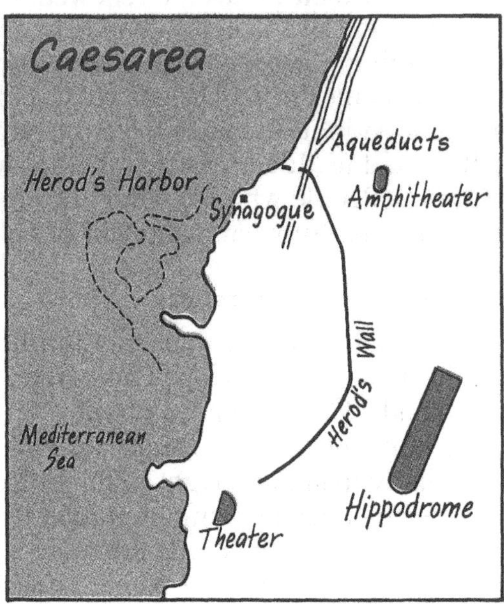

From 22–10 B.C. Herod the Great built the city of Caesarea, including a new stacked-stone harbor, on the site of an old Phoenician port. The capital of Roman government in Palestine for over six hundred years, Caesarea was a thriving travel center in Paul's time, the main port of arrival and departure for Paul's missionary journeys. He was in prison there for two years before he went to Rome (Acts 23:31-35; 24:27).

at sundown on sabbath. Some said special prayers on Yom Kippur or Passover. Some recited the Jewish laments at funerals. Some got up early to say Resurrection prayers each Sunday. Some were vegetarians, not eating meat. Some would touch no wine. Let them be (Romans 14:4). Paul's point is this: Whatever the practice, respect it because each person is trying to live that way "in honor of the Lord" (14:6).

The danger is not in scruples or customs; it is in violating community. "Why do you pass judgment on your brother or sister?" (14:10). Paul's concern is that a person can cause someone else to lose salvation. How? By provoking the scrupulous to eat even if they do not believe they are free to do so. "We will all stand before the judgment seat of God" (14:10). God is merciful; let us be merciful.

Therefore, not only refrain from judging, but more, "never . . . put a stumbling block or hindrance in the way of another" (14:13). Don't violate your own conscience. In your freedom, don't trample on the sensitive conscience or weakness of others. "It is good not to . . . do anything that makes your brother or sister stumble" (14:21). Remember, "Christ has welcomed you"—Jew and Gentile, with all your differences in belief and practice. Therefore, "welcome one another" (15:7). Paul quotes the Psalms, Deuteronomy, and Isaiah (Wisdom, Law, Prophets) to show salvation extended to everyone (15:9-12). God indeed is holding out welcoming hands all day long (10:21; Isaiah 65:1-2).

Mission to Spain

Paul has "written . . . rather boldly" to a congregation he has never met (Romans 15:15). His reason? He has been called "to be a minister of Christ Jesus to the Gentiles in the priestly service of the gospel of God" (15:16). The Roman church did not ask for the letter; they didn't ask for Paul's advice. Paul is simply living out his mission that came directly from the Lord.

But now we learn something about Paul we have not known before. He has preached all over Asia Minor, throughout Greece (15:19). His ambition was to start new work. He did not want to "build on someone else's foundation" (15:20). He was an evangelist, a missionary. Paul wanted to teach people who had never heard the gospel. He quotes part of the Servant passage from Isaiah 52:15:

> "Those who have never been told of him shall see,
> and those who have never heard of him shall
> understand" (Romans 15:21).

Now we know. Paul wants to go to Rome to set up a base of operations for the west, to go where no evangelist has gone, to take the gospel to Spain.

Without the projected mission to Spain, Paul would not have written the Letter to the Romans. But why Spain? Spain was his ultimate goal because it was Gentile territory. Spain

NOTES, REFLECTIONS, AND QUESTIONS

had few Jews. A mission there would fulfill his call to be an apostle to the Gentiles. Then, in the divine economy, the conversion of the Gentiles would stir up jealousy among the Jews, and eventually bring their conversion. That prize would satisfy his spiritual quest to bring his people home to God in Christ.

A western base of operations in Rome required two things—a sound theology (Romans 1–11) and a harmonious relationship between Jewish and Gentile Christians (Romans 14–16).

Spiritually grounded, the church in Rome would support Paul's missionary enterprise. He would go to the edge of the map, completing his life by creating wholly Gentile churches.

Describe opportunities you have had to teach the gospel to those who have never heard it or do not know or understand it.

Paul closes his letter with his travel hopes (15:28-29) and with a poignant plea for prayer. God willing, he will take the offering to Jerusalem, then set sail for Rome on his way to Spain. His prayers usually ask only for boldness to proclaim the gospel; but now he prays about human situations, people's attitudes. In the name of Jesus, by the love of the Holy Spirit, please pray with me "that I may be rescued from the unbelievers in Judea" (Paul knew he was going into trouble in Jerusalem) "and that my ministry to Jerusalem may be acceptable to the saints" (15:30-31). Paul was afraid the offering from Gentile hands might be rejected by Judean Jewish Christians and that unity would be shattered. What an appeal for prayer! What was the outcome? (See Acts 21:7–28:31.)

Greetings to Rome

Twenty-seven people are named in the greeting in Romans 16:1-16. Many we know nothing about; others, we know only what the text tells us. Paul urges the people to greet one another for him with a holy kiss of peace (16:16). Others, including his secretary, Tertius, join him in sending greetings, for Paul not only wants harmony within a congregation but fellowship throughout the worldwide church.

Paul ends his profound letter of witness and encouragement with a soaring benediction: "To the only wise God, through Jesus Christ, to whom be the glory forever! Amen" (16:27).

MARKS OF OBEDIENT COMMUNITY

The faith community looks and acts differently from the world. We are motivated by grace to handle financial affairs

NOTES, REFLECTIONS, AND QUESTIONS

Obedient community, renewed in mind and transformed in purpose, offers itself daily in joyful service to others—a fragrant sacrifice of obedience to Christ.

with integrity, sexual relationships with fidelity, negotiations with honesty. We care about the welfare of children and the strength of family life. We perceive the human body to be a temple of the Holy Spirit and therefore resist all that would damage it. Possessions are a gift to be used to help a needy world.

Our sacred moments—baptism, Holy Communion, weddings, and funerals—underline our teachings and our practices. We fail to live out Christ's way, but we never stop trying.

What are some ways the faith community thinks and acts differently from the world?

Caring for the neglected / marginalized folks.

In what areas of living do you sometimes experience a pull back to old habits, to unchristian behavior?

unforgiving, uncharitable, thoughts, acts

Tell of an experience, yours or someone else's, of a life transformed by a renewed mind.

Sermons transform lives through thoughts refinement.

Tell another experience of a congregation transformed by a renewed mind.

As you grow older, where have you encountered new challenges to the Christian life, fresh temptations?

What helps you most in trying to live out Romans 12?

Staying close to body of church.

IF YOU WANT TO KNOW MORE

Letter: Write a few paragraphs in your own words that summarize characteristics of Christian living. Turn them into a letter to a young person.

NOTES, REFLECTIONS, AND QUESTIONS

GROW

"The fruit of the Spirit is love, joy, peace, patience, kindness, generosity, faithfulness, gentleness, and self-control. There is no law against such things."

—Galatians 5:22-23

27 Fruit of the Holy Spirit

OUR HUMAN CONDITION

We long for a presence, a power, or a purpose in our lives that will bring peace and contentment. We try so hard, but joy escapes us.

ASSIGNMENT

Galatia was a Roman province in the middle of Asia Minor. Paul started several churches there. They dated to his first missionary journey with Barnabas. This letter was designed to be circulated among the fledgling churches in that area. Read passionately, noting the poignant personal plea for them to remain free in Christ and to exhibit the glorious fruit of the Spirit.

Memorize Galatians 5:1 or 5:22-23.

Day 1 Acts 13–14; 15:36–16:10; 18:22-23 (missionary journeys involving Galatia)
Day 2 Galatians 1–2 (Paul's defense of his apostleship, recognized in Jerusalem, rebuke of Cephas)
Day 3 Galatians 3 (salvation by faith or Law, promise to Abraham, purpose of the Law)
Day 4 Galatians 4 (slavery under the Law, Hagar and Sarah allegory)
Day 5 Galatians 5–6 (called to freedom, fruit of the Spirit)
Day 6 Read and respond to "The Word of the Lord" and "Marks of Obedient Community."
Day 7 Rest

PRAYER

Pray daily before study:

"You will show me the path that leads to life;
your presence fills me with joy
and brings me pleasure forever" (Psalm 16:11, TEV).

Prayer concerns for this week:

GROW

Day 1 Acts 13–14; 15:36–16:10; 18:22-23 (missionary journeys involving Galatia)

Day 2 Galatians 1–2 (Paul's defense of his apostleship, recognized in Jerusalem, rebuke of Cephas)

Day 3 Galatians 3 (salvation by faith or Law, promise to Abraham, purpose of the Law)

3:30 He redeemed us from the curse of the law by become a curse for us
Mark 15: My God, my God, why have you forsaken me?

Day 4 Galatians 4 (slavery under the Law, Hagar and Sarah allegory)

Adoption: until you inherit, you are childlike, a minor
God so loved the world, that He sent his son. God's initiative.

Day 5 Galatians 5–6 (called to freedom, fruit of the Spirit)

5:1 For freedom Christ has set us free stand firm therefore, and do not submit again to the yoke of slavery.

Christ + is bad.

Day 6 "The Word of the Lord" and "Marks of Obedient Community"

THE WORD OF THE LORD

The believers were first called "Christians" in Antioch of Syria (Acts 11:26). "While they were worshiping the Lord and fasting, the Holy Spirit said, 'Set apart for me Barnabas and Saul for the work to which I have called them.' Then after fasting and praying they laid their hands on them and sent them off" (13:2-3).

Paul's first missionary trip started by ship to Cyprus, continued up the southern rim of Asia Minor (Turkey) into the south-central region called Galatia. On the second and third missionary journeys, Paul left Antioch of Syria by land, walked or rode a donkey to his home city of Tarsus, then went through the mountain pass called the "Cilician Gates," and on to the fertile plain of Galatia. Paul started churches in ancient towns like Derbe, Lystra, Iconium, and Antioch of Pisidia. These churches were the first fruits of his labor. No wonder he loved them so much. He felt like a mother giving birth to her children (Galatians 4:19).

Letter to the Galatians

We could have studied Paul's letter to the Galatian churches before we studied Romans, for surely it was written earlier. But now, after Romans, we have a strong understanding of Paul's theology to help us. Galatians differs from other letters because Paul is so upset. This is no courteously composed letter to people he did not know. Galatians is an angry, abrupt letter from a spiritual father to his children. Paul loved the Galatians so much; he wished the tone of his letter could be different, but he was deeply troubled (Galatians 4:20).

Even the opening of Galatians is different. Paul alludes to his concerns in the salutation, then skips the usual thanksgiving and prayer and launches immediately into his concern with an intense burst of feeling.

Other preachers were modifying the gospel he had so carefully proclaimed (1:6). Paul could be tolerant of preachers who were vain or competitive or self-serving if they were faithful to the gospel (Philippians 1:15-18). But concerning those who twisted Christian freedom so people were again slaves to rules and sin and wrath, Paul wrote, "I wish those who unsettle you would castrate themselves!" (Galatians 5:12).

Why was circumcision such a big deal? For Paul it was the make-or-break issue of salvation. Judaizers were Jewish Christians who said, "Yes, but." They insisted that Gentiles must become proselytes to Judaism as well as believers in Christ. They said it would be better if the Gentile male converts were circumcised. Then they would, for sure, be a part of Judaism's promises. It seemed a rather easy way to be a first-class Christian.

NOTES, REFLECTIONS, AND QUESTIONS

This silver chalice, probably used in early celebrations of the Eucharist, was found in Antioch of Syria and shows Christ and the apostles. It dates from the fourth or fifth century A.D.

The Cilician Gates, a narrow pass through the Taurus Mountains, and probably a footpath in prehistoric times, provided a corridor through Cilicia between the Mediterranean Sea and the interior of Asia Minor. The commerce that flowed through the pass provided the wealth for Paul's hometown of Tarsus.

The Whole Law

In addition to becoming moralists who are "justifying" themselves, the Judaizers are walking right back under the Law (Galatians 5:3). If they want to live under part of the Law, they must live under all of the Law and therefore under the curse when they fail. "Cursed is everyone who does not observe and obey all the things written in the book of the law" (3:10; see Deuteronomy 27:26). "If you will only obey the LORD your God, by diligently observing all his commandments," then you will be justified (28:1). Once you walk back under self-justification, you are back in sin, in wrath, under the law of perfect righteousness. Paul insists we are either under one authority or the other. There is no middle ground, no compromise, no possibility of having a little self-justification and a little grace (Galatians 2:16).

If salvation under the Law were possible, "Christ died for nothing" (2:21). Paul recalled that Torah links wrath to an execution: "Anyone hung on a tree is under God's curse" (Deuteronomy 21:23). Jesus experienced that curse. "Christ redeemed us from the curse of the law by becoming a curse for us" (Galatians 3:13). But his death was futile if we can earn our righteousness. Not only is Jesus' crucifixion in vain; so is our "death" in him. Paul's preaching is in vain!

Promise to Abraham

The issue is this: How are Gentiles included in the promise to Abraham and his "seed"? Judaizers said, by becoming part of the ethnic people of God, by circumcision. Paul said, by being incorporated into the seed, that is, into Christ, by baptism (Galatians 3:26-27).

The apostle reminds the Galatians that righteousness was reckoned to Abraham by faith (3:6). Abraham's offspring, "seed" (singular), refers to Christ, says Paul (3:16); and Abraham's faith and Christ Jesus are for the Gentiles, the nations of the world (3:8, 14). A legal will, once it is ratified and notarized, cannot be changed by other people. The law of Moses, which is holy, was given four hundred thirty years after Abraham, but did not nullify the original covenant promise (3:17). The Law was added to hold down transgressions; but salvation would come, as promised, through Abraham's seed, Jesus, and through faith alone (3:19, 29).

Paul illustrates. Children, heirs to but not yet holders of property, under the rules of parents or guardians, are really like slaves. So too those under the Law. But in Christ we are no longer slaves to sin; we are in relationship to "Abba! Father!" and heirs to all the glories of the coming Kingdom (4:6-7). Do you want to go back to being under the guardianship of the Law? Already you are worried about which Jewish holidays to honor, which foods to eat, which traditions to follow. "I am afraid that my work for you may have been wasted" (4:11).

NOTES, REFLECTIONS, AND QUESTIONS

The long discussion of Sarah and Hagar (4:21-31) is confusing. As Paul states, this reference is an allegory, a way of reading a story where its details stand for deeper meaning; so to hear Paul's point, disregard the original story. In this allegory Hagar, Abraham's slave wife, and her son Ishmael symbolize slavery under the Law. Sarah, wife of promise, and her son Isaac symbolize freedom under the gospel. "Drive out the slave [legalism]" (4:30). "We are children, not of the slave but of the free woman [grace]. For freedom Christ has set us free" (4:31–5:1).

Paul is devastated that his churches, once so full of joy, of prayer, of Jew and Gentile together, are now led astray. "You were running well; who prevented you from obeying the truth?" (5:7).

What upset Paul so much was that he thought circumcision for Gentile converts had been laid to rest by the Jerusalem Council (Acts 15). He thought he had settled it again when he confronted Peter in Antioch of Syria (Galatians 2:11-14). Now, probably under the influence of some Jewish Christians from Jerusalem or Damascus, Jewish law was being advocated in Galatia.

When Paul speaks of living by the flesh, he does not mean merely sins of passion such as sexual sins or acts of violence. "Flesh" is the old Adam, subject to the law of sin and death, the reality of humanity living to serve the creature. Notice that Paul's list of sins of the flesh includes mental, physical, and spiritual sins—a caution to those who in arrogance condemn physical or gross sins of passion and gloss over spiritual sins. If we live in the Spirit of Christ, we cannot live in the spirit of selfishness.

Paul believes each Christian receives the Spirit, the power to live in Christ. By dying to sin and being raised in Resurrection hope, the Christian lives in a new Spirit-filled realm.

The Galatians received the Holy Spirit when they believed. That gift is an important element in Paul's appeal. "Did you receive the Spirit by doing the works of the law or by believing what you heard?" (Galatians 3:2). Apparently the Galatians valued the Spirit, but Paul points out that "if you are led by the Spirit, you are not subject to the law" (5:18) and implies that it is the Spirit, not the Law, that deals effectively with "the desires of the flesh" (5:16).

Fruit of the Spirit

In other letters, Paul identified *gifts* of the Spirit for serving the community. "We have gifts that differ according to the grace given to us: prophecy, in proportion to faith; ministry, in ministering; the teacher, in teaching; the exhorter, in exhortation; the giver, in generosity; the leader, in diligence; the compassionate, in cheerfulness" (Romans 12:6-8). A similar list of gifts of the Holy Spirit was sent to Corinth: apostles, prophets, teachers, workers of miracles, healers, speakers in tongues,

NOTES, REFLECTIONS, AND QUESTIONS

interpreters of spiritual experience (1 Corinthians 12:28-30).

Paul now stresses the *fruit* of the Spirit (Galatians 5:22-23). Paul describes Christians as those in whom the Spirit is free to bear fruit. That fruit is not to be confused with virtues Christians can select and cultivate on their own. The fruit of the Spirit is a package of benefits that comes with the gift of the Spirit. Christians receive the Spirit as the source from which the fruit can grow and develop. Since the fruit has not been given with the Spirit, Christians cannot claim to possess it. Rather, as they live by the Spirit, they will come to know the delectable fruit that the Spirit produces with their active involvement.

What fruit has the Spirit produced in your life?

The Spirit within, like sap within a tree, brings forth fruit. Paul's own life and letters reflect the spirit of each one of these authentic marks of the Christian life.

Love. Each letter contains deep affection for the churches. Paul understood that love is an attitude, not an emotion. Love is a way of looking at life, not a feeling. "Love is patient; love is kind; love is not envious or boastful or arrogant or rude. It does not insist on its own way; it is not irritable or resentful; it does not rejoice in wrongdoing, but rejoices in the truth. It bears all things, believes all things, hopes all things, endures all things" (1 Corinthians 13:4-7).

Love, the first-named *fruit* of the Spirit, weaves all the *gifts* of the Spirit into a perfect harmony (13:1, 8). Can we love unless we first receive love? No. We drink deeply of Christ's love, and then we become more loving. "In this is love, not that we loved God but that he loved us. . . . since God loved us so much, we also ought to love one another" (1 John 4:10-11).

Joy. No higher note of joy is sounded than Paul and Silas's singing hymns at midnight in the Philippian jail (Acts 16:25). Paul wrote back to Philippi from another jail, "Rejoice in the Lord always; again I will say, Rejoice" (Philippians 4:4). Paul encouraged Christians to "give thanks in all circumstances," for praise and thanksgiving seem to walk hand in hand with joy (1 Thessalonians 5:18).

Peace. In a worldly sense, Paul seldom had a moment's peace. In a heavenly sense, he was at peace with God, at peace with his calling, at peace with all eventualities. "I have learned to be content with whatever I have. I know what it is to have little, and I know what it is to have plenty. In any and all circumstances I have learned the secret of being well-fed and of going hungry, of having plenty and of being in need. I can do all things through him who strengthens me" (Philippians 4:11-13). The Holy Spirit gives us an inner peace with life, because right relationships bring harmony. Peace is not a

NOTES, REFLECTIONS, AND QUESTIONS

stagnant backwater sheltered from the mainstream of life. Peace happens in life's excitement when we live God's way.

"The fruit of righteousness will be peace;
the effect of righteousness will be quietness
and confidence forever" (Isaiah 32:17, NIV).

Patience. One suspects Paul was impatient by nature. As a student he "advanced in Judaism beyond many . . . of the same age" (Galatians 1:14). As a young Pharisee, he was impatient to drive out believers. He certainly was driven to preach the gospel in as many places as possible. Yet filled with the Spirit, he did not rail at his jailers while in prison or complain of God's providence when doors of opportunity closed. To the Romans he wrote, "Be patient in suffering" (Romans 12:12). Clearly, Paul daily expected the return of Christ Jesus in glory. Yet he patiently warned against setting a date. Patience waits for *kairos,* God's good time.

Kindness. One of Paul's great acts of kindness was to send the slave Onesimus back to his master, Philemon, with a letter so gracious, so appealing in love and generosity that Philemon had little choice but to forgive the slave and receive him into his household as a Christian brother. "Love is kind," wrote Paul (1 Corinthians 13:4). Kindness often comes in tiny deeds. No law forbids it (Galatians 5:23). Anyone can do an act of kindness.

Generosity. Paul gave up marriage and children. He offered himself totally for the gospel. He extended hospitality wherever possible. His concern for the poor in Jerusalem caused him to implore the Corinthians to be generous, "for God loves a cheerful giver" (2 Corinthians 9:7). His commitment to this offering took him back to Jerusalem though trouble awaited him there.

Faithfulness. Here the word means fidelity. Of all the fruit, none expresses Paul so well as steadfast, unwavering faithfulness. Second Timothy 4:7 might well speak for him: "I have fought the good fight, I have finished the race, I have kept the faith." "Faithfulness" in the Bible mostly refers to God. The psalmist praises God's "steadfast love in the morning" and God's "faithfulness by night" (Psalm 92:2). In faith, believers lean their full weight on the faithfulness of God.

Gentleness. This word means humility, or gentleness in dealing with others, as in Galatians 6:1: "My friends, if anyone is detected in a transgression, you who have received the Spirit should restore such a one in a spirit of gentleness." Paul could breathe fire (as shown in his Letter to the Galatians); yet he could be as gentle as "a nurse tenderly caring for her own children" (1 Thessalonians 2:7).

Self-control. God does some things; we do some things. We must not be "tossed to and fro and blown about by every wind of doctrine, by people's trickery" (Ephesians 4:14). Our anger or impulsiveness cannot be allowed to take us off track. Paul treated his body as if he were a soldier or an athlete, totally under control. "Athletes exercise self-control in all

NOTES, REFLECTIONS, AND QUESTIONS

things. . . . So I do not run aimlessly, nor do I box as though beating the air; but I punish my body and enslave it" (1 Corinthians 9:25-27). The Spirit, divine power given, produces not irresponsibility as in "the Spirit made me do it" but self-control, power over the self.

Paul pushes his point to the maximum. None of these qualities is against the Law! (Galatians 5:23). In the fruit of the Spirit, you can go to excess!

MARKS OF OBEDIENT COMMUNITY

We, in the faith community, receive the Holy Spirit like a gentle rain from heaven. The Spirit frees us from legalism and nurtures within us the Christlike fruit of the Spirit.

What could take away our freedom and lead us back into a restrictive legalism?

Which is the greater danger to our church today—legalism or lack of moral restraint? Say why you think so.

What avenues are open for your congregation to be freshly energized by the Holy Spirit?

Which fruit of the Spirit do you especially wish would grow in your life?

What do you need to do to allow the Spirit to produce that fruit in you?

IF YOU WANT TO KNOW MORE

Observe a Christian who reveals a fruit of the Spirit in a special way. Talk with that person and ask where the fruit comes from, how it is nourished.

Letter: Write a letter telling a friend about the Holy Spirit. Describe the gifts and the fruit of the Holy Spirit. Tell how you have received the Spirit and how the Spirit is helping you grow. Or indicate you would like to experience the Holy Spirit.

NOTES, REFLECTIONS, AND QUESTIONS

Obedient community opens itself to the Holy Spirit's working freely in its midst.

NEW LIFE

"Seek the things that are above, where Christ is, seated at the right hand of God. Set your minds on things that are above, not on things that are on earth, for you have died, and your life is hidden with Christ in God."

—Colossians 3:1-3

28 Christ Above All

OUR HUMAN CONDITION

We are fascinated by zodiac signs and new age ideas, biorhythms and crystals, generic spirituality. We want to know how our lives are ordered, whether this is a good day or not. There must be secret wisdom out there to guide us.

ASSIGNMENT

Pretend you are Tychicus (Colossians 4:7), accompanied by former slave Onesimus (4:9), out from Ephesus, hand-delivering this letter and reading it to the river churches in Asia Minor. Read the letter aloud to someone else. Look for philosophical struggles, the cosmic authority of Christ.

Day 1 Colossians 1–4
Day 2 Colossians 1:1–2:5 (supremacy of Christ)
Day 3 Colossians 2:6-23 (warning against false teaching); Psalm 81 (summons to festival worship)
Day 4 Colossians 3–4 (new life in Christ, duties of the new life)
Day 5 Philemon (Paul's plea for Onesimus)
Day 6 Read and respond to "The Word of the Lord" and "Marks of Obedient Community."
Day 7 Rest

PRAYER

Pray daily before study:

"All your creatures, LORD, will praise you,
and all your people will give you thanks.
They will speak of the glory of your royal power
and tell of your might,
so that everyone will know your mighty deeds
and the glorious majesty of your kingdom.
Your rule is eternal" (Psalm 145:10-13, TEV).

Prayer concerns for this week:

New Life

Day 1 Colossians 1–4

Day 4 Colossians 3–4 (new life in Christ, duties of the new life)

Day 2 Colossians 1:1–2:5 (supremacy of Christ)

Day 5 Philemon (Paul's plea for Onesimus)

Day 3 Colossians 2:6-23 (warning against false teaching); Psalm 81 (summons to festival worship)

Day 6 "The Word of the Lord" and "Marks of Obedient Community"

THE WORD OF THE LORD

Colossae was a small market town on the Lycus River in Asia Minor, just a few miles from the more important towns of Laodicea and Hierapolis. Colossae was a center for wool trade; Laodicea, capital of the Phrygian region; and Hierapolis, a trade city strategically situated at the juncture of the Maeander and the Lycus rivers.

Paul, in his missionary travels, consistently bypassed these towns. He pioneered farther east in the great cities of the Galatian plain and farther west in the seaport area of Ephesus. These three towns were evangelized by Paul's convert and co-worker, Epaphras (Colossians 4:12-13), who was part of the beehive of missionary activity in and out of Ephesus.

Tradition says this letter, one of the "prison letters," came from Paul in Rome near the end of his ministry—an older, seasoned apostle. The anger he had focused on his intimate friends in Galatia is not pointed at strangers in Colossae. New problems, more Gentile than Jewish, required new interpretations. The fresh theological emphasis in Colossians 1:15-20 is an early Christian hymn glorifying Christ, much like the hymn Paul quoted in Philippians 2.

Some scholars think someone other than Paul wrote Colossians and Ephesians (which address similar problems). They argue that Paul's thoughts, thoroughly saturating the minds of co-workers, have been placed in this letter to honor their teacher and address church issues ten to twenty years after Paul's death. Certainly our Bible would be impoverished without Colossians, for it sets forth the whole system of heavenly doctrine of Christ.

Problems in Colossae

The form is Paul: Greetings from Paul and Timothy to God's people in Colossae, grace and peace. The prayers of gratitude mention their faith and love. As usual, the prayers start the theme. The new converts are playing with new wisdom, special "knowledge" and "philosophy," prompting the prayer "that you may be filled with the knowledge of God's will in all spiritual wisdom and understanding" (Colossians 1:9). The prayer says God "has rescued us from the power of darkness" (1:13), the power of Satan overcome by Christ. "Forgiveness of sins" (Colossians 1:14), not normally Paul's phrase, is fully imbedded in the gospel, implicitly included in justification, and strong in Jesus' ministry.

The problem in Colossae appears to have been a blend of various influences. (Recall the prophets preached against syncretism—blending pagan religions with Israel's religion.)

Neo-Platonic philosophy (2:8) left God perfect and aloof, pure reality but totally inaccessible. God showers the world with random resemblances—angels, divinities who give hints of God. Jesus could have been one of these.

Gnosticism, from the Greek *gnosis,* means "knowledge."

NOTES, REFLECTIONS, AND QUESTIONS

This philosophy, growing in influence in first and second centuries A.D., taught a separation between God, who is spirit, and matter, which is evil. If the created world is evil, the spirit's task is to escape. If the body is evil, the soul must be freed. Centuries before, Plato had taught that the body, including sexuality, emotion, hunger, and pain, is holding us back. These things are not from God.

How foreign these notions were to Judaism and Christianity, both of which insisted God is Creator of all that is. Gnosticism led Christians astray in two ways: (1) The body was to be subdued, denied, creating a form of asceticism. Severe fasting, abstinence from meat or wine, sexual chastity, rough clothing marked the ascetic Christian. These ideas not only led strict Christians away from Christian freedom but induced them toward spiritual pride, self-congratulation, and separation from community. (2) Gnosticism caused some people to say the body was not important. They were saved spiritually; so whether they ate or drank, had sex or not, did not matter. Using this thinking as an excuse, libertine Christians drank wine to debauchery, ate to gluttony, fornicated, and committed adultery.

Greek mystery religions mixed with "knowledge" or "secret wisdom" from various philosophies. Participating in a special ritual, a secret initiation, took a person to a higher spiritual plane; in fact, the experience promised immortality. Again, this "knowledge," for Christians, led to elitism.

Astrology, the study of the sun, moon, and stars, had roots in ancient Persia and ancient Egypt. Astrology studied celestial occurrences to read omens, learn a person's destiny based on birth date, and discern influences on human affairs. The Greeks studied the zodiac as a science and associated stars, moon, planets, and signs with colors, plants, parts of the body, and precious stones. Stars were messengers from the gods. Stoic philosophy allied with astrology to create a fatalistic outlook. Modern concepts of biorhythms and theories of heredity and environment in some social sciences are similarly controlling. So are some theological views that God has ordained all that is and is to be. If we are totally controlled by forces acting upon us, all human freedom is taken away, all responsibility gone.

A final influence had a Jewish flavor, perhaps combining astrology with biblical references to the moon-based calendar and food laws. This strange blend of lore, law, and practice expressed an attitude that salvation in Christ was fine as far as it went. But there are other things that one must reckon with in order to be really saved. Such attitudes appear again and again among Christians.

Colossians Responds

The theological attack is total. Jesus Christ is the *eikon* (from which we get *icon*), the image of God. He is God made

NOTES, REFLECTIONS, AND QUESTIONS

NOTES, REFLECTIONS, AND QUESTIONS

visible. Moreover, God made everything through him. John's Gospel, perhaps also combatting the gnostics, declares, "In the beginning was the Word [*Logos*]. . . . He [Christ, the Word] was in the beginning with God. All things came into being through him, and without him not one thing came into being" (John 1:1-3). John affirms the biblical faith that "in the beginning . . . God created the heavens and the earth" (Genesis 1:1). Christ is preexistent, greater than any angel, and God through Christ (through the Word) created the universe, which is therefore good (1:31). Christ is the Lord over all other forces "visible and invisible, whether thrones or dominions or rulers or powers" (Colossians 1:16). He is Lord over them because he created them. So why go to them for knowledge? Go directly to him, for "in him all the fullness of God was pleased to dwell" (1:19).

Colossians does not mention the Word, but the thinking is much the same. The eternal Son mentioned in 1:18 became the human Jesus, in whom God's fullness dwelt. The preexistent one holds all things together. Yet somehow the cosmic powers rebelled; but in the Incarnation, cross, and Resurrection, Christ reconciled all things. In other words, the universe is no longer a hostile place. Christians do not have to placate the "powers" (1:16), and they can put away their horoscopes.

The Mystery of Christ

Now Christian gnostics who believed the body is evil began to say that Jesus couldn't have been completely human. He would have been a god who only looked like a human. He must have been an illusion, an "acting out" by God. Or else the divine Spirit left that human shell before the agony of the cross. Not so, declared Paul and the Gospel writers. He was "born of a woman" (Galatians 4:4). In the garden, his sweat became like blood (Luke 22:44). On the cross he cried, "I am thirsty" (John 19:28). Colossians says he made "peace through the blood of his cross" (Colossians 1:20). The estranged "he has now reconciled in his fleshly body through death" (1:22).

Not only did God's wisdom and truth (the Word) create the world; it entered the world in human form and accepted suffering and death. This concept was abhorrent to Jewish ideas of a triumphant Messiah, and it was foreign to Greek ideas of a perfect (and remote) God who neither touches nor experiences human frailty.

You talk about mystery? The mystery of Christ is to be proclaimed openly to the whole world. "The mystery that has been hidden throughout the ages and generations . . . has now been revealed to his [God's] saints" (1:25-26). The "mystery," full of glory, full of riches, is "Christ in you, the hope of glory" (1:27). The mystery is "Christ himself" (2:2)—the coming of God in human form, the Crucifixion and Resurrection, the believer's death and resurrection in Christ, the power of the Holy Spirit indwelling the believer's heart, and the promise of participation in Christ's final victory. In him "are hidden all the treasures of wisdom and knowledge" (2:3).

Do you need to go elsewhere to find knowledge? "See to it that no one takes you captive through philosophy and empty deceit" (2:8). How? By appealing to elemental spirits (probably not the four elements, earth, fire, air, and water, as in Greek thought, but heavenly spirits or powers such as angels, spiritual mysteries, rhythms of the calendar, constellations that affected life on earth). In Christ, God dwells in "fullness" (2:9). Christ is not one of many, needing completion. Christ is "head of every ruler and authority," including angels, constellations, rhythms of moon and planets (2:10). When you were spiritually circumcised (2:11), when you were baptized (2:12), you put off all fears, frustrations, and anxieties about your past and future. Christ nailed all the demands of the Law and all our fears about the future to the cross (2:14).

Therefore, don't be led astray by those people who want you to abstain from food, or observe new moons or festivals in order to be first-class religious people who cope successfully with cosmic powers (2:16).

"If you have been raised with Christ, . . . set your minds on things that are above" (Colossians 3:1-2). Some things must die—the self-seeking, self-glorifying sin of your old nature. The old self has corrupt sexual desires and angry, bitter attitudes. That old self is greedy (for power or money or sex); and greed is the worst form of self-worship, idolatry (3:5).

And the new self? Colossians 3:17 asks for a life that is wholly oriented to Christ. The cosmic powers are irrelevant.

Christian Households

The Letter to the Colossians addresses three elements of the social order—marriage, family, and slavery. To do so, it relies on a well-known pattern in Greco-Roman culture—the table (or list) of household duties, which mentions wives, husbands, slaves, children. Ephesians and First Peter also have such lists. But the New Testament writers modify the tradition by referring repeatedly to Christ and to Christian motivation.

Has the revolution gone too far? In the revolution, particularly among the Gentiles, some thought the second coming of Christ would be so soon that marriages should be dissolved. Women and men were together in the church, in Christ. But Christ's coming was delayed. Now some semblance of order was important. Marriage should be honored; social customs of propriety should be observed. For a patriarchal society, the instructions have an amazingly level hand. Wives are to be subject to their husbands "as is fitting in the Lord"; husbands are to love their wives (Colossians 3:18-19).

In a Gentile world where children were chattel, where their lives were literally under their parents' control, family life takes on the sanctity of a Jewish home. Christian children are to obey "in the Lord" (3:20). But again the balance. Fathers

NOTES, REFLECTIONS, AND QUESTIONS

Tables of household duties such as the list in Ephesians 5:21–6:9 are called *Haustafeln,* a scholarly term that means "rules of the house." Such lists were widely used in the first and second century A.D. to teach proper behavior. The New Testament writers used the traditional form but made their lists specific for Christian behavior. Two other lists are in Colossians 3:18–4:1 and 1 Peter 2:18–3:7. Lists in a similar style are in 1 Timothy 2:8-15; 5:1-2; 6:1-2; and Titus 2:1-10; 3:1.

(and mothers) are not to "provoke" (3:21, NRSV), "irritate" (3:21, TEV), or "embitter" (3:21, NIV) their children, because the children may be spiritually damaged. "They may lose heart" (3:21, NRSV) or "become discouraged" (3:21, TEV, NIV).

Slaves and Masters

When Paul wrote to Philemon requesting that his slave Onesimus be received back home, that home was Colossae (Colossians 4:9). Paul appealed to Philemon for grace and forgiveness "for my child, Onesimus" (Philemon 10). Observe the tenderness: "I am sending him, that is, my own heart, back to you" (verse 12). Then this amazing logic: "Perhaps this is the reason he was separated from you for a while, so that you might have him back forever, no longer as a slave but more than a slave, a beloved brother . . . both in the flesh and in the Lord" (verses 15-16).

Slavery was institutionalized all over the world in Old Testament and New Testament times. Runaway slaves could be punished and killed. Paul does not overtly condemn slavery, but he wrote, "There is no longer . . . slave and free; but Christ is all and in all" (Colossians 3:11). That truth will be actualized some day, but for now the instruction for slaves is to serve wholeheartedly as if serving Christ (3:22-24). When judgment comes, any wrongdoing you have received will be punished. You will stand on an equal footing before Christ, for "there is no partiality" with God (3:25). Again the balance. Masters, be just and fair "for you know that you also have a Master in heaven" (4:1).

Make Good Use of Every Opportunity

Colossians concludes with moral guidance. Pray. Keep alert. "Conduct yourselves wisely." One phrase jumps out—"making the most of the time" (Colossians 4:5), "making good use of every opportunity you have" (4:5, TEV). Is this not a parting volley at those who study the stars, waiting for a propitious time? Colossians says we do not need to read signs to know when to do good. Do the things of Christ today—full measure, with enthusiasm.

The greetings at the end are interesting: Tychicus, "faithful minister" who had been with the apostle in Macedonia (Acts 20:4; Colossians 4:7), will deliver the letter, give words of encouragement, and read the letter aloud in Colossae, Laodicea, and Heirapolis. Onesimus is joining him (4:9). If this is the slave, formerly of Philemon's household in Colossae, he is now free and a "beloved brother." Did Philemon do "even more" than Paul had asked and free Onesimus (Philemon 21)? Aristarchus (Colossians 4:10) is in jail with Paul. So is John Mark, who deserted Barnabas and Paul on their first journey but who has now received Paul's forgiveness, a fresh start, and full affirmation. These men, including Justus (Colossians 4:11),

NOTES, REFLECTIONS, AND QUESTIONS

In Paul's time, slaves constituted as much as twenty percent of the population of the Roman Empire. This first-century Roman slave badge reads, "Seize me if I should try to escape and send me back to my master."

were Jewish Christians. Epaphras (4:12), their founding evangelist, greets them. He is always praying for his churches (4:13). Luke the physician and Demas send greetings (4:14). All send greetings to a woman named Nympha and "the church in her house" (4:15). These were all Gentile Christians.

MARKS OF OBEDIENT COMMUNITY

The faith community is aware of philosophical fads, ancient or modern, that would take away our freedom in Christ. We work to understand and explain these heresies. We teach the sound doctrine of new life in Christ, helping others avoid idea traps that would enslave them. Disciples are learners, not "the wise ones."

How does the zodiac confuse Christian thinking?

In what ways does "new age" spirituality muddy Christian doctrine and morality?

How is it possible for us to be influenced by environment and heredity without being determined by them?

Identify notions or ideas that lead people astray today.

How do we use the gifts of the Spirit that come when we put on the "new self" to build up the body of Christ?

IF YOU WANT TO KNOW MORE

To understand the social revolution in Paul's time, read about family life in the Roman Empire.

Letter: Write a letter to the group or to yourself, comparing philosophical ideas currently circulating with the heresies alluded to by Paul.

NOTES, REFLECTIONS, AND QUESTIONS

Obedient community, spiritually centered in Christ the wisdom of God, gives first place to Christ in all things.

STAND

"Take up the whole armor of God, so that you may be able to withstand on that evil day, and having done everything, to stand firm."

—Ephesians 6:13

29 Whole Armor of God

OUR HUMAN CONDITION

The world seems not an orderly, dependable world but a world of massive outpourings of hatred and violence, holes in the ozone, planets crashing, birds and animals in conflict with bulldozers, rivers running yellow with chemicals or red with soil erosion. Hurricanes, tornadoes, earthquakes, and fires defy human sufficiency. Is the cosmos in chaos?

ASSIGNMENT

The sentences in Ephesians are long and complex. Break them into phrases. Compare particular verses in several translations. "The Word of the Lord" section requires the same sentence by sentence, phrase by phrase reading to get the richness. Notice Ephesians 1–3 is God's work; Ephesians 4–6 is our response.

Day 1 Ephesians 1 (spiritual blessings and power)
Day 2 Ephesians 2 (from death to life, one in Christ)
Day 3 Ephesians 3 (prayer for wisdom, gospel for the Gentiles)
Day 4 Ephesians 4:1–5:20 (unity in the body of Christ)
Day 5 Ephesians 5:21–6:24 (the Christian household, the whole armor of God)
Day 6 Read and respond to "The Word of the Lord" and "Marks of Obedient Community."
Day 7 Rest

PRAYER

Pray daily before study:
"All who find safety in you will rejoice;
they can always sing for joy.
Protect those who love you;
because of you they are truly happy.
You bless those who obey you, LORD;
your love protects them like a shield"
(Psalm 5:11-12, TEV).

Prayer concerns for this week:

Day 1 Ephesians 1 (spiritual blessings and power)

Day 2 Ephesians 2 (from death to life, one in Christ)

Day 3 Ephesians 3 (prayer for wisdom, gospel for the Gentiles)

Day 4 Ephesians 4:1–5:20 (unity in the body of Christ)

Day 5 Ephesians 5:21–6:24 (the Christian household, the whole armor of God)

Day 6 "The Word of the Lord" and "Marks of Obedient Community"

THE WORD OF THE LORD

NOTES, REFLECTIONS, AND QUESTIONS

Ephesians is perhaps the crown and climax of the New Testament. It sings about God, Jesus Christ, human salvation, the church, God's victory over demonic powers that tear life apart, the unifying of the cosmos by the power of Christ's love, and the ultimate inheritance designed for God's people.

Wedged between the opening salutation (Ephesians 1:1-2) and later prayers of thanksgiving (1:15-23) is a doxology praising "the God and Father of our Lord Jesus Christ" (Ephesians 1:3-14, one Greek sentence!). Bits of hymns, prayers, confessions, and early Christian liturgy are woven into this opening song of praise. Notice the Trinitarian structure: God the Father (1:3); Jesus Christ, who has redeemed us (1:4-13); and the Holy Spirit, "the pledge of our inheritance" (1:13-14).

Ephesians is more a tract designed to be circulated and read aloud in church after church, all through Asia Minor, than a letter addressed to a particular church with specific problems. Just as Epaphras had carried the gospel to Colossae, Laodicea, and Hierapolis, so other missionaries, teachers, evangelists, and Christian workers had moved in and out of Ephesus, converting Gentiles and Jews throughout the region. Some early manuscripts do not contain the word *Ephesus* (Ephesians 1:1) as if that blank were to be filled in by the name of the town where the letter was being read.

The letter is a treasure of Paul's thought, yet it contains style differences from Paul's known writings and fresh theological concepts. Like Colossians, it addresses the cosmic warfare and lifts up the preexistent Christ. Perhaps disciples in Ephesus, remembering Paul's sermons and reading his letters, wrote this tract to address the churches under his influence. Some scholars have suggested Ephesians was a "cover letter" for the collected letters of Paul.

Chosen Before the Foundation of the World

Ephesians does not begin with evil; it begins with Jesus Christ. It does not start with "cosmic powers" (6:12); it first focuses on Christ, who is bringing every spiritual blessing from the heavenly places (1:3). Christ expresses the plan of God, in whom God chose us "before the foundation of the world" (1:4) and "destined us for adoption as his children through Jesus Christ" (1:5). That thought is mind-boggling. It goes further than Jeremiah who believed he was called while still in his mother's womb (Jeremiah 1:5). The salvation wrought in Jesus was not the result of historical circumstances that emerged in time but the accomplishment of God's eternal intent. All this unmerited love has been poured upon us, "freely bestowed" (Ephesians 1:6). Through Christ we are daughters and sons (1:5). That is the relationship God purposed when "the earth was a formless void" (Genesis 1:1).

NOTES, REFLECTIONS, AND QUESTIONS

God's Mystery Made Known

In a world of mystery religions, Ephesians whispers a "mystery." In a society seeking spiritual "knowledge," Ephesians speaks the truth previously hidden. God "has made known to us the mystery of his will" (Ephesians 1:9). People are always asking about the purpose of God, always groaning to know "the will of God." Ephesians tells us: It is to gather up the entire universe in harmony. God's will, gradually, in "the fullness of time," is to bring into perfect unity "all things," everything, "things in heaven and things on earth" (1:10).

To those early Christians addressed in Ephesians, the letter declares they are the fruit of the gospel, the first to set their "hope on Christ" (1:12). They are part of the unifying action of Christ's redeeming love. How do they know? They have received "the seal of the . . . Holy Spirit" (1:13), like the stamp of a king's ring in hot wax. They have received the "pledge," like the earnest money in a business transaction, guaranteeing God's promised inheritance (1:14).

Christ Is Head of the Church

Ephesians says God has placed Christ at God's "right hand" in "the heavenly places" above all the fates, all the angels, all the devils, "far above all rule and authority and power and dominion, and above every name that is named, not only in this age but also in the age to come" (1:21). That covers everything! In the great cosmic warfare, Christ has won, is winning, will ultimately prevail. Notice, in earlier letters, the emphasis is on *time*. Christ's return was imminent: Be ready. Now the category is *space*. Christ's authority rules the universe. For Christ is "the head"—of the church and of everything (1:22-23). Head means authority. Head means leadership. But head also refers to a column of figures. What is the implication? In a world of confusion where things just don't add up, Christ is bringing the numbers into a meaningful relationship.

How is Christ doing this mighty work? Through the church! In referring to the church, Paul had written, "You are the body of Christ" (1 Corinthians 12:27). Ephesians puts it, "the church, which is his body" (Ephesians 1:23). Christ is head of the church. That leadership occurred when Christ brought us out of our trespasses. Before, we followed "the ruler of the power of the air" (Satan) (2:2). But now, under Christ's headship, we are "alive together with Christ" (2:5).

A New Humanity

The gulf between Jew and Gentile in the ancient world was deep. The division was not mere social prejudice; it was theologically grounded. By religious law, traditions, and practice, Jews set themselves apart, avoided Gentile contact. For Gentiles the issue was different. From the standpoint of the covenant, they were outsiders.

NOTES, REFLECTIONS, AND QUESTIONS

Now comes the Ephesian letter. Gentiles, remember that once you were "without Christ," apart from God but also "aliens from the commonwealth of Israel" (2:12). Remember, God in Christ has "grafted" outsiders into the olive tree that is Abraham and his descendants (Romans 11:17-18).

You Gentiles "once were far off" (Ephesians 2:13). What has brought you near? "The blood of Christ" (2:13)! God in Christ "has broken down the dividing wall, that is, the hostility between us," between Jew and Gentile (2:14). The blood, the divine unmerited love, brings peace (2:15).

Now a new humanity has been created, Jews and Gentiles together—one humanity. Hostility is replaced by peace, peace to those "far off" (Gentiles) and peace to those "near" (Jews). Both have full and complete access, not to idols or laws but "in one Spirit to the Father" (2:17-18). No aliens; all are full citizens, "members of the household of God" (2:19).

Ephesians has the highest view of the church in the New Testament. The church, filled with Christ's Spirit, is seen as the instrument for building the unity of all humanity. As the Temple held Judaism together, so the church will hold the new humanity together—with Christ the cornerstone.

Our Responsibility

The first half of Ephesians tells us what God has done; the second half tells us what we must do.

Again the bridgelike *therefore* (Ephesians 4:1). What God has done culminates in a benediction: "Now to him who by the power at work within us is able to accomplish abundantly far more than all we can ask or imagine, to him be glory in the church and in Christ Jesus . . . forever and ever. Amen" (3:20-21). Give some examples.

By now we understand the distinction between abandoning Jewish traditions and practices we no longer need and accepting the clear moral imperatives that are part of the new life in Christ, to lead lives worthy of the gospel.

When speaking of "Christ's gift" (4:7), Ephesians echoes Psalm 68:18. The psalm says God *receives* gifts. But Ephesians turns it around to say that God ascends to the throne *giving* gifts. The writer of Ephesians sees Christ in the psalm. He conquered "captivity" (Ephesians 4:8)—all "the cosmic powers" and "spiritual forces of evil" (6:12) that hold humankind in bondage. Christ even descended into the underground of sin and death to take those forces captive too (4:9-10). Then God in Christ poured forth gifts of the Holy Spirit upon Christ's people (4:11-12).

God gives a rich diversity of gifts to build up "the body of Christ" (4:12). The gifts in Ephesians are more formal than

Ephesians 4:7-10 assumes that Christ, the preexistent one, descended from heaven and ascended again; moreover, 4:9 may well be an allusion to Christ's "descent into Hades" (like 1 Peter 3:19); if so, these references provide the New Testament basis for the line in the Apostles' Creed.

those in 1 Corinthians 12. In Corinthians the gifts of the Spirit are functions, capacities released in the congregation; in Ephesians they are specific "offices" in the church. "Some would be apostles, some prophets, some evangelists, some pastors and teachers" (Ephesians 4:11). Notice pastor and teacher are one office. Obviously the churches were being organized. But this organization is not merely to do ministry; it is "to equip the saints" (4:12), "to prepare God's people" (4:12, NIV) *for* the work of ministry.

In churches today professionals often do "the work of ministry." What can we do to train, to equip, to mobilize the whole people of God for ministry?

Too many people, ignorant of Scripture and sound Christian teachings, are "tossed to and fro" (4:14) by every faddish idea, by trickery, by self-serving people. Without being presumptuous or obnoxious, how can we speak "the truth in love" to help people take their powerful place as part of Christ's body (4:15-16)?

Imitate Christ

For sure, we are not to live as the world lives, with veiled eyes and hard hearts. Old lusts, greediness, insensitivity, sexual impurity, telling lies, thievery, bad-mouthing, bitterness, holding grudges—all of these impurities are to be cast aside, replaced by newness of mind and self (4:22-24). Anger is human, sometimes justified. But Ephesians stresses understanding and forgiveness. "Do not let the sun go down on your anger" (Ephesians 4:26). How do we know how to behave? We are to imitate God in Christ, who "gave himself up for us" (5:1-2).

Wives, husbands, children are to defer to one another "out of reverence for Christ" (5:21). In a highly patriarchal Roman society, Ephesians calls for balance, mutual respect. Still, we must acknowledge Ephesians does think in terms of hierarchical order. A good paraphrase of Ephesians 5:21 would be, "Be responsive to one another's needs." Christ begins in humility, the act of love. Husbands should lead in loving. Wives should offer, in return, respect and love, as unto Christ himself. Both bodies are one, therefore care for the other is like care for one's own body. Does not Christ tenderly care for his body, the church? "A man will leave his father and mother and be joined to his wife, and the two will become one flesh" (5:31; see Genesis 2:24).

NOTES, REFLECTIONS, AND QUESTIONS

In the Ephesians metaphor, marriage and church move back and forth. Just as Jesus will present his bride, the church, holy and without blemish, so the husband seeks to care for his wife. Both husbands and wives should love and respect (be supportive of) each other (Ephesians 5:33).

Stand

In the cosmic struggle, won yet not completed, each Christian, alone and in community, must battle. God gives power, yet believers must be brave too (6:10). We fight, not against other human beings but against "evil in the heavenly places" (6:12). Those forces still have power. We must use all our spiritual resources.

The writer's mind is filled with messianic descriptions of God dressed in military attire. He urges believers to "put on the whole armor of God" (6:11). Stand. Stand. Stand.

"Fasten the belt of truth around your waist" (6:14). Truth is from God. Hold fast to truth.

> "I the LORD speak the truth,
> I declare what is right" (Isaiah 45:19).

God goes to war. The divine war will be won by righteousness, justice. God put on "the breastplate of righteousness" (Ephesians 6:14; Isaiah 59:17). A soldier of God puts on righteousness. It protects the heart.

"As shoes for your feet put on whatever will make you ready to proclaim the gospel of peace" (Ephesians 6:15). Our writer puts Roman sandals on the warrior and pleads with believers to be ready "to proclaim the gospel of peace." Every Christian should be a witness.

A shield (6:16) is defensive. A large Roman shield, covered with leather soaked in water, protected against flaming arrows.

For head covering, Ephesians again speaks of God. God puts "a helmet of salvation on his head" (Isaiah 59:17). So should the Christian (Ephesians 6:17).

The sword goes on the offensive (6:17). The spoken word of witness has power. A person can be saved by a word well spoken. "He made my mouth like a sharp sword" (Isaiah 49:2). The Scriptures have immense power. "Indeed, the word of God is living and active, sharper than any two-edged sword, piercing until it divides soul from spirit, joints from marrow; it is able to judge the thoughts and intentions of the heart" (Hebrews 4:12).

How has your DISCIPLE group discovered this power in Scripture?

The general point of this description of armor is that Christians are to be outfitted with aspects of salvation, and so can do battle against the spiritual powers.

NOTES, REFLECTIONS, AND QUESTIONS

In Paul's time, the everpresent Roman soldiers were stationed in every town and city to ensure peace and to keep citizens aware that they lived under Roman authority. Early Christians who heard or read Ephesians instantly understood its references to armor—breastplate, belt, shoes, shield, and helmet.

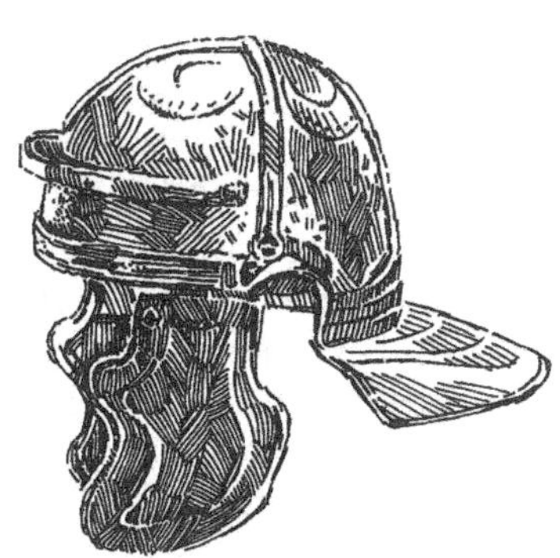

This helmet of a Roman soldier, found near Hebron, dates from the second century A.D.

MARKS OF OBEDIENT COMMUNITY

God "has made known to us the mystery of his will" (Ephesians 1:9)—to bring all things in the universe into harmony. What can we do to help?

We use fresh inspiration, new converts, diverse gifts to strengthen or build up the fellowship which is the body of Christ. We remember that the body is not the end but the means, not the goal but the servant of God to do the work of Jesus in the world. Our small fellowship is part of the body of Christ around the world and across the centuries.

What can we do together to exhibit "church"?

What did Jesus do in his earthly ministry that we, his body, are not effectively doing now?

What would equip us to go into difficult places unafraid?

Picture not one "soldier" but a group of "soldiers" putting on the whole armor of God. What battles do we face in which we need this protective equipment?

IF YOU WANT TO KNOW MORE

Study the geography of western Asia Minor (including sea routes) to see how Ephesus was the hub for extensive missionary activity.

Letter: If unity is God's purpose, what can we do to help bring people together? Write a letter that affirms racial or ethnic harmony or supports a cause of social justice. Or write a more personal letter aimed at breaking down walls of hostility, perhaps to someone within your church, urging forgiveness, reconciliation, restoration of fellowship.

NOTES, REFLECTIONS, AND QUESTIONS

Obedient community enters the struggle against evil, equipped with truth, righteousness, peace, faith, salvation, and God's Word.

GODLINESS

"If you put these instructions before the brothers and sisters, you will be a good servant of Christ Jesus, nourished on the words of the faith and of the sound teaching that you have followed."

—1 Timothy 4:6

30 Leadership in the Church

OUR HUMAN CONDITION

Our vision is stunted and our energy sapped by unclear expectations, trust and support withheld, and no encouragement to take risks.

ASSIGNMENT

First and Second Timothy and Titus are called the Pastoral Letters because they address duties and problems that face pastors of congregations. Traditionally, the three letters have been attributed to Paul. More recent scholarship views them as coming from a disciple of Paul after his death.

As a leader of a class, a group, or a church, as an active servant of Christ, listen to this letter from one who has "been there" and now shares his wisdom with you.

Day 1 1 Timothy 1 (defense of the truth)
Day 2 1 Timothy 2–3 (prayer, qualifications of church leaders)
Day 3 1 Timothy 4 (a good minister)
Day 4 1 Timothy 5 (honor widows and elders)
Day 5 1 Timothy 6 (godliness with contentment)
Day 6 Read and respond to "The Word of the Lord" and "Marks of Obedient Community."
Day 7 Rest

PRAYER

Pray daily before study:

"You are my God, so be merciful to me;
I pray to you all day long.
Make your servant glad, O Lord,
because my prayers go up to you.
You are good to us and forgiving,
full of constant love for all who pray to you"
(Psalm 86:3-5, TEV).

Prayer concerns for this week:

Godliness

Day 1 1 Timothy 1 (defense of the truth)

Day 2 1 Timothy 2–3 (prayer, qualifications of church leaders)

Day 3 1 Timothy 4 (a good minister)

Day 4 1 Timothy 5 (honor widows and elders)

Day 5 1 Timothy 6 (godliness with contentment)

Day 6 "The Word of the Lord" and "Marks of Obedient Community"

THE WORD OF THE LORD

NOTES, REFLECTIONS, AND QUESTIONS

For centuries, the church has called First and Second Timothy and Titus the Pastoral Letters or the Pastorals. The tone, the feel, is different from the undoubted letters of Paul. New issues are addressed, new struggles faced. Instead of enthusiastic evangelism in fledgling churches, the mood reflects pastoral care and order for established congregations. Earlier letters were written to churches; the Pastorals are addressed to pastors. Yet the content, how to care for the church, affects every believer. Emphasis on the soon-coming of Christ has receded into the background. Concern for creedal theology, solid Christian behavior, and good order in the church has surfaced.

Third-Generation Correspondence

Timothy was nurtured by his grandmother Lois and by his mother Eunice. Many believers now were born of Christian parents. So these letters hold special help for us, for they swirled amid church life much like ours today.

Timothy and Titus were spiritual sons of Paul, as alike yet as different as brothers. Timothy was Jewish, circumcised at Paul's insistence to render him effective in the synagogues (Acts 16:1-3). Titus was Gentile, an exemplar of the faith when Paul faced Peter and James in Jerusalem (Galatians 2:1-3). These two young "pastors" represent the two-pronged Jewish-Gentile thrust of the gospel. Paul sent Timothy to Ephesus, left Titus in Crete.

Paul and Barnabas saw Timothy in Lystra on their first missionary trip. Timothy's father was Greek, his mother Jewish. Even as a child, Timothy, like Paul, had been well instructed in the Hebrew Scriptures. When Paul returned to Lystra, Timothy had matured, was obviously gifted, and was highly regarded by believers in Lystra and nearby towns. Paul took him with the entourage to Europe. According to 1 Timothy 4:14, Timothy was ordained. Thus began a "father-son" working relationship that continued until Paul's martyrdom. Timothy was among the first Christians to set foot on European soil. He helped Paul start new congregations in Macedonia, and stayed to care for the churches there while Paul went to Athens. Whenever a crisis arose, Paul tapped Timothy. Paul sent him to Thessalonica, Ephesus, Corinth, and Philippi. Paul took him to Jerusalem and was grateful to have him by his side in Rome.

One of the most severe and widespread persecutions of the early Christians occurred under the emperor Nero (A.D 54–68), who is shown here in a gold coin that dates from the time of his rule. Nero was emperor at the time of Paul's death around A.D. 64.

Timothy in Ephesus

Although the Christian community in Ephesus was relatively small, it was the fountainhead of missionary activity in Asia Minor. Furthermore, every brand of Greek philosophy, Jewish mythology, and Persian mysticism floated through the air in Ephesus. The purpose of First Timothy was to reinforce sound teachings amid threatening ideologies and to provide guidance for governing the church.

False teachings have two results: They confuse Christian thinking, and they lead to immoral behavior. Heretical teachers had infiltrated the Ephesian church with endless, far-fetched stories; wild Jewish apocalyptic myths; strange genealogies of Jewish ancients; meaningless talk; and constant arguments.

Timothy was tempted to move on. Any pastor would be. Stay put is the counsel. "Remain in Ephesus so that you may instruct" (1 Timothy 1:3). Confront the false ideas, not with a sharp tongue but with sound teachings. Do it patiently, persistently; "fight the good fight" (1:18).

Persistent Problems in the Church

"Knowledge," or "gnosticism," took a strange twist. If matter is evil, wouldn't people try to be "spiritual"? Some did, but others denied this world by reveling in it. What appeared to be worldly was actually a death wish. Deny life by taking drugs. Reject reality by getting drunk. Spurn sexual commitment by fornication. Today's "in" groups may rock to a despair beat, party in a life-denying musical rhythm, space out with mind-altering chemicals. The music often focuses on despair and death. We misread the times if we see them as "worldly." Instead they are "gnostic," life-denying.

What are some other examples of life-denying attitudes and actions?

The Old Testament prophets labeled idolatry the Number 1 sin against the Number 1 commandment. Idolatry is worshiping the creature rather than the Creator (Romans 1:25). Some people spin human philosophies that lead to worshiping the mind of the creature. These ideas, like the baals of old, do not hold the believer accountable to God's righteousness. Philosophies can become a form of idolatry, leading to self-designed behavior. If the philosophy is world-denying, it leads to despair or immorality.

Now some, of course, took the ascetic route (1 Timothy 4:1-3). Stoics, certain Jews, zealous Christians who were influenced by this "knowledge" that the world is evil abstained from certain foods and wine, avoided marriage. Even Timothy was so conscientious that he got sick drinking the impure water. "Take a little wine for the sake of your stomach" (5:23). Timothy was to teach patiently about the Jewish-Christian God of creation. Life taken with gratitude is good. Food is meant to be eaten with thanksgiving. Sex is meant to be enjoyed in marriage. God created the world and saw that it was good (4:4; Genesis 1:31).

NOTES, REFLECTIONS, AND QUESTIONS

NOTES, REFLECTIONS, AND QUESTIONS

Instructions for Worship and Prayer

Every revolution is followed by a settling down. In a world where Jewish women did not speak in synagogue and where some Gentile wives remained secluded in the home, Christian joint participation in worship was socially explosive. As in Corinth, proper hair arrangements and modest clothing were suggested for Christian meetings (1 Timothy 2:9-10). For men, the Jewish form of lifting hands in prayer, like incense, was appropriate but should stress praise rather than anger (2:8). Women should dress suitably for worship, avoiding a show of luxury or undue pride.

Women, shown even in this restrictive passage (2:11-12, and in 1 Corinthians 14:33-36), joined in prayer and testimony. But worship services had become bedlam. Now the gift of gentleness is praised. Silence suggests the quiet, peaceful soul, not the rebellious spirit under restraint. The guidelines do not mean "don't teach," for teaching by women was performed throughout the church. (Prisca taught Apollos, and Romans 16 lists several women prominent in ministry.) Rather, in that social context, women should not take over, but exhibit a gracious manner. Those who would destroy the integrity of the home should remember the dignity and honor of motherhood; rejoice in faith, love, and holiness; and be respected within the unity of the church for modest behavior.

Though we may find this counsel outdated, even offensive to some persons, the letter's concern is for the integrity of the church as an institution.

Those Who Serve

How soon the church developed officers and designated leaders we do not know. We saw that the Holy Spirit gifts listed in 1 Corinthians 12:27-28 (healing, teaching) were without office. Holy Spirit gifts in Ephesians 4:11 were by office (pastors, evangelists). The salutation to the Philippians mentions "bishops and deacons," but some scholars think that phrase may have been added to manuscripts as they circulated.

The word *bishop* (*elder, presbyter*) is literally "overseer" (1 Timothy 3:1-2). The image carries modest authority but more strongly implies caring, superintending, shepherding, teaching. The word *pastor* is suitable, and the shepherd's crook is an appropriate symbol. The guidelines are clear (3:2-7). Because believers should give respect to elders, such persons must not be new converts (3:6); for that respect must not turn their heads. It is a reflected honor, like "Be subject to one another out of reverence for Christ" (Ephesians 5:21). Notice the relationship between overseeing the household and overseeing the church (1 Timothy 3:4-5).

The fellowship should be like family. Sex and money must be under Christ's strong control. Outsiders should respect the "overseer's" integrity and grace; such character strengthens the church's witness.

The word *deacon* means "one who serves" (3:8). Jesus' washing the disciples' feet is the example; the towel is the symbol. Deacons include women like Phoebe (Romans 16:1) and men like Stephen (Acts 6:5, 8). The first deacons were chosen by the community in Jerusalem to help with equitable distribution of food (6:1-6). The Twelve wanted the deacons to help so the elders could continue teaching, preaching, praying, and healing. Dangers for deacons include loose talk, alcohol, concern about money, sexual promiscuity, and lack of self-discipline. Deacons should be given small tasks ("tested") before being given greater responsibilities. In their hearts they should have "great boldness in the faith that is in Christ Jesus" (1 Timothy 3:13).

Creeds to Fight False Teaching

The word *herald* (1 Timothy 2:7) refers to a special emissary or messenger of the king or other high civil authority. The herald went from city to city announcing a special message, giving full weight to the announcement—not a word less, not a word more. First Timothy quotes liturgical creeds to be heralded (2:5-6). These will help in the fight against false teachers.

"There is one God," Creator of spirit and matter.

"There is also one mediator between God and humankind." Jesus had to be man in order to reach us; Jesus had to be God in order to save us.

He "gave himself a ransom for all." His cross redeemed and justified everyone who stands in sin and under wrath.

Another creed expresses our "mystery" (3:16).

"He was revealed in flesh" (3:16)—the Incarnation; disputed the gnostics. God entered "matter," took on the human condition; so matter cannot be evil and rejected.

"Vindicated in spirit"—Jesus' status as Son of God seen in the Resurrection.

"Seen by angels"—angels testified to his ascension (Acts 1:9-11).

"Proclaimed among Gentiles"—a gospel for the nations, for everyone.

"Believed in throughout the world"—a reality to be amazed at, thankful for.

"Taken up in glory"—Christ is Lord and will come again in power and victory.

Spiritual Discipline

The letter advises Timothy the pastor to discipline himself spiritually and mentally like an athlete. "Train yourself in godliness, for, while physical training is of some value, godliness is valuable in every way" (1 Timothy 4:7-8). If you are going to be a tough-minded teacher, you must be disciplined (4:11-16). Keep teaching. Read the Scriptures to others who cannot read or do not understand. Exhort. Preach. Witness. Elders recognized your special "gift," so they ordained you

NOTES, REFLECTIONS, AND QUESTIONS

(4:14). "Guard what has been entrusted to you" (6:20). Just because you are young, don't let others put you down. Show maturity "in speech and conduct, in love, in faith, in purity" (4:12). These gifts are not limited to a particular age.

Taking Care

First Timothy 5–6 provides a host of practical, Jewish-Christian teachings. They are everyday but so desperately needed in every congregation.

Respect one's elders (5:1-2). First Timothy 5:3-16 is a response to abuses in the church's care for widows. The passage provided guidelines that are both caring and fair.

Take care of your family, even your extended family (5:3-8, 16). Take relatives, like widows and orphans, under your wing. Don't leave them dependent on the church or public welfare. Even unbelievers are that considerate. In Timothy's society, a woman alone had to be attached to a family to survive. After Pentecost, the Jerusalem church immediately provided love and food for destitute Hebrew-speaking and Greek-speaking widows (Acts 6:1-3). If family members could care for a widow, even a distant relative, they should. The church already carried a heavy load. Younger widows should marry if they could, becoming productive and related to a family (1 Timothy 5:11-14). The goal was to see that all the women were cared for so they did not sell themselves into slavery or prostitution and so they did not lose their faith in Christ.

Money

Church workers should be paid, but they should not be greedy. Be careful not to bring a careless charge against them; but if two or three witnesses declare that they persist in sin, rebuke them publicly (1 Timothy 5:19-20). Be thoughtful and deliberate before ordaining elders and deacons (5:22).

Be content—an admonition to Timothy and presumably to all Christians. We ought not to be greedy, for we will take nothing material with us from this world (6:7). Desire for riches can plunge people into "ruin and destruction. For the love of money is a root of all kinds of evil" (6:9-10). Already some people, including the evangelist Demas, had deserted because of love for worldly things (2 Timothy 4:9).

"Take hold of the eternal life, to which you were called and for which you made the good confession in the presence of many witnesses" (1 Timothy 6:12). As the years go by, a church worker can forget, can let the fire grow dim, can drift into anxiety about food and clothing. Don't envy the rich. They have a tough responsibility. They must trust God rather than their riches. Day by day, without holding back, they are to be "rich in good works," always generous, always eager to share with others (6:17-19). The hope for the rich is that they will "take hold of the life that really is life" (6:19).

NOTES, REFLECTIONS, AND QUESTIONS

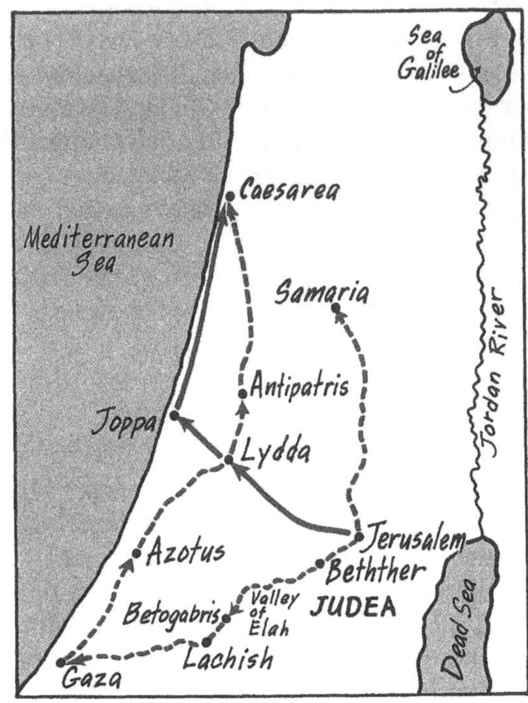

After Pentecost the gospel quickly spread outward from Jerusalem through the efforts of the apostles and other early Christians (Acts 8:1, 4). The broken line shows the route of Philip the Evangelist in 8:5-40. The solid line shows the route of Peter in 9:32–10:33.

As you contemplate your relationship to material things, where do you see signs you are anxious, envious, or always restless for more? see signs you are maintaining a balance?

NOTES, REFLECTIONS, AND QUESTIONS

MARKS OF OBEDIENT COMMUNITY

The faith community affirms its leaders with both respect and accountability. We undergird them with prayer, encouragement, and consolation. Reproof takes the form of instruction and gentle guidance. We make sure our leaders have their spiritual and material needs met.

How do we sometimes isolate our spiritual leaders, causing them to feel alone?

The faithful community offers its leaders respect and accountability, encouragement and nurture.

What is godliness? How would you describe a godly leader?

How can we can discuss mutual expectations with our pastors, officers, teachers, and group leaders?

What could your DISCIPLE group do to encourage your pastor(s)? Provide time away for a spiritual retreat, a family vacation, a fellowship meal? offer babysitting, funds for an outing? honor a pastor's need and time for prayer?

You may wish to send a trusted friend to discover a hidden need that, if met, could revitalize your pastor's(s') spirit.

IF YOU WANT TO KNOW MORE

Letter: Write a letter to your pastor, either affirming ministry or offering to fulfill some need the pastor and family have.

Find out what your church believes about ordination. Get a copy of the ordination liturgy and read it. Attend an ordination service if possible.

TEACH

"Hold to the standard of sound teaching that you have heard from me, in the faith and love that are in Christ Jesus. Guard the good treasure entrusted to you, with the help of the Holy Spirit living in us."

—2 Timothy 1:13-14

31 From Generation to Generation

OUR HUMAN CONDITION

Without memory, we lack identity. Who are we? What will shape us? What will guide us? What can we build on?

ASSIGNMENT

Compare key ideas in First and Second Timothy and Titus. Notice the emphasis (like Deuteronomy 6) on teaching, learning, doctrine, and Scripture, as if the church were a school dedicated to handing down the heritage. Like the writings of the prophets, these Pastoral Letters help us remember who we are.

Day 1 2 Timothy 1 (thanksgiving and encouragement)
Day 2 2 Timothy 2 (be strong in grace, a worker approved by God)
Day 3 2 Timothy 3 (godlessness in the last days, the power of Scripture)
Day 4 2 Timothy 4 (the good fight of faith)
Day 5 Titus 1–3 (teach sound doctrine, pastor and flock, Christian conduct)
Day 6 Read and respond to "The Word of the Lord" and "Marks of Obedient Community."
Day 7 Rest

PRAYER

Pray daily before study:

"LORD, how happy is the person you instruct, the one to whom you teach your law! (Psalm 94:12, TEV).

Prayer concerns for this week:

our services won't save us, but we are saved to serve

Humility: having an honest estimate of ourselves before God.

TEACH

Day 1 2 Timothy 1 (thanksgiving and encouragement)

Day 2 2 Timothy 2 (be strong in grace, a worker approved by God)

Day 3 2 Timothy 3 (godlessness in the last days, the power of Scripture)

Day 4 2 Timothy 4 (the good fight of faith)

Day 5 Titus 1–3 (teach sound doctrine, pastor and flock, Christian conduct)

Day 6 "The Word of the Lord" and "Marks of Obedient Community"

THE WORD OF THE LORD

NOTES, REFLECTIONS, AND QUESTIONS

Second Timothy is the most intimate of the Pastoral Letters, remembering "tears" at times of separation; requesting cloak, parchments, and books be sent (2 Timothy 4:13); and speaking kindly of the young pastor's grandmother and mother (1:5). Many of Paul's heaviest theological thoughts infuse the letter, 1:8-10 for example. Yet it also contains some new and different thoughts, perhaps added by later missionaries.

Timothy was in Ephesus (1 Timothy 1:3). From our earlier studies, we know Ephesus was a Roman seaport metropolis, a headquarters for Christian evangelization. Timothy was responsible for a network of churches in Asia Minor. These churches faced fierce and growing external persecution. But worse, they experienced strong internal dissension. The letter advises Timothy to be strong; stay put; teach, teach, teach.

Every word, every analogy in Second Timothy urges strength, courage, boldness. The Holy Spirit will give Timothy power and love and self-discipline (2 Timothy 1:7). He must not be distracted by silly arguments or strange philosophical debates, but should be as focused as a soldier (2:4), as disciplined as an athlete (2:5), as hard-working as a farmer (2:6). Some suffering should be expected. "Join . . . in suffering for the gospel, relying on the power of God" (1:8). Above all, "Do not be ashamed . . . of the testimony about our Lord" (1:8).

Philosophical Idolatries

Timothy must maintain loyalty to the apostolic tradition against those who would dilute or compromise it. Some people fell away over gross sins—Demas with money, some Corinthian church members over sex—but a more subtle temptation came from human philosophies that had power to confuse the mind, then lead to immorality. Although they were not visible to the eye, like images of stone or wood, philosophies could be idolatrous. The prophets of ancient Israel would have spotted them right away. Of human craft rather than from God's revelation, they attracted attention, energy, and human devotion; but they laid no obligation on the devotee, neither to Torah nor to Christ. What were these philosophical idolatries? Since they are so prevalent in our present world, let us use modern terminology.

• Some people sat around and talked religion for hours. They quoted poets and philosophers, referred to religions of the East, debated theological viewpoints. Not serious students in a seminary, they were coffee-cup philosophers, spending their days in meaningless "chatter" (2 Timothy 2:16-18). Acts reports that such people gathered daily in Athens. Few converted. "All the Athenians and the foreigners living there would spend their time in nothing but telling or hearing something new" (Acts 17:21). They did not work in a soup kitchen, spend time in prayer, or teach children. Their gods were an endless stream of words. Pastor Timothy, avoid these people!

• Some people, like Hymenaeus and Philetus, said the Resurrection had already happened or that it happened in the case of Jesus because he was the Son of God, but there is no future resurrection for us (2 Timothy 2:17-18). Or they claimed we already live resurrection lives, and so do not need moral guidelines. Influenced by Greek philosophy, they believed in the immortality of the soul but not the resurrection of the body. Among the unbelievers, that posture is understandable. The Crucifixion and Resurrection are "a stumbling block to Jews and foolishness to Gentiles" (1 Corinthians 1:23). But among believers, the cross, which includes Jesus' resurrection and ascension, is the heart of revelation.

• A few moralizers insisted on adding some extras to Christian faith. Some added Jewish rites and rituals. Some of them were "circumcisers" (Titus 1:10), Gentiles who took on Jewish practices, like those in Galatia (Galatians 2:12-13). They told unscriptural Jewish myths (1 Timothy 4:7; Titus 1:14). They wove speculative genealogies of famous Jewish personalities. Some punished the body. Some developed exclusive groups based on special knowledge or mysteries. Some false teachers infiltrated Christian homes, preyed on weak believers, even manipulated their minds for financial gain (1:11).

Titus

Titus, "loyal child in the faith" (Titus 1:4), was Greek, born of Gentile parents. When Paul and Barnabas traveled to the dramatic Jerusalem Council (Acts 15; Galatians 2) for a face-off with James and Peter, they took Titus as a case in point (2:1). Paul refused to have him circumcised. Titus was the first test case of freedom from the Jewish Law. His witness was a watershed in taking Christianity to the whole world. When Jerusalem Christians affirmed Titus, Paul's view of the gospel was vindicated.

Paul dispatched Titus on two urgent missions to Corinth, first with the "severe" letter (2 Corinthians 7:6-16) and later with the sensitive task of gathering the gift for the poor in Jerusalem (8:16-24). Not surprisingly, Paul gave Titus the tough assignment to Crete, island home of poor, despised Gentiles (Titus 1:12-16). As a pastoral assignment, Crete stood at the bottom of the list. No preacher yearned to go to Crete. Yet Paul chose one of his best pastor-teachers to take one of his toughest churches.

The island of Crete, south of the Greek Peloponnesus, forms the southern border of the Aegean Sea. During the Bronze Age (3000–1200 B.C.), the Minoans developed a high culture on Crete, building ornate palaces with superb frescoes. The Cretans were known as the Sea Peoples. But a

NOTES, REFLECTIONS, AND QUESTIONS

volcanic eruption at nearby Santorini was followed by a great earthquake in 1450 B.C., devastating Crete, scattering its people, and precipitating cultural decline. Many of these dispossessed Sea Peoples emigrated to the coast of Palestine, evolving into the Philistines of Gaza and the Phoenicians of Tyre.

By New Testament times, neighboring peoples looked down on the people left on Crete, stereotyping them as rude and lacking in moral fiber. They were the outcasts, the marginalized poor. One of Crete's own poets, Epimenides, described his fellow citizens as "liars, vicious brutes, lazy gluttons" (Titus 1:12). The Greeks dismissed them as barbarians. The Cretans claimed Zeus was buried on the island, that they had found his tomb. The Greeks said that was a lie. In the Greek language the word *Cretanize* meant to lie.

Some Cretans were converted at Pentecost, so the church there was not new (Acts 2:11); but it was struggling. So, to guard against the church's succumbing to the island's legendary reputation, Titus, young but experienced Gentile missionary, is to attack the problem head-on: "Rebuke them sharply, so that they may become sound in the faith" (Titus 1:13). History records that, in such an unpromising society, Christianity took root and flowered into a great tradition.

Teach the Faith

What should Timothy and Titus do in these established churches? They should teach sound doctrine (1 Timothy 4:6-11; 2 Timothy 3:14-17; Titus 2:1). They should teach the same apostolic faith that brought them their salvation. "When the goodness and loving kindness of God our Savior appeared, he saved us, not because of any works of righteousness that we had done, but according to his mercy, through the water of rebirth and renewal by the Holy Spirit. This Spirit he poured out on us richly through Jesus Christ our Savior" (3:4-6). Titus may have heard Paul's sermon to the mob in Jerusalem when Paul testified that Ananias in Damascus had said to him, "Get up, be baptized, and have your sins washed away, calling on his [God's] name" (Acts 22:16). Titus, "insist on these things" (Titus 3:8).

What should Timothy and Titus emphasize? The orthodox teaching learned from Paul and confessed already in the early creeds. "Remember Jesus Christ, raised from the dead [a corrective to the immortal-soul people], a descendant of David [a rebuttal to gnostics]"; that is gospel (2 Timothy 2:8).

The Pastorals are interested in "sure sayings" (Titus 3:8)—solid theological tradition. Second Timothy quotes a liturgical profession:

> "If we have died with him, we will also live with him;
> if we endure, we will also reign with him;
> if we deny him, he will also deny us" (2 Timothy 2:11-12).

NOTES, REFLECTIONS, AND QUESTIONS

Only people steeped in the Hebrew prophets would draw the upside-down conclusion:

"If we are faithless, he remains faithful—
for he cannot deny himself" (2:13).

The God of the Bible will be faithfully righteous and merciful no matter what we do. "Remind them of this," Timothy (2:14).

Pastor Also Teacher

The preacher is to be teacher. Why? Because of the distressing times. We're reminded of Amos's saying there is a famine in the land,

"not a famine of bread, or a thirst for water,
but of hearing the words of the LORD" (Amos 8:11).

The teacher should "do your best to present yourself to God as one approved by him, a worker who has no need to be ashamed, rightly explaining the word of truth" (2 Timothy 2:15). The pastor-teacher must study. Timothy must "rekindle" the flame, the gift of God, he felt at his ordination (1:6). Pastors must stoke the fires, mentally and physically. The teacher needs to feed on God's Word. The pastor or teacher must distinguish truth from error, gospel from heresy. "You have heard of this hope before in the word of the truth, the gospel. . . . it is bearing fruit and growing in the whole world" (Colossians 1:5-6).

As a carpenter carefully builds with plumb and level and a skilled artisan proudly submits work to a supervisor, a teacher of the gospel will present learners in the faith as a present to God.

But Titus and Timothy cannot do the work alone. Pastors need teachers, lots of teachers. "What you have heard from me through many witnesses [converts who testify to joy and peace in Christ] entrust to faithful people who will be able to teach others as well" (2 Timothy 2:2).

Older men should teach younger men. Older women must teach younger women. Teenagers can help teach children. Mothers will teach their children something. So will fathers. What will it be? The letter to Titus says, "Teach what is consistent with sound doctrine" (Titus 2:1). Timothy was fortunate to have been raised by a godly grandmother and mother. He was taught the Scriptures. Wouldn't it be wonderful if it could be said of every child, "From childhood you have known the sacred writings that are able to instruct you for salvation through faith in Christ Jesus" (2 Timothy 3:15)? The command of Moses still instructs us: "Recite them [the words of the great commandment] to your children and talk about them when you are at home and when you are away, when you lie down and when you rise" (Deuteronomy 6:7). And the words from Second Timothy assure us: "All scripture [Hebrew and Christian] is inspired by God and is useful for teaching, for reproof, for correction, and for training in

NOTES, REFLECTIONS, AND QUESTIONS

righteousness, so that everyone who belongs to God may be proficient, equipped for every good work" (2 Timothy 3:16-17). How desperately today we need a multiplication of teachers of the words of God!

No teacher can teach what he or she does not know. Teachers cannot take people where they themselves have not been. Paul testified, "I know the one in whom I have put my trust" (1:12). Timothy and Titus had that faith in Christ required of anyone who would teach the gospel. "Guard the good treasure entrusted to you, with the help of the Holy Spirit" (1:14).

Teaching is tough. Children wiggle; youth rebel; adults procrastinate. Teaching requires mental toughness, dedication, self-discipline, enthusiasm. Are you willing to give of yourself? In some societies, the teacher is highly respected. How highly respected are teachers in your area?

In some churches, the teacher is highly honored. How highly honored are teachers in your church?

We shouldn't be surprised at difficulties in teaching. We have been warned: "People will be lovers of themselves, lovers of money, boasters, arrogant, abusive, disobedient to their parents, ungrateful, unholy, inhuman, implacable, slanderers, profligates, brutes, haters of good, treacherous, reckless, swollen with conceit, lovers of pleasure rather than lovers of God, holding to the outward form of godliness but denying its power" (3:2-5). What a time to be a teacher of Scripture in Crete or Ephesus! What a time to be a teacher where we are!

MARKS OF OBEDIENT COMMUNITY

The church is a learning community where study, shared inquiry, and tested experience go on all the time. Just as the Shema, the great commandment, "Hear, O Israel: The LORD is our God, the LORD alone" (Deuteronomy 6:4), was contained in the community of memory, to be shared with the children's children, so the church teaches the gospel from generation to generation. The task expands, never ends, requires us all.

What ingredients characterize a vital "learning" congregation?

NOTES, REFLECTIONS, AND QUESTIONS

Obedient community, entrusted with the treasure of the gospel, teaches it to its children and its children's children.

How are you growing as a learner?

as a teacher?

What will inspire others to teach?

What constitutes "the good treasure" entrusted to us to be passed on to future generations?

How is teaching of sound doctrine going on for children, youth, and adults through your church's teaching ministry?

What would strengthen your "learning community"? After-school programs for children? confirmation classes? home study for families? tutoring? adult classes? youth study? Bible study? study of doctrine?

IF YOU WANT TO KNOW MORE

Read Psalm 78:1-7, which beautifully expresses the importance of passing on God's teaching from generation to generation.

Plan a way you can teach children or grandchildren, yours or someone else's, so they will get excited about the Christian faith.

Talk to some young Timothy in your church about what he or she is learning in your church school. Could she or he become a helping teacher?

Letter: Write a letter offering to help in some educational phase of your church. Offer to teach DISCIPLE for youth. Offer to help teach children.

NOTES, REFLECTIONS, AND QUESTIONS

CLAY JARS

"We have this treasure in clay jars, so that it may be made clear that this extraordinary power belongs to God and does not come from us."

—2 Corinthians 4:7

32 Remember Who You Are

OUR HUMAN CONDITION

Most of us feel inadequate to tell others about God's love in Christ. We lack confidence. We fear revealing too much about ourselves. We fear invading the privacy of others. We may offend. We may be rebuffed. Or we might succeed; then what would we do?

ASSIGNMENT

Our readings recap the entire study. Our purpose is to strengthen our ability to be messengers, to be witnesses, to be carriers of this gospel treasure. Notice how each Scripture selection focuses on a major motif. A theme throughout the study is the assurance of God's faithfulness and the call to messengers to proclaim it.

Day 1 Lamentations 3:1-40 (return); Deuteronomy 4:15-40; 5:1–6:9 (remember); Deuteronomy 30 (obey)
Day 2 Isaiah 6 (call to witness); Jeremiah 1:4-10 (call to courage); Ezekiel 1; 3:1-15; 33:1-9; 37 (call to be a sentinel)
Day 3 Isaiah 52 (the feet of the messenger); Isaiah 53 (the suffering servant); Isaiah 55 (seek the Lord); Isaiah 56:1-8 (covenant extended to all who obey)
Day 4 Romans 5 (grace abounds); Romans 8 (Christ is Lord); Romans 10 (messenger needed); 2 Corinthians 4 (treasure in clay jars)
Day 5 Ephesians 1:15-23 (the church—Christ's body); 2–3 (the household of God); 4:1–5:20 (giving thanks at all times)
Day 6 Read and respond to "The Word of the Lord" and "Marks of Obedient Community."
Day 7 Rest

PRAYER

Pray daily before study:

"I will remember your great deeds, LORD;
I will recall the wonders you did in the past.
I will think about all that you have done;
I will meditate on all your mighty acts"
(Psalm 77:11-12, TEV).

Prayer concerns for this week:

CLAY JARS

Day 1 Lamentations 3:1-40 (return); Deuteronomy 4:15-40; 5:1–6:9 (remember); Deuteronomy 30 (obey)

Day 2 Isaiah 6 (call to witness); Jeremiah 1:4-10 (call to courage); Ezekiel 1; 3:1-15; 33:1-9; 37 (call to be a sentinel)

Day 3 Isaiah 52 (the feet of the messenger); Isaiah 53 (the suffering servant); Isaiah 55 (seek the Lord); Isaiah 56:1-8 (covenant extended to all who obey)

Day 4 Romans 5 (grace abounds); Romans 8 (Christ is Lord); Romans 10 (messenger needed); 2 Corinthians 4 (treasure in clay jars)

Day 5 Ephesians 1:15-23 (the church—Christ's body); 2–3 (the household of God); 4:1–5:20 (giving thanks at all times)

Day 6 "The Word of the Lord" and "Marks of Obedient Community"

NOTES, REFLECTIONS, AND QUESTIONS

THE WORD OF THE LORD

Return

The devastated remnant of Jews in Jerusalem wept over the tragedy that had overtaken them. Through their tears they could see the hand of God who had punished them and the face of God who loved them still.

They could hear the call of God that had been the clear and constant theme of the prophets before the destruction: Remember, repent, return.

> "Let us test and examine our ways,
> and return to the LORD,"

says Lamentations 3:40. Not mere tears of remorse, not prayers of regret, not acts of penance, but a return to righteousness and compassion is God's expectation.

Remember

But do we know what God expects? Yes, certainly. Deuteronomy clearly voices the prophets' definition of righteousness as expressed by Moses. "You shall have no other gods before me" (Deuteronomy 5:7). God knocks every idol from its throne. Idolatry is the foundation of wickedness. Paul understood our inclination to leave God and adore ourselves when he underscored that all people tend to serve the creature rather than the Creator (Romans 1:25). He pleaded that we "put to death . . . greed (which is idolatry)" (Colossians 3:5). Idolatry is our relentless desire to grab, to please ourselves, to do things our way. Remember that.

And teach it. Teach the heartbeat of holiness, stated by Moses, reiterated by Jesus: "Hear, O Israel: The LORD is our God, the LORD alone. You shall love the LORD your God with all your heart, and with all your soul, and with all your might" (Deuteronomy 6:4-5; compare Mark 12:29-30). Remember these words and "recite them to your children." Part of remembering is to remember collectively. The task of community recall is an unending recital of the faith lest the community forget.

Obey

Obedience leads to life; disobedience points to death. "See, I have set before you today life and prosperity, death and adversity. If you obey the commandments of the LORD your God. . . , then you shall live. . . . But if your heart turns away and you do not hear, but are led astray . . . you shall perish" (Deuteronomy 30:15-18).

Paul never intended faith or trust to be devoid of right living. His words on being made right with God through Jesus Christ always point to a radical transformation of human nature and conduct. "Do not be conformed to this world, but be transformed by the renewing of your minds, so that you may discern what is the will of God" (Romans 12:1-2).

The Call to Witness

Into a world of not seeing, God shines light. To unhearing humanity, God speaks the Word. How? By calling messengers, by opening their minds to truth, and by commissioning them to speak.

Isaiah was given a tough task—to point to a reality people would not see, to speak truths they would not hear or comprehend. No wonder Isaiah, in promising a Messiah, spoke of a people who walked without light (9:2).

When have you felt you were part of a people who could not see, would not hear, refused to comprehend?

Jeremiah's call demanded much courage on the young prophet's part. He was tested by danger and discouragement again and again. He loved his people so much, the people he had to denounce, that he is called the weeping prophet. Often he wanted to give up, quit. But the fire of truth burned in his bones, both when he foretold "violence and destruction" (20:8) and when he bought the family farm to symbolize hope in God's promises (32:9-15).

Ezekiel ate the scroll, at least in his mind's eye (Ezekiel 3:1-3). He was to be a sentinel, a watcher positioned to warn the people (3:16-17). His job was to cry out, to be faithful to the message. The outcome was up to God and to others. The same was true when he foresaw hope, restoration, return.

What is the difference between being a faithful witness and trying to guarantee success of the gospel as if the outcome were your responsibility?

When have you done either or both?

The Messiah

Out of the experience of exile, Isaiah foresaw a servant different from tradition (Isaiah 52:13–53:12). Common wisdom described a king, a descendant of David, a soldier who would throw off the yoke of the enemy. But a different image was hinted at by the prophets. Messiah would be born in the tiny village of Bethlehem (Micah 5:2). He would ride humbly on a donkey (Zechariah 9:9). He would suffer innocently on behalf of a sinful people (Isaiah 53:12). His feet would bring the good news of peace and salvation (52:7). How "beautiful"

NOTES, REFLECTIONS, AND QUESTIONS

the feet of all messengers who carry his word of good news.

In your experience, who has brought to you the good news, announced peace and salvation to you?

Urgent Witness

We are to tell others, witnessing with a sense of urgency. With hints of Messiah came thoughts of inclusiveness. The Gentile as well as the Jew shall be included in God's grace.

"The foreigners who join themselves to the LORD . . .
and hold fast my covenant—
these I will bring to my holy mountain" (Isaiah 56:6-7).

It is happening in the prophets! God's grace is broadcast in all directions to all nations. Salvation will come from the Jews, and it will reach all people. Isaiah sensed it. "From the ends of the earth we hear songs of praise" (24:16).

"I will bring your offspring from the east,
and from the west I will gather you;
I will say to the north, 'Give them up,'
and to the south, 'Do not withhold' " (43:5-6).

What a foundation the prophets laid for Paul. What a foundation for the words of Jesus: "Then people will come from east and west, from north and south, and will eat in the kingdom of God" (Luke 13:29).

Grace Abounds

We have learned that Paul saw the work of Christ as the fulfillment of prophetic insight. Righteous trust was demanded; but sin was pervasive, powerful. The Law was holy, but the Law became a stimulus to sin all the more. So God, faithful to an unending desire to save, sent Jesus as the obedient breakthrough. Now we can be brought into right relationship with God. "Therefore, since we are justified by faith [not by our own works], we have peace with God through our Lord Jesus Christ" (Romans 5:1). This grace is for sinners—for all of us. It is a free gift and abundantly available for all.

Why are we continually tempted to believe we either "deserve" or must "earn" God's love?

Christ Is Lord

We no longer stand under condemning wrath, although certain kinds of suffering are still ours. We are freed from the rebellious desire to sin, free from a debilitating moralism, and

NOTES, REFLECTIONS, AND QUESTIONS

open to love God. We live energized by the Spirit, free to anticipate a resurrection like Jesus' and a kingdom of harmony like that dreamed of by the prophets. No power on earth or in heaven is as great as the power of Jesus. He will be with us in love always.

Messengers Needed

Just as God called Isaiah, Jeremiah, and Ezekiel to speak the word, just as God in Christ called Paul to be an apostle to the Gentiles, so God calls a continuous stream of people to be witnesses, messengers of good news. So many people in the world simply do not know the good news because no one has told them.

"How are they to call on one in whom they have not believed? And how are they to believe in one of whom they have never heard? And how are they to hear without someone to proclaim him?" (Romans 10:14).

With whom are you sharing the good news?

What further call from God are you hearing?

Clay Jars

Of course we are weak and inadequate. With great insight Paul claims that our weakness gives more power to the gospel. He told the Corinthians he did not preach with worldly wisdom or oratory. He did not attribute changed lives to some natural charisma (1 Corinthians 2:1-5). God's grace is even more obvious, more powerful, when clothed in human weakness. Therefore, we who witness are like clay jars; but that does not diminish the glory of the treasure we hold; it emphasizes it (2 Corinthians 4:7).

The Church—Christ's Body

The church is Christ's body (Ephesians 1:22-23). To live in Christ is to live in fellowship with other Christians. Dividing walls of hostility are torn down by the sacrificial death of Christ (2:13-14). "You are one in Christ Jesus" (Galatians 3:28).

Paul insisted the fellowship meal and the Lord's Table were for everyone. If a person was or wasn't circumcised, if people drank wine or didn't, observed special prayers or holidays, ate meat or didn't—no matter. If anyone was in Christ, that person sat equally at table in the household of God.

Thanks to God

Thanksgiving is not a season but a way of life. Praise is not an occasional act of an individual, not a periodic ritual by a congregation. Praise is a rich perfume always permeating the people of God.

NOTES, REFLECTIONS, AND QUESTIONS

Obedient community witnesses with confidence because God has touched our lives.

Love Feast

Several Christian traditions, from time to time, observe a Love Feast. Sometimes eating a fellowship meal is part of it. Often it closes with the Lord's Supper. But essential ingredients are singing, prayer, Scripture, and personal expressions of faith and joy. It is a feast of agape, of acceptance, understanding, and affirmation.

The community is so supportive that a person can feel free to tell of struggles, hurts and healings, longings and fulfilled hopes, sins and mercy. A love feast is a moment of mystery in which it is safe to glorify God, safe to tell one's personal story. It is a time in which the Spirit guides the witnessing. Love is so strong a person is free to be silent, to pray, to affirm others.

CALL TO OBEDIENT COMMUNITY

ONE: Awake, my people, pay attention.
The Holy One has a point of contention:
At the marketplace they measure with false weights.
They sell the needy for a pair of shoes.
They indulge their appetites,
ignoring the hungry at the door,
deaf to the cry of the poor.
They have ears but do not hear.
ALL: Everything's fine. Peace. Peace.
ONE: The houses are splendid, the monuments secure.
They revel in their success, saying,
"By our own hands we built this!"
"The Temple will never be destroyed!"
They have hearts to discern but do not perceive.
ALL: Everything's fine. Peace. Peace.
ONE: They silence the prophets whose voices trouble the peace.
They cling to the law that gives them security
or to the special knowledge that makes them elite.
They have eyes but do not see.
ALL: Everything's fine. Peace. Peace.
ONE: They bow at the altars of their gods.
They indulge in ecstasies without responsibilities
and sensation without sensibility.
They have veiled their faces from faithfulness.
ALL: Everything's fine. Peace, peace.
NORTH: We are rich!
EAST: We are strong!
SOUTH: We are right!
WEST: We're having fun!
NORTH: But isn't it strange
how you just can't trust anyone anymore?
No one's word is good. Everyone is out for themselves.*
EAST: Why are the cities crumbling?
And why are there so many poor?*
SOUTH: What about all the violence? And fragmented families?*
WEST: Life is empty, meaningless.
Nothing we do really satisfies.
It takes bigger thrills to excite us, more drama to entertain us.
We're not even sure who we are anymore.*
ALL: Everything is not fine.
We are cut off from one another.
We are distant from ourselves.
We are alienated from earth.
We are exiled from God.
NORTH: Our sin is greed.
EAST: Our sin is pride.
SOUTH: Our sin is arrogance.
WEST: Our sin is dissipation.
ALL: It is idolatry—worshiping the creature, not the Creator.
NORTH: We have killed Truth and sacrificed Integrity.
EAST: We have crucified Compassion and written off Patience.
SOUTH: We have ravaged Respect and restricted Vision.
WEST: We have buried Faithfulness and trivialized Love.
ALL: We have sowed the wind and reaped the whirlwind.
There is no peace. No life, no hope.
No holiness, no wholeness. Only dead and scattered bones.
(*Silence*)
ONE: Come from the four winds, O Breath.
Breathe upon these that they may live.
ALL: Rise upon us, O Gracious One,
with healing in your wings.
ONE: Turn to me, and I will welcome you home
—as a mother the child of her womb—
I will not forget you!
—as a father the long-lost young—
I will not reject you!
—as a spouse the beloved one—
I will not forsake you! Turn to me. **
And you will live!
And my children shall come home
from the north and from the south,
from the east and from the west,
bringing gifts and treasures with them.
The Holy One was buried but is risen!
Was dead but is alive!
ALL (*to North*): Come to the banquet!
We have need of you.
May your ears hear the cries of creation,
your minds plan justice,
dispense generous mercy.
May you hear the truth and live with integrity.
ONE: Your chief administrator shall be called Righteousness.
ALL (*to East*): Come to the banquet!
We have need of you.
May your hearts discern the call to action,
attentive to the needs of all,
your hands work with tender strength
and build with patient perseverance.
And may you walk with humble hearts before God.
ONE: Your strong walls shall be called Salvation.
ALL (*to South*): Come to the banquet!
We have need of you.
May your speech guide with graciousness
and imaginations inspire to hopefulness.
May your eyes see the Vision and make it plain.
ONE: Your overseer shall be called Peace.
ALL (*to West*): Come to the banquet!
We have need of you.
May your unveiled face shine with human kindness
and divine care,
and the fullness of your attentive presence
grace us with the hospitality of humor and dignity
and deep meaning.
May your unveiled face shine with faithful love.
ONE: Your gates shall be called Praise.
ALL: And people will come from east and west,
north and south, and eat with all the saints
at the heavenly banquet.
ONE: The dividing wall of hostility is broken down.
You who were far off are brought near.
ALL: We are all one in Christ Jesus
who unites us as one household of faith and freedom—
one body, one blood, one family.
ONE: Go into the world then, beloved of God,
remembering who you are,
NORTH: with ears to hear,
EAST: hearts to discern,
SOUTH: eyes to see,
WEST: unveiled faces.
ONE: And may your words and deeds,
being and doing, loving and serving,
be a witness to the presence of the resurrected Christ,
the unbounded grace of God,
and the renewing power of the Holy Spirit.
ALL: Amen.

A SERVICE OF WORD AND TABLE

GATHERING

GREETING
The grace of the Lord Jesus Christ be with you.
And also with you.
The risen Christ is with us.
Praise the Lord!

HYMN
"Immortal, Invisible, God Only Wise"

OPENING PRAYER
Almighty God,
to you all hearts are open, all desires known,
and from you no secrets are hidden.
Cleanse the thoughts of our hearts
by the inspiration of your Holy Spirit,
that we may perfectly love you,
and worthily magnify your holy name,
through Christ our Lord.
Amen.

PRAYER FOR ILLUMINATION
Lord, open our hearts and minds
by the power of your Holy Spirit,
that, as the Scriptures are read
and your Word proclaimed,
we may hear with joy what you say to us today.
Amen.

SCRIPTURE LESSON
Deuteronomy 6:1-13

SCRIPTURE LESSON
Isaiah 55:1-11

SCRIPTURE LESSON
Colossians 1:11-20

HYMN
"Break Thou the Bread of Life"

GOSPEL LESSON
John 1:1-14

SERMON
Let this be a time of witness by group members.

CONCERNS AND PRAYERS
Let opportunity be given for prayers for others.

INVITATION
Christ our Lord invited to his table all who love him,
who earnestly repent of their sin
and seek to live in peace with one another.
Therefore, let us confess our sin before God and one another.

CONFESSION AND PARDON
Merciful God,
we confess that we have not loved you with our whole heart.
We have failed to be an obedient church.
We have not done your will,
we have broken your law,
we have rebelled against your love,
we have not loved our neighbors,
and we have not heard the cry of the needy.
Forgive us, we pray.
Free us for joyful obedience,
through Jesus Christ our Lord.
Amen.

All pray in silence.

Leader to people:

Hear the good news:
Christ died for us while we were yet sinners;
that proves God's love toward us.
In the name of Jesus Christ, you are forgiven!

People to leader:

In the name of Jesus Christ, you are forgiven!

Leader and people:

Glory to God. Amen.

THE PEACE
Let us offer one another signs of reconciliation and love.

All exchange signs and words of God's peace.

THE GREAT THANKSGIVING
The Lord be with you.
And also with you.
Lift up your hearts.
We lift them up to the Lord.
Let us give thanks to the Lord our God.
It is right to give our thanks and praise.
It is right, and a good and joyful thing,
always and everywhere to give thanks to you,
Father Almighty, creator of heaven and earth.
You formed us in your image
and breathed into us the breath of life.
When we turned away, and our love failed,
your love remained steadfast.
You delivered us from captivity,
made covenant to be our sovereign God,
and spoke to us through your prophets.
And so,
with your people on earth
and all the company of heaven
we praise your name and join their unending hymn:

Holy, holy, holy Lord, God of power and might,
heaven and earth are full of your glory.
Hosanna in the highest.
Blessed is he who comes in the name of the Lord.
Hosanna in the highest.

Holy are you, and blessed is your Son Jesus Christ.
Your Spirit anointed him
to preach good news to the poor,
to proclaim release to the captives
and recovering of sight to the blind,
to set at liberty those who are oppressed.
and to announce that the time had come
when you would save your people.
He healed the sick, fed the hungry, and ate with sinners.
By the baptism of his suffering, death, and resurrection
you gave birth to your church,
delivered us from slavery to sin and death,
and made with us a new covenant
by water and the Spirit.
When the Lord Jesus ascended,
he promised to be with us always,
in the power of your Word and Holy Spirit.
On the night in which he gave himself up for us,
he took bread, gave thanks to you, broke the bread,
gave it to his disciples, and said:
"Take, eat; this is my body which is given for you.
Do this in remembrance of me."
When the supper was over, he took the cup,
gave thanks to you, gave it to his disciples, and said:
"Drink from this, all of you;
this is my blood of the new covenant,
poured out for you and for many
for the forgiveness of sins.
Do this, as often as you drink it,
in remembrance of me."
And so,
in remembrance of these your mighty acts in Jesus Christ,
we offer ourselves in praise and thanksgiving
as a holy and living sacrifice,
in union with Christ's offering for us,
as we proclaim the mystery of faith.

Christ has died; Christ is risen; Christ will come again.

Pour out your Holy Spirit on us gathered here,
and on these gifts of bread and wine.
Make them be for us the body and blood of Christ,
that we may be for the world the body of Christ,
redeemed by his blood.
By your Spirit make us one with Christ,
one with each other,
and one in ministry to all the world,
until Christ comes in final victory
and we feast at his heavenly banquet.
Through your Son Jesus Christ,
with the Holy Spirit in your holy church,
all honor and glory is yours, almighty Father,
now and for ever.
Amen.

THE LORD'S PRAYER
All pray the Lord's Prayer.

BREAKING THE BREAD
The pastor breaks the bread in silence, or while saying:

Because there is one loaf,
we, who are many, are one body, for we all partake
of the one loaf.
The bread which we break is a sharing in the body of Christ.

The pastor lifts the cup in silence, or while saying:

The cup over which we give thanks is a sharing in the blood of Christ.

GIVING THE BREAD AND CUP
The bread and wine are given to the people, with these or other words being exchanged:

The body of Christ, given for you. **Amen.**
The blood of Christ, given for you. **Amen.**

PRAYER AFTER COMMUNION
Eternal God, we give you thanks for this holy mystery
in which you have given yourself to us.
Grant that we may go into the world
in the strength of your Spirit,
to give ourselves for others,
in the name of Jesus Christ our Lord,
Amen.

HYMN
"Here I Am, Lord"

DISMISSAL WITH BLESSING
Go forth in peace.
The grace of the Lord Jesus Christ,
and the love of God,
and the communion of the Holy Spirit
be with you all.
Amen.

Litany by Kathleen Joy Leithner.